Remind Me Today

*Reflections on Life
Through the 23rd Psalm*

A DAILY DEVOTIONAL

Wanda Hood

Copyright 2015 by Wanda Hood

All rights reserved. No part of this publication may be reproduced or transmitted in any form or by any means electronic or mechanical, including photocopy, recording, or any information storage and retrieval system now known or to be invented, without permission in writing from the publisher.

Cover photograph by Wanda Hood © 2015. All rights reserved.

Cover design by Steve Mellon © 2015. All rights reserved.

Scripture quotations taken from the *Holy Bible*, New Living Translation (NLT), second edition, ©1996, 2004, 2007 by Tyndale House Foundation. Used by permission of Tyndale House Publishers Inc., Carol Stream. Illinois 60188. All rights reserved.

Scripture quotations marked *The Message* (MSG) are taken from *The Message* by Eugene H. Peterson, ©1993, 1994, 1995, 1996, 2000, 2001, 2002. Used by permission of NavPress Publishing Group. All rights reserved.

Scripture quotations marked NIV are taken from the Holy Bible, *New International Version*. Copyright ©1973, 1978, 1984, 2011 by Biblica, Inc. Used by permission of Zondervan. All rights reserved worldwide. www.zondervan.com.

Scripture quotations marked NKJV are taken from the New King James Version, © 1982 by Thomas Nelson, Inc. Used by permission. All rights reserved.

Scripture verses marked Phillips are taken from *The New Testament in Modern English* by © J. B. Phillips, copyright 1958, 1959, 1960, 1972. All rights reserved.

Published and distributed by

Encourage Publishing, LLC
New Albany, Indiana
812.987.6148
www.encouragebooks.com

ISBN 978-0-9962067-1-6

Printed in the United States

Remind Me Today

Contents

Acknowledgments	4
About the Author	6
Introduction	7
Remind Me Today 8	
January	9
The Argument 41	
February	43
March	73
April	105
A Forgotten Memory 136	
May	137
June	169
The Marriage 200	
July	203
August	235
September	267
A Thankful Heart 298	
October	299
November	331
Is it December already? 362	
December	363
Final Thoughts	395

Acknowledgments

First and mostly importantly, I am so thankful for the leading of the Holy Spirit. Without his guidance and inspiration, I could not have written this book. There were many nights I struggled with ideas and would awaken with one on my heart that could have only come through him. God has been faithful in keeping me motivated and committed to finishing what I started. It is really the Lord's work; I was just chosen to put it on paper.

Secondly, I want to thank my husband, Jack, who has patiently put up with my two years of writing. Many times I was so distracted by my thoughts that I only seemed to be with him in body but not in mind. He was so generous in allowing me to use him as examples over and over again, sometimes divulging personal details of our life together. When we married in 1998, he truly became my soul mate and I have been so blessed to be with him.

I also express gratitude to my children, grandchildren, great-grandchildren and a nephew for giving me permission to share their experiences in some of my posts. They allowed me to use their personal, sometimes painful trials in my devotions. They'll all agree that the valleys were hard and lonely, but they were what led to and strengthened the growth of their own faith.

I especially want to thank my three good friends, Waneta, BoBo and Shannon for allowing me to use them as examples of courage and perseverance. They have been an inspiration for me and I admire all of them so much. I know God has special rewards waiting for each of them.

Thank you to my son, Steve Mellon, for your encouragement and help through this process. Your cover design is beautiful and offers a sense of peace.

Thank you Steve Mellon and Anne Milam for the guidance and advice that helped me make the right publishing decisions.

Last of all, a heartfelt thank you to all my friends for putting up with my endless chatter about the book. I am especially grateful for the encouragement I received from so many of you. It helped more than you will ever know.

About the Author

Wanda Hood began writing a daily devotional and posting it on Facebook in July of 2013. As an accomplished poet, her daily heartfelt and carefully crafted prose was a completely new and rewarding experience for her and her followers. Initially intending to post her devotions for a year or so then move on to a new writing experience, Wanda began receiving encouragement from friends, comments from her followers and suggestions about putting her devotions into a book.

Thus began a two-year journey of personal reflections on her life experiences and those of her family and friends, culminating in "Remind Me Today", an easy-flowing and poignant daily devotional, each day illuminated by carefully selected scriptures from a refreshing variety of Bible versions, and every month carried forward with excerpts from the 23rd Psalm.

Wanda resides in Kokomo, Indiana with Jack, her husband of almost twenty years, whom you will get to know through her writing. You will also become acquainted with her children, Debbie, Steve and Jeff, Jack's children, Steve and Karen, and with their many grandchildren, Tyler, Morganne, Drew, Mikeh, Elizabeth, Chloe, Brooke, Jessie, Petar, Anna, Austin and Emily, and great-grandchildren, eight so far: Emme, Riley, Gunnar, Harper, Cash, Malachi, Paige and Stella.

Introduction

This book offers a daily spiritual reflection on life's victories, joys, trials, frustrations, heartaches, illnesses, grief and any other experiences you may have. You may not encounter the same ones I chronicled, but some will strike a chord and bring to your mind what you have already lived through and offer some thoughts on what may lie ahead on your path.

Our journey through life is a story being written with every new experience we encounter, each one leaving a footprint on our memory and shaping us in some way. We'll often have choices to make which ultimately determine how we mature in our faith and develop our character.

My prayer is that through "Remind Me Today" you'll find the strength to embrace life with its challenges and learn to cherish your victories through the power and peace the Holy Spirit brings to each of us. We have a loving and merciful God who walks with us through every step of our faith journey and offers a personal relationship that no one else can supply.

Writing these daily devotions and poems resulted in a great deal of personal growth. I had to recall and reflect on some painful experiences of my own life and those of my family. Some moments I've wished I could relive and redo, but I've come to realize that who I am today is a result of where I've been. This was not a job, but became a passion leading me to a new and exciting spiritual awakening. Most pages have space for you to note your own reflections, thoughts and questions. By the end of the year, I hope that you are able to look back on your own writing and find that you, also, have grown.

Remind Me Today

*Remind me today
that there's more to life
than laundry, cooking and cleaning.
I have a Savior who died for my sins
so my journey on earth has meaning.*

*Every day I look around and see
all the loneliness pain and despair.
Remind me, Lord, that you love us all,
and nothing is beyond your repair.*

*Remind me again of what I have
and who you designed me to be.
Use the words I pen to tell the world,
there's a Savior that can set them free.*

Wanda Hood

January

*The Lord is my shepherd,
I shall not want.*

*Lord, help me remember that
you are my (personal)
shepherd, that you care for me,
and will meet my needs.*

*Remind me that what I want is
not always what I need.*

January 1

Staying balanced

"How well God must like you - you don't hang out at Sin Saloon, you don't slink along Dead End Road, you don't go to Smart Mouth College. Instead you thrill to God's Word, you chew on scripture day and night. You're a tree replanted in Eden, having fresh fruit every month, never dropping a leaf, always in blossom."

Psalm 111:3 (MSG)

When I began exercising at the gym a few years ago, my instructor had me stand on a balance ball to gain balance skills. The first few times I had to hold on to someone's hand or be by a wall where I could place my hand. Once I mastered the balancing, it became easier. However, if I leaned too far either way, I'd lose my balance and have to get off and start over. The secret to maintaining that balance was watching my image in the mirror. When I looked around, I lost my balance.

As we begin this New Year, our focus should be on keeping a balance in our life. God desires for us to have a full life, but we need to spend time with him first. When we keep our spiritual eyes on him, everything else falls into place. We need to set aside time for family, work and other activities but if all our energy is spent on them our life soon becomes out of balance.

Like focusing on my image at the gym, keeping our eyes on our Lord and being in his Word ensures a balanced, blessed and happy year.

Oh Father of my past, present and future, help me keep my priorities straight as I begin a new year. I want to keep you on the throne of my life every day.

January 2

Overdue

"Create in me a clean heart, O God, and renew a steadfast spirit within me."

Psalm 51:10 (NIV)

"That is why we never give up. Though our bodies are dying, our spirits are being renewed every day."

II Corinthians 4:16 (NLT)

I used to go to the library on a regular basis and would check out a couple of books at a time. Occasionally I wouldn't be able to finish one of them by the due date and I would return to the library to renew it. However, I couldn't continue to renew it over and over. If I didn't take the book back, I was fined. The book was never mine and eventually had to be returned to the library.

We live in an earthly body that is not going to last indefinitely. In reality, it dies a little every day and there isn't anything we can do about it. But the part of us that is spirit lives for eternity. As believers, we're renewed every day. We don't have to go anywhere to be renewed, for it's done through the Holy Spirit. Having that assurance helps us deal with our physical body that is wearing out. The inner spirit that defines who we are belongs to our Lord, and will be in his safe keeping forever.

Father, thank you for your Spirit who renews and strengthens me every day.

January 3

Pressing out wrinkles

"Because of the Lord's great love, we are not consumed, for his compassions never fail. They are new every morning; great is your faithfulness. I say to myself, 'The Lord is my portion; therefore I will wait for him.'"

Lamentations 3:22-24 (NIV)

Before dryers and permanent press were invented, most clothes had to be ironed. Once a week I devoted most of my day standing at the ironing board with three small children to deal with as well. The job often seemed overwhelming for, along with the clothes of our children and myself, I had my husband's six white shirts to iron. Sometimes I'd look at the basket full of wrinkled clothes and think "How am I going to get all this done?" Somehow I always did and then felt a sense of pride once they were neatly folded and hung at the end of the afternoon.

Often our busy lives make our days seem like a basket full of wrinkled clothes. Nothing goes right, we have interruptions, our mood sours and we just want the mess to go away! If we offer up our day before God, he will smooth out the hours before us with his gentle guidance, removing the wrinkles in our schedules. Then when evening arrives we can reflect with thanksgiving on the wonder of our Lord's touch and how he led us through, restoring calm and peace to our soul.

Father, help me recognize the small blessings that brighten up a too busy day.

January 4

Anger

"Don't sin by letting anger control you. Think about it overnight and remain silent. Offer sacrifices in the right spirit and trust in the Lord."

Psalm 4:4-5 (NLT)

Occasionally I have a stressful day. There may be too much to do and not enough time, I might be discouraged about something that's not going the way I'd hoped, or it might be an unresolved disagreement. When I finally get to bed and have time to reflect on the day, my attitude can affect my prayers that night. I'll have trouble clearing my mind so I can unwind. However, if I lay still long enough and focus on God's love and forgiveness, peace returns and I am able to drift off to sleep.

There's a good reason why the Bible instructs us not to go to bed angry. Don't carry anger or frustrations to bed with you. I'm learning to "get over it" and move on. Not overreacting in frustrating situations is a hard skill to learn. We don't always have to agree with everyone or have a problem-free day; in the midst of those situations we can still find that elusive peace when we spend time with our Lord.

Father, you know all my imperfections and still you love me. Help me develop my patience and practice forgiveness.

January 5

Conversations

"But you know better now, so make sure it's all gone for good; bad temper, irritability, meanness, profanity, dirty talk."

Colossians 3:8 (MSG)

"Be an example to all believers in what you say, in the way you live, in your love, your faith and your purity."

I Timothy 4:12 (NIV)

While looking through an antique Bible one day, I found an article that had been clipped from a newspaper over 100 years ago. What it said convicted me and caused me to do some serious thinking. The title of the article was "What Will We Talk About in Heaven?" Even among committed Christians, our conversations aren't always the kind we would have if God was sitting there with us. We tell off-color jokes, lash out in anger, criticize, make disparaging remarks about others and use language we know is wrong. We talk as though God doesn't hear us, but he does.

Maybe we've become so comfortable with it that it's ingrained in us. Do you think God will want us to talk in heaven the way we talk here on earth?

Remember, our Lord does hear all our words. He's there beside us every time we speak. What will we talk about in heaven? I don't know, but I'm going to practice daily so that my words will be pleasing to him now.

Father, sometimes my speech reflects the world instead of the Creator of the world. I'm sorry.

January 6

Remodeling

"Now may the God of peace make you holy in every way, and may your whole spirit and soul and body be kept blameless until our Lord Jesus Christ comes again."

I Thessalonians 5:23 (NLT)

One of my favorite TV shows is "Property Brothers." I enjoy watching the transformation of a house with multiple problems into a home that is a place of beauty. The people having the remodeling done usually have a long list of things they want. Part of their responsibility is to help in removing old flooring, walls and cabinets. After all the problems have been corrected they may not get everything on their list, but the important aspects of the home have been corrected and they fall in love with it.

When we accept the Lord as our Savior, he begins a remodeling process in us. We may have a list of things we want added or changed, but our Lord knows what we need. We have to work during the process as we weed out old habits and attitudes. The changes aren't always easy, in fact sometimes they can be painful, but the end result is worth it, as he transforms us into a new creature, perfect in his sight.

Father, thank you for the remodeling process you are performing in my life every day. Remind me that I have a responsibility to toss out the bad attitudes and sinful habits that keep me from becoming the person you designed me to be.

January 7

Illness and grief

"For God is my witness, whom I serve with my spirit in the gospel of His Son, that without ceasing I make mention of you always in my prayers, making request, if by some means, now at last I may find a way in the will of God to come to you."

Romans 1:9-10 (NKJV)

I have seen amazing changes take place in my family when others were praying for them. Relationships have been healed, marriages restored, illnesses cured, houses sold, jobs obtained, help sent for every physical need. Consequently, prayer has become a very necessary component of my daily life.

The past year brought illnesses and grief to many of our friends. Sometimes trials can nearly overwhelm us and we feel as though we can't take any more. We're guaranteed trials in our life, but God promises to walk with us through every one of them and bring us peace in the valleys we'll face in our lives.

Many times Paul expressed his concern and distress over situations his beloved friends were experiencing. When he wasn't able to go to them to help, he assured them that he prayed for them always.

The most effective tool we have for helping others is our prayers on their behalf. God may or may not answer the way we hope, but he will bring peace to those we pray for.

Lord, comfort and heal my family and friends who are buried in mountains of grief and sickness. Comfort them as only you can.

January 8

A road less traveled

"You can enter God's Kingdom only through the narrow gate. The highway to hell is broad, and its gate is wide for the many who choose that way. But the gateway to life is very narrow and the road is difficult, and only a few will find it"

Matthew 7:13-14 (NLT)

When we're traveling somewhere and aren't in a hurry, Jack likes to explore "the road less traveled." We enjoy exploring little towns and sharing lunch at a mom-and-pop restaurant. The pace is slower on these roads and the scenery is a lot more interesting. When you're on the interstate, everyone is in a hurry and there's not a lot to look at. You have to be alert all the time because traffic is often heavy, cars are switching lanes and the only places to eat are fast food restaurants at the exits.

As Christians, we are on a road not traveled by many of this world. Most people don't realize or care where their wide road is taking them. They don't have a destination in mind, and they like the road they are traveling on because they have so much company.

We have a destination that we know will be more wonderful than we can even imagine, so when the road seems uneven and rough at times the hope we have keeps us moving forward. The truth is, everyone on both roads will reach a destination some day!

Thank you Father for the people you've placed in my life who help steer me toward the right road and keep me grounded.

January 9

My legacy

"For I am not ashamed of the gospel of Christ, because it is the power of God that brings salvation to everyone who believes; first to the Jew, then to the Gentile. For in the gospel the righteousness of God is revealed, a righteousness that is by faith from first to last, just as it is written, 'The righteous will live by faith.'"

Romans 1:16-17 (NIV)

As I draw closer to the end of my journey on this earth, I wonder what kind of legacy I'll leave behind. It won't be for my spotless house or beautiful garden. I haven't achieved fame or fortune, nor have I won any awards or trophies. In the eyes of the world, I would seem to be pretty insignificant.

What I pray I will be remembered for is my faith. I want others to know beyond any doubt that I'm a Christian, saved by grace.

How sad it is when someone dies and their relatives and friends don't know about their beliefs. I've lost close family members that never shared whether they had a faith so I'll never know if they received grace. My hope is that I will see them in heaven someday.

Make sure your relationship with Christ is visible to those you love so they'll be assured of your faith. You don't have to preach to display your trust in The Lord. They'll know it by how you spend your time, how you talk, your behavior and the love you display towards others.

Lord, help me be a bold witness so others will see my faith. More than anything else, I want others to know I have faith in my Savior, Jesus Christ.

January 10

Exercise pain

"Consider it a sheer gift, friends, when tests and challenges come at you from all sides. You know that when under pressure, your faith-life is forced into the open and shows its true colors. So don't try to get out of anything prematurely. Let it do its work as you become mature and well-developed, not deficient in any way."

James 1:2-4 (MSG)

When I begin an exercise machine at the gym, stretching muscles in a new way, I'll be sore for a few days. If I continue with the machine the muscles grow stronger and the pain finally leaves. I have also learned that I need to increase the weight every now and then so my muscles can grow even stronger. Although I sometimes dread going to the gym, I'm always glad I did, for I know it makes me healthier and keeps me mobile.

We will face trials in our life which can cause us pain as well. If we only focus on the challenges, it's easy to complain and even deny the hurt it causes. But, like my physical exercise, the trial develops our strength and character. After we go through these difficult times, our faith is stronger and we're able to find joy in our victory. Until I experienced this in my own life, I had a hard time believing we could rejoice in our suffering.

You are the Father of mercy and strength. Thank you for supplying what I need every day.

January 11

Adjustments

"'My kingdom,' said Jesus, 'doesn't consist of what you see around you.'"

John 18:36 (MSG)

"But there's far more to life for us. We're citizens of high heaven! We're waiting for the arrival of the Savior, the Master, Jesus Christ, who will transform our earthy bodies into glorious bodies like his own. He'll make us beautiful and whole with the same powerful skill by which he is putting everything as it should be, under and around him."

Philippians 3:20-21 (MSG)

I think I have a condition that I call VAS (vacation adjustment syndrome). When we first arrive at our destination, I go through a couple days of feeling a little down and unsettled. I adjust, and after a short time I am fine. Basically I'm a home body and there's nothing like the familiarity and security you feel when you're in your own home.

While we're here on this earth we are never completely satisfied because this is not our home. We settle in and have a life here but, just like my time away from home, we will never feel like we belong because we are foreigners and aliens. There is a longing within us to be where we have our citizenship. Our biggest challenge is to enjoy our time here but never let it diminish our hope in the unimaginable wonders of our real home.

Heavenly Father, I am thankful for my home on earth, but I long for the home you have waiting for me in heaven.

January 12

My sanctuary

"O Lord, hear me as I pray; pay attention to my groaning. Listen to my cry for help, my king and my God, for I pray to no one but you. Listen to my voice in the morning Lord. Each morning I bring my requests to you and wait expectantly...But let all who take refuge in you rejoice; let them sing joyful praises forever. Spread your protection over them, that all may be filled with joy. For you bless the godly, O Lord; you surround them with your shield of love."

Psalm 5:1-3, 11-12 (NLT)

We have a small sitting room off our kitchen. Whenever my children come to visit, that's where we gather for our morning coffee and conversation. It's small enough to provide closeness and offers a feeling of tranquility. This is where I spend time with my Lord each morning, bringing my cup of freshly brewed coffee and settling into my favorite chair. I can gaze out the window at the day opening up before me, and have my personal time with him. It's become a sanctuary where I go to calm my heart when I'm troubled. There, in quiet and peace, I am able close my mind to the rest of the world and linger in the presence of my Lord, feasting on his Word and listening to him as he speaks to my heart.

If you don't have a room you can call your sanctuary, at least find a quiet place and a time that allows you to be alone and away from the TV and other distractions. God doesn't care if it's morning or evening. He's already there, waiting for you to stop and rest in his presence. You'll soon find yourself looking forward to that special time.

Lord, I know that. anywhere I am, I can reach out to you and I will be in your sanctuary.

January 13

Tyler's marathon

"Keep your eyes on Jesus, who both began and finished this race we're in. Study how he did it. Because he never lost sight of where he was headed--- that exhilarating finish in and with God --- he could put up with anything along the way: cross, shame, whatever. And now he's there, in the place of honor, right alongside God."

Hebrews 12:2 (MSG)

One weekend my grandson, Tyler, participated in a marathon at Disney World. He had been training for this event for almost a year, but a few months before the race, he began experiencing pain in his knee. It was diagnosed as a small tear in his meniscus, and the doctor strongly suggested he not participate in the marathon. After prayer and consideration, Tyler decided to go ahead and compete. He successfully completed the marathon in spite of pain and won a medal, reaching the goal he had set. Of course, many prayers were going up on his behalf.

All of us face pain in our lives and sometimes the goal we have set will seem nearly impossible to attain. Satan tries to discourage us by telling us we can't do it, we're not good enough, it'll take too much time, it's not that important or people won't understand. If we've prayed about what we want to accomplish, God will honor our prayers and equip us for the task. Our Lord strengthens us along the way. Tyler's race is an example of how we can achieve our goal, looking beyond the pain we endure for the prize we will one day receive.

Father, help me remain strong in my afflictions and setbacks so I can finish my race in victory.

JANUARY

January 14

Flaws

"For God did not call us to be impure, but to live a holy life."

I Thessalonians 4:7 (NIV)

"Create in me a clean heart, O God. Renew a loyal spirit within me."

Psalm 51:10 (NLT)

We were sitting in the sanctuary one evening at church and the spotlights were illuminating the area behind the choir. Jack noticed small imperfections in the finish on the wall. Being a meticulous painter, he notices things like that. When the lights are dim, those little places are nearly invisible to most of us.

We all struggle with little sins that we barely notice and consequently we don't deal with them. If we observe others struggling with the ones that are more obvious, we may pat ourselves on the back, thinking "at least I'm not guilty of that kind of behavior." As believers, we have the Holy Spirit within us and he's an expert in discovering those "little sins" that can so easily derail us. The light of the Holy Spirit illuminates those imperfections so we see more clearly. Then we can conquer them and become more Christ like.

Merciful Gad, forgive me when I step out of your will. Help me not to be so focused on finding fault in others but to concentrate on showing the fruits of the spirit in my own life.

January 15

I want your attention

"For I know the plans I have for you," declares the Lord, "plans to prosper you and not to harm you, plans to give you hope and a future. Then you will call on me and come and pray to me, and I will listen to you."

Jeremiah 29:11-12 (NIV)

My daughter has always been a talker. Anyone who knows her will attest to that. Jack tells me she inherited this from her mom. When she was small and wanted my attention, she tugged on my sleeve and say "Mommy" over and over again until I answered. It didn't matter how busy I was, or if I was talking to someone; she had a way of getting me to respond.

Isn't it wonderful that we can call on God and have his attention immediately? He's never too busy and, even if someone else needs his help at the same time, he still responds to us as soon as we whisper "Father." He's just waiting for us to reach out, for he's already aware of our need. Many of us pray at night when we go to bed - maybe millions all at once - yet he listens to everyone. We don't receive "divided attention" for he is totally focused on every prayer offered. How amazing is that?

Lord, your attention to my needs never ceases to amaze me.

January 16

A bottle of tears

"You keep track of all my sorrows, you have collected all my tears in your bottle. You have recorded each one in your book."

Psalm 56:8 (NLT)

As I was reading one of the Psalms the other day, I saw something I've never noticed before. I was familiar with the scripture telling us that God has numbered the hairs on our head, but in this psalm I learned that He counts our tears as well. I must have a pretty big bottle of them. I had a lot of scraped knees and bumped heads that brought tears as a child. I've cried tears in anger, frustration, disappointment and hurt. I'm in awe that God counted and recorded each of them.

I was always sympathetic and offered comfort to my children in their hurts, but I didn't count their tears, nor even keep a record of how many times they cried. I loved them all in ways only a parent can understand, but God's love is so much more than that.

All those times when I felt all alone in my sorrow and hurt, God was collecting and counting the tears I shed. I want to carry this revelation with me for comfort when I grieve or am hurt again. Just knowing he loves me that much is overwhelming.

Father, thank you for sharing my sorrow and hurt during the trials of my life.

January 17

Wars

"So now there is no condemnation for those who belong to Christ Jesus. And because you belong to him, the power of the life-giving Spirit has freed you from the power of sin that leads to death."

Romans 8:1-2 (NLT)

Our country is less than 250 years old and yet we have been involved in multiple wars. The war that caused perhaps the most heartache was the Civil War. It's hard to imagine that our country was so divided that relatives would war against each other. Traveling from one state to another could put you in enemy territory. Their ideas and values were worlds apart and the people were willing to sacrifice their time and lives to defend them.

We have a civil war going on within us. We want to please God, but our sinful nature leads us astray. We say and do things that grieve our Lord, and don't do the things that would help us grow spiritually. We face choices all the time and don't always make good ones. It seems as though we will never be free from the war waging within us. When we only focus on these daily battles, we'll always feel like we're losing.

Praise God, that battle has already been won. We have victory over the sin in our life because of our Savior, Jesus Christ. His death, burial and resurrection conquered sin and offers the hope of an eternity in heaven with him. His Spirit is always there to lead, strengthen and help us to stand strong in the battles we face.

Father, no enemy can stand up to your wrath. Remind me daily that you will win the final battle with the enemy.

January 18

Making a deposit

"Blessed is the man who trusts in The Lord, and whose hope is in the Lord. For he shall be like a tree planted by the waters, which spreads out its roots by the river, and will not fear when heat comes; but its leaf will be green, and will not be anxious in the year of drought, nor will it cease from yielding fruit."

Jeremiah 17:7-8 (NKJV)

Jack and I try to add to our savings account on a regular basis. Then, if we have an unexpected expense, there's enough money saved to take care of it. Until I started doing this, I sometimes had to be creative to find the needed funds and that could be stressful.

We have an account with God called a "Trust Account." Each time you place your trust in God's provisions or let him direct your path, you're making a deposit in that account. I think he even pays interest on your balance, for when you have to make a large withdrawal there's always more trust than you thought.

Sometimes I made small deposits when I trusted for little trials and once in a while I had a large deposit, but it always seemed like there was more than enough to meet my need when I made a withdrawal.

Father, thank you for holding my little faith deposits in your safe-keeping.

January 19

Growing

"Like newborn babies, crave spiritual milk, so that by it you may grow up in your salvation."

I Peter 2:2 (NIV)

"But grow in the grace and knowledge of our Lord and Savior Jesus Christ."

II Peter 3:18 (NIV)

When our granddaughter Chloe was about nine she wasn't growing the way the doctor thought she should, so he prescribed a growth hormone. She had a shot every day for several years and gradually began to grow. Now she has reached a normal height and weight for her age. All of us were grateful there was something the doctor could do to correct that deficiency.

Many Christians have a spiritual growth deficiency. When they first accepted their Savior, they experienced some growth but then it slowed and they stayed on a plateau, not reaching the level God planned for them. There is a prescription for that growth just as there was for Chloe. They need to visit the Great Physician. His solution for their problem will be a daily dose of his Word. Feeding on his Word and consulting with him regularly will create the growth they need. Otherwise they will remain baby Christians.

Chloe eventually was able to stop taking her shots, but our spiritual growth will only continue when we stay in God's Word and talk to him daily.

Father, your Word supplies the solution for my failure to grow the way I should. Remind me to get my daily dose.

January 20

News experts

"I don't think the way you think. The way you work isn't the way I work 'God's Decree.' For as the sky soars high above the earth, so the way I work surpasses the way you work, and the way I think is beyond the way you think."

Isaiah 55:8-9 (MSG)

Whenever I watch unfolding news on TV, I'm quickly bored with so-called experts going into endless detail, attempting to explain reasons for what has happened. Whether it's unusual weather patterns, school shootings, drug problems or the increasing flood of illegal immigrants, the newscasters all seem to feel the need to give us their opinions and explanations. Realistically, these self-proclaimed "authorities" don't know why these things happen, but they fill up endless hours of time with their ramblings.

As believers, we're also tempted to seek reasons for why things happen, especially if we're personally affected. We question why God allows bad things to happen to good people or why those of the world seem to experience so few problems. We struggle with unanswered prayer and unexpected trials. We want to believe that God has reasons for all that we go through but we wish he would enlighten us as well. However, those unanswered questions develop our faith. Even though we may never fully understand why certain things happen, we can walk our path with confidence, one step at a time, trusting that our Lord is in control and is walking beside us all the way.

All powerful God, the horizons I see are often clouded with questions and concerns. Help me learn to trust more and accept your plans for my life.

January 21

Facing storms

"The Lord is my shepherd; I shall not want. He makes me to lie down in green pastures; He leads me beside the still waters. He restores my soul; He leads me in the paths of righteousness for His names sake. Yea though I walk through the valley of the shadow of death, I will fear no evil; Your rod and Your staff, they comfort me."

Psalm 23:1-4 (NKJV)

"Then Jesus said, 'Come to me all do you who are weary and carry heavy burdens, and I will give you rest. Take my yoke upon you. Let me teach you, because I am humble and gentle at heart, and you will find rest for your souls. For my yoke is easy to bear, and the burden I give you is light.'"

Matthew 11:28-30. (NLT)

A few times, early in my faith walk, I was nearly brought down by the storms I faced in my life. During one of those occasions I cried out to God, "Lord, I can't do this anymore, please help me." As I sat there, alone and in despair, a feeling of calm washed over me. I felt his arms encircling me while he led me safely through and out of that overwhelming feeling of hopelessness. He has never left me. Therefore, I can face my future knowing that, no matter what comes along, he will still be by my side, leading, comforting and guiding me. I have peace for I know he supplies what I need to walk strong in my faith.

As we walk our own individual paths in life, we'll encounter mountains that block our way, but he leads us safely around them. When the strong winds of adversity nearly blow us down, his hand holds us tight so we can stand firm without fear. Satan throws his fiery darts of pain, worry, temptation, sickness and grief at us, but our Lord stays with us through them all. He alone can give us what we need to endure and be victorious. We can overcome, for his wings of love shelter us.

Protector Father, thank you for sheltering me with your umbrella of love when I walked through the storms in my life.

JANUARY

January 22

God knows us

"You know what I am going to say even before I say it, Lord....Such knowledge is too wonderful for me, too great for me to understand."

Psalm 134:4, 6 (NLT)

It seems like some couples who have been married for many years know instinctively what the other one is going to say and sometimes finish one another's sentences.

God knows us inside and out. He knows what we're thinking, which should give us pause. There are times our thoughts are not clean or loving and we wouldn't want others to know them. But God does. He knows what we're going to say before the words are even formed in our mind. He is already aware of the kind and encouraging words we are going to say to someone as well as the hurtful words we will speak in anger. He hears the lies and gossip, but even when our words disappoint him, he loves us anyway.

Lord, help me to consider carefully what I say. I want to speak in love but sometimes I don't and I know that hurts you. Help me tame my tongue so I can reflect your love to others.

January 23

Coincidences

"How abundant are the good things that you have stored up for those who fear you, that you bestow in the sight of all, on those who take refuge in you."

Psalm 31:19 (NIV)

It has been said, "Coincidences are the miracles where God remains anonymous." I can think of many of them in my life. Whenever I had one of those "coincidences," I would reflect on what had occurred and see God's orchestration in everything that took place. My friends said I was lucky but I knew better!

Time after time, God has placed me where I needed to be to help someone else, and he has put the right people in my path, at the exact moment when I needed help. There was someone there when my car broke down, employment when I needed a job, boarders when I needed extra income and best of all, an amazing man in my life when God knew I was ready. His timing is perfect.

Take the time to reflect on your own life. You will be amazed at the number of times God had a hand in everything that happened! Then trust him whenever you face the uncertainties in your life.

Father, you see every need I have and you already have a plan in place. Thank you for the manna you supply me with every day.

January 24

A new body

"But there's far more to life for us. We're citizens of high heaven! We're waiting the arrival of the Savior, the Master, Jesus Christ, who will transform our earthly bodies into glorious bodies like his own. He'll make us beautiful and whole with the same powerful skill by which he is putting everything as it should be, under and around him."

Philippians 3:20-21 (MSG)

I've noticed as I get older that I'm not able to walk as fast as I used to. Using a cane isn't bad, but it can be inconvenient, because I'm frequently looking for somewhere to prop it, or hang it if I need both hands free. I can't eat some of the foods I used to enjoy. As many of you have probably figured out by now, growing older can be a challenge. I've heard it said that it's "not for wimps". How can we still think and feel inwardly like we did forty or more years ago, yet our bodies don't cooperate?

We have hope, though. We are promised new bodies when we get to heaven. No more canes, walkers or wheelchairs. No more diets, trips to the doctor or any of the other efforts we exert to stay healthy and fit. We won't age – now, won't that be awesome? Doctors, dentists and pharmacists will have to find something else to do in heaven! The Great Physician will have healed us permanently!

Father of surprises, I am looking forward to the new body you are preparing for me. While I am waiting, teach me to appreciate and accept my limitations.

January 25

Because I said so

"God, our God, will take care of the hidden things, but the revealed things are our business. It's up to us, and our children to attend to all the terms in this Revelation."

Deuteronomy 29:29 (MSG)

When my children were young, they wanted a reason for everything I asked them to do, so I heard the word "why" a lot. It didn't matter if they already knew the answer; they would still ask. I guess my stock answer was, "Because I said so." Even as teenagers, their question "why" came in the form of a look or attitude.

When our prayers aren't answered the way we want, or when we face unexpected trials that we don't understand, we question God and he usually chooses not to reveal the reason. Sometimes we'll never know why some things happen in our life. He doesn't promise that we'll understand, but he does promise that he will see us through it. All that he asks of us is to believe he is in control. Our responsibility is to follow in faith.

Lord, I'm sorry for the times I question how you are working in my life. I don't always understand why, but I want to stand on my faith that your answer is right.

January 26

Knickers in a knot

"If you are angry, be sure that it is not out of wounded pride or bad temper. Never go to bed angry - don't give the devil that sort of foothold."

Ephesians 4:26-27 (Phillips)

Recently I heard the phrase "Don't get your knickers in a knot, because it solves nothing and it makes you walk funny." For your information, knickers are pants that come right below the knee. They are finished off with a band that fits snugly around your leg, overlapping socks that come up to your knee. I was amused by the statement as I tried to imagine wearing knickers so messed up that they made you walk differently.

When we get our "nose out of joint" or we're "bent out of shape" about what someone said or did, we have our "knickers in a knot." Then we "get out of step" in our faith walk and witness. Two very important fruits of the spirit are patience and self-control.

Reacting in anger or retaliating will make non-believers question our Christianity, for they notice that what we say about our faith and what we do don't match. It is wise to pause before speaking out in response to someone or something that upsets us so we don't get our heart out of step with the Holy Spirit.

Sweet Jesus, wash me with your Spirit today so I won't react in anger or impatience. Help me to display the fruits of the spirit in my walk and talk.

January 27

Bad days

"No, despite all these things, overwhelming victory is ours through Christ who loved us."

Romans 8:37 (NIV)

Did you ever have one of those days when everything seems to go wrong? We had a day like that in Florida. The weather was nice so we decided to drive to a nearby town and nearly had a collision as we exited the interstate. That was stressful but we tried to relax and enjoy the day anyway. A little while later, we made a return at Sam's and had a long, challenging wait. After making our purchases we were in a checkout lane and had another long wait - and, of course, all the other lanes moved faster. Finally we stopped for dinner at a Longhorn Steakhouse and when we returned to the truck, Jack opened the back door and one of our purchases fell out on the parking lot and broke. On our way home, Jack asked "Do you feel like this has been one of those days?" Fortunately, days like this don't happen very often, but we all experience them sometime, those days where we're just waiting for the other shoe to drop.

If we have times where one challenge occurs right after another, we're tempted to feel like everything is out of control, or we're being punished. Troubling times come to everyone, often in multiples. They may not be major trials, but when they pile up they can seem overwhelming. In trust and faith, we can rise above them with the assurance that "this too will pass" and let his Spirit bring us peace.

Father, thank you for the good days I have. Help me move beyond the bad ones.

January 28

Gift cards

"For the wages of sin is death, but the gift of God is eternal life in Christ Jesus our Lord."

Romans 6:23 (NKJV)

"Thanks be to God for His indescribable gift."

II Corinthians 9:15 (NKJV)

Gift cards are wonderfully convenient alternatives to purchased gift items that are often not the right fit or what the recipient would like. During the time I grew up, there was no such thing as a gift card. The only cards I knew about were greeting cards, post cards and a deck of cards. I can't remember the last time I received a post card and many people now send e-cards in place of greeting cards.

For me, Christmas shopping has become a challenge, so I have resorted to purchasing gift cards. The upside to this is the ease of mailing and the fact that I can get all the Christmas shopping done in less than an hour. The recipient then gets to pick out what he or she wants after Christmas.

God has given us a gift (card) which we will redeem in the future when we get to heaven. We don't have an actual card to hold in our hand, but God has recorded it in his Book. The gift cards we use here on earth can be lost, stolen or expire but our gift from God is guaranteed. It's a gift card no one would be able to afford so Jesus bought it for us. That's the best gift we could ever receive!

Father of all good gifts, I can never thank you enough for the best gift of all: my Savior.

January 29

Challenges

"Then the angel said to me, "Write this: 'Blessed are those who are invited to the wedding supper of the Lamb!" And he added, "These are the true words of God."

Revelation 19:9 (NIV)

When I was a Mary Kay consultant, our senior director offered us a challenge at one of the meetings. Any consultant who sold $2000 of Mary Kay product in one month got to share a day with her, consisting of a ride in a limo, having lunch at The Macaroni Grill and finishing up the outing with a shopping trip to Rodeo Drive, a popular boutique in Louisville. I managed to meet that goal and made the special trip. We had the added benefit of bringing a guest, so I took my daughter as well. There were only ten or twelve of us attending that day so I felt very special!

We are invited to a very special banquet as guests of our Savior. We don't have a date on our calendar for it, but it has been promised to all who are in God's family. A special invitation is extended to every believer. We will be celebrating with the One who made all this possible.

I was allowed to join the other Mary Kay consultants on the limo ride because I worked very hard to qualify. Our banquet with our Lord is a gift. We don't have to work hard to be invited. What an awesome invitation!

Father of Feasts, I rejoice that I have an invitation to the best feast of all.

January 30

Life changes

"Let every detail in your lives - words, actions, whatever - be done in the name of the Master Jesus, thanking God the Father every step of the way."

Colossians 3:17 (MSG)

Have you ever thought about how the focus of your life changes over the years? As a teenager my thoughts were on my friends, activities, boys and school. As a young parent, my focus was on meeting the needs of my family. When our children were grown, I had more time and I began to grow spiritually. After my husband died and the children had moved on with their own lives, my focus had to shift again. I re-entered the work force, adjusted to life on my own and my faith journey began to grow in earnest. Then, when I married Jack, my thoughts and focus changed again. This time I was able to share that journey with my husband who was a committed Christian. What consumed me when I was young no longer drives me. The most important thing in my life has become my relationship with the Lord.

God understands if we don't have as much time to spend with him while we're raising our families. He rewards and honors the care and guidance we give our families while they're in our charge. God has blessed us with a responsibility that involves demonstrating his love to our family. The reward comes in raising Godly children. When you focus on that goal, God is in the center of your life.

God, you created the seasons of our lives and worked through the changes we experienced. Thank you for the constant in the midst of newness.

January 31

Help, I've fallen

"The Lord upholds all who fall, and lifts up all who are bowed down."

Psalm 145:14 (NIV)

There is a familiar commercial featuring a woman who has fallen and is crying out "Help, I've fallen and I can't get up!" My mother once fell in her back yard after tripping over a shovel. Fortunately, she was seen by a neighbor who called 911. Falling physically can be traumatizing, and sometimes we do need help.

Usually our falls are not physical but emotional or spiritual. We allow ourselves to sink into worry pits or we wander down Stress Street. We saturate our minds with everything but God's Word, over extend ourselves in our jobs, our activities and sometimes our work in the church. When that happens, God is shifted from the center of our life to the sidelines. Then when we're faced with a trial, we're overwhelmed and no longer feel his presence. He's still there but we've held him at arm's length.

Staying close to our Lord doesn't take a lot of time, but it does take an open heart that is willing to listen for guidance from the Holy Spirit. He will keep you grounded and steady in your journey so you won't fall.

Father, you promise that I will never fall out of your reach. I take comfort in the assurance that you are there even when I do stumble or fall because I know you'll help me stand strong again.

The Argument

It wasn't that important
yet words had been hurled like rocks
thrown at a can.

Now he sat
stone faced and silent, staring at nothing
while I stood,
lost in a sea of emotions.

How had this erupted into a battle over
such a small thing?

Silently we lingered,
each lost in our own thoughts.

I wanted to erase
the whole afternoon and start over but
it was too late.

Deep inside,
forgiveness struggled to surface through
swirling waves of anger.

Someone has to make
the first move.

Would he or
should I?

I knew the answer
but still I resisted, wanting to be right.

Finally,
I reached out and touched his arm.
He looked up.

"I'm sorry", we both mumbled.
We had forged a treaty
sealed by love.

February

*He makes me to lie down
in green pastures*

*Lord, you gently settle me down
in my life with the peace and
security that can be found only
in the safety of your care.*

February 1

Learning patience

"I waited patiently for the Lord to help, and he turned to me and heard my cry. He lifted me out of the pit of despair, out of the mud and the mire. He set my feet on solid ground and steadied me as I walked along."

Psalm 40:1-2 (NLT)

Every Sunday a group of us from church eat out at a local restaurant. On one occasion everyone's food was served but mine. The waiter assured me it was almost ready, but all the others had finished their meal before my food was finally brought to the table. Understandably, I was a little upset. I felt as though the waiter was concerned about everyone but me.

Many times I have had to wait on God to answer a prayer. When you're praying earnestly, it can become discouraging if you see others rejoicing about answered prayers and you're still waiting. Nevertheless, I have learned when the answer does come, it's either exactly what I need at just the right time, or he gives me a peace so I can accept a "No" or "Not now."

The restaurant didn't consider how unsettling it was when I received my food late, but God does care when our prayer answers don't come when, or like we had hoped. That's when his Spirit lifts us up and fills us with something better.

Father, help me overcome the temptation to be upset over things that aren't important and to focus on the promise that you have everything under control.

FEBRUARY

February 2

Guarantees

"I've wiped the slate of all your wrongdoings. There's nothing left of your sins. Come back to me, come back. I've redeemed you."

Isaiah 44:22 (MSG)

A number of years ago I was waiting in line at a Sears store in Southern Indiana. The gentleman in front of me was holding a brown paper bag in his hand. When he got to the checkout he turned the bag upside down and dumped the contents on the counter. There lay an assortment of old Craftsman tools, some broken and all well-worn from use. He told the clerk he wanted to turn them in for new ones. To my surprise, the clerk replaced them all at no charge to the customer. Sears had guaranteed all Craftsman tools, and replaced them if they broke or were so worn they were no longer usable. They were so confident of the quality of their tools that they were willing to replace them.

God's guarantee tops that one! He replaces our flawed, sinful life with a brand new one that will never have to be replaced again. Even when we're nicked, scarred, and broken because of our sinfulness, God covers us with the salve of forgiveness. We don't have to go back and ask for another new life because the new one he gave us will last for all eternity. That guarantee gives me complete peace and confidence.

Lord, thank you for replacing my flawed, broken life with a new one guaranteed for eternity.

February 3

Piano lessons

"But if you look carefully into the perfect law that sets you free, and if you do what it says and don't forget what you heard, then God will bless you for doing it."

James 1:25 (NLT)

I took piano lessons for three years when I was in grade school. During that time I learned to read music and managed to play some fairly advanced pieces by the time I finished, but I was by no means a pianist. I memorized two or three songs but then other interests became more important. I did manage to master a few popular pieces but I had the most fun with chopsticks, learning to build on the original tune. A couple of times my friend Susan and I played a chopsticks duet on her piano and it sounded better when we played it together.

Sometimes what we do in our Christian walk may feel like we're just playing chopsticks. On our own it will be nothing, but with God offering his accompaniment, our witness and work becomes a melody of beauty reflecting his glory. He is pleased with it and applauds our efforts when we include him. If we allow him to use us, our work will never be boring or mediocre and will turn out to be a masterpiece.

Father, walk with me through my work and witness so it resonates with the richness of your love.

February 4

Maintaining your house

"When an evil spirit leaves a person, it goes into the desert, searching for rest. But when it finds none, it will say, "I will return to the person I came from." So it returns and finds that its former home is all swept and in order. Then the spirit finds seven other spirits more evil than itself and they all enter the person and live there. And so that person is worse off than before."

Luke 11:24-26 (NLT)

After Jack and I were married, I sold my house in Clarksville. I had always worked hard to keep it up and looking nice but once I sold it the house fell into disrepair. The people who bought it didn't seem to care about its appearance and it eventually went into foreclosure in a neighborhood that was deteriorating.

When we become a Christian, God cleans us up and we become a new person. However like keeping up a house, we have a responsibility to keep our hearts and minds clean, maintaining our souls with God's Word, for if we don't we'll soon slip back into old habits and ways of thinking. The Bible is our instruction manual on how to take care of every corner of this new home we're in.

We're to fill this new home with God's Spirit so there's no room for anything that's out of his will. Throw away those worries that have piled up in the corner of your heart. Sweep out any greed and discontent that clutter your mind. Polish up the window of your soul so you can see your Lord more clearly. Then your home will have a curb appeal that draws others who are searching for a new home.

Father, I want to display true Christian love and values so others will be drawn to you.

February 5

Air compressor

"I pray that from his glorious, unlimited resources he will empower you with inner strength through his Spirit. Then Christ will make his home in your hearts as you trust in him. Your roots will grow down into God's love and keep you strong."

Ephesians 3:16-17 (NLT)

Jack keeps an air compressor in the garage so he can pump up his bicycle tires when they're deflated. On a few occasions he had to pump up one of the trailer tires. I've learned that driving on a tire that is too low in pressure causes premature wear and can be risky as well. Consequently, we never pull our fifth wheel anywhere without everything he might need in the event we have tire problems

There are times we become deflated spiritually. Even when we think we're trusting God and are doing our best to walk in faith, someone may say or do something that rattles us or pulls us down. Watching and hearing too much negative news can create a slow leak in our trust, causing us to lose the quiet peace we long to have.

The Holy Spirit becomes like an air compressor to our soul, refilling us and restoring the peace we feel we've lost. He gives us what we need to withstand the temptation to worry, become prideful, and give in to those distractions that undermine our trust.

Holy Spirit, fill my empty spiritual tank with your guidance and power.

February 6

Reservations

"...Only those whose names are written in the Lamb's Book of Life will get in."

Revelation 21:27 (MSG)

A few months after my husband's death in 1983, my daughter, grandson, one of my sons and I drove from Southern Indiana to Florida. What I hadn't taken into consideration was spring break. I didn't make reservations ahead so when we stopped in Atlanta around dinner time, no rooms were available. Fortunately the motel was gracious enough to locate a room for us in Macon, but it would be another three hours before we were able to check in and relax. It was a very long day.

When we, as believers, finally arrive at our destination in heaven, we won't have to be concerned about our reservation. The moment we accept Christ as our Savior, our names are recorded in the Lamb's Book of Life. God is preparing a place for us and it'll be ready when we arrive.

He has an unlimited supply of rooms still available. We should be inviting others to join us. They won't find anyplace on this earth that will measure up to the mansions that will be prepared for them in heaven.

Father, thank you for your faithful promises which never fail.

February 7

Unused gifts

"Don't cherish exaggerated ideas of yourself or your importance, but try to have a sane estimate of your capabilities by the light of the faith that God has given to you all. For just as you have many members in one physical body and those members differ in their functions, so we, though many in number, compose one body in Christ and are all members of one another. Through the grace of God we have different gifts."

Romans 12:4-6 (Phillips)

In 1955 my husband and I visited his granny in Prestonsburg, KY. As she was showing me around her house, she pointed out several sets of towels and linens she had received as gifts. They were still in the gift boxes and had never been used. She'd had them for several years and was saving them for a special occasion. I had an uncle who did the same thing with shirts and ties that he had been given. They were all neatly stored in their boxes, also waiting to be used. Both my uncle and my husband's granny were still holding on to their gifts when they died, never enjoying what someone had purchased for them.

Each one of us has been given gifts from our Lord that we call talents. Our gifts are specifically chosen to fit us. We have the responsibility of discovering and using the gifts he has given us, for they were given to us for a reason. Our gift may allow us to reach one person in a way no one else could. Don't let your gift waste away on the shelf like Granny and my uncle did. How tragic it would be if there were people you didn't help, souls who never heard the gospel, or songs that were never sung because of your unused gifts.

Giving Father, help me remember that everything I have is a gift from you.

February 8

Rehearsals

"Can all of your worries add one single moment to your life? So don't worry about tomorrow, for tomorrow will bring its own worries. Today's trouble is enough for today."

Matthew 6:27, 34 (NLT)

"Give all your worries and cares to God, for he cares about you."

I Peter 5:7 (NLT)

For many years I sang with the choir at my church in Clarksville. One Easter we put on a program with the choir playing the parts of people who were involved in the last week before the crucifixion. It seemed like we had endless rehearsals, but our director wanted everything to be as close to perfect as possible. Going over and over the parts insured that they would be firmly planted in our memory.

Sometimes though, rehearsing isn't good. If I've had a bad day, or have a fear about possible news, I tend to replay those concerns over and over again in my mind, wasting time and energy trying to figure out how they can be fixed. As a rule I'm not a worrier, for I've learned worry has never changed anything. However, when I'm tired or stressed the problems seem bigger than they actually are and I begin focusing on them instead of God's faithfulness. As a result, they become firmly entrenched in my mind like the music I rehearsed.

Lord, help me to free my mind from nagging concerns and worries that I can't do anything about so I can rest in the peace that you alone can give.

February 9

On second thought

"He said, 'Come ahead.' Jumping out of the boat, Peter walked on the water to Jesus. But when he looked down at the waves churning beneath his feet, he lost his nerve and started to sink. He cried, 'Master, save me!'"

Matthew 14:29-30 (MSG)

There have been times that I've had an urge to try something different, maybe "out of my comfort zone" so to speak. Occasionally it would be an impulse decision; then, "on second thought," I would be afraid or unsure of myself and would abandon the idea. If the choice was a worldly one, it needed careful consideration because the consequences could outweigh the benefits. But if the Lord was calling me for a reason, I needed to follow his leading.

Two or three years ago, I was approached about writing something for a booklet that our church was preparing for the women. At first I was enthused about being asked, then a wave of insecurity swept over me and "on second thought" I declined. At the time, I had no confidence in my ability to write anything that the women would want to read. Thankfully, God gave me another opportunity to explore this gift.

When Peter climbed out of the boat, he walked on the water. Only when he "gave it a second thought" did he begin to sink. If God plants a desire in your heart to serve him in a new way, pray about it. If you still have that longing, DON'T give it a 'second thought'. DO IT and God will guide you and reward your efforts.

Lord, forgive me when I overthink the opportunities you offer me and hesitate in fear. Help me to move forward in faith and trust you for the results.

February 10

Moving again

"I'm asking God for one thing, only one thing: to live with him in His house, my whole life long. I'll contemplate his beauty; I'll study at His feet."

Psalm 27:4-5 (MSG)

When I'm in the mood to reminisce, I think about all the times I've moved in my life. As I calculate it, I've lived in 25 different homes over the years, and have memories of all but the one we lived in when I was a baby. Most of the memories are wonderful, but a few are painful. At the time, I never thought about the moves a lot. We just dealt with it and settled in to our next house, trying to make it home.

Occasionally Jack and I discuss what we'll do when we no longer feel like keeping up our property, but we're both confident that God will lead us at that point in our life. More often, though, I dream about the permanent home that's waiting for me when my journey on earth is finished. Then I'll never have to move again. Maybe it will never have to be dusted or swept and perhaps the grass won't need to be cut or leaves raked, but if I do have those responsibilities, my new body will be more than able to do whatever needs to be done. Won't that be amazing and wonderful?

Jesus, my Savior, I am eternally grateful for the promise that I will live with you for eternity.

February 11

Music idols

"Shout for joy to the Lord, all the earth. Worship the Lord with gladness; come before him with joyful songs."

Psalm 100:1, 2 (NIV)

Fifty years ago one of the most widely acclaimed groups in our pop music culture made their first appearance in the United States. When Ed Sullivan introduced them. they were greeted by hordes of screaming fans; from that day forward they were worshipped by adoring followers who couldn't get enough of them. The Beatles followed in the footsteps of two other singers who also stirred up crowds of fans who screamed and cried in all their excitement, reaching out to touch them and treasuring any souvenir they could get from their idols. No other groups or singers have since drawn the same kind of adulation as did Frank Sinatra, Elvis Presley and the Beatles.

We rarely see that type of emotion displayed when we're singing and worshipping our Lord and Savior. King David had moments when he sang and danced for joy in his worship. Occasionally I am so moved by the words of a song that I'll raise my hand and I will experience a joy seeking to be released. I love that feeling - almost a tingling inside. God designed us so we would have a need to express our worship of him.

When we finally get to heaven, we will worship without restraint. We won't be concerned about offending anyone because all of his children will be worshipping in their own way.

Father, thank you for giving us the music that enables us to fully express joy in our worship.

February 12

Playing house

"You will show me the way of life, granting me the joy of your presence and the pleasure of living with you forever."

Psalm 16:11 (NLT)

Jack often tells people about playing house with me when we were six years old. He especially enjoys mentioning the grass soup and mud pies that I would fix him. By the time we decided to get serious and play house again in 1998, I had honed my cooking skills, so he didn't have to endure my childhood menu. Through many years of preparing meals for a family of five, I had become a fairly good cook and I enjoyed trying foods that were out-of-the-ordinary and experimenting with new recipes. Never being satisfied with "ordinary", I would add spices to create something different and more flavorful.

It is tempting to be content with having a mundane, unexciting faith journey. Our Savior wants our walk with him to be fresh and fulfilling. He challenges us to spice it up by allowing him to open up new and different ways of seeing him. He is our creator, but he is also as near as the tip of your finger, where he stands ready to take your hand and lead you on a spirit-filled walk of faith. That's what adds the spice to your journey. When I get up in the morning I want to say to him, "What are we doing today?" Then I'll wait for opportunities to be opened up to me. Don't let yourself be content with an ordinary, unexciting faith journey!

Father, thank you for opening up new paths for me to explore. Help me keep my faith journey fresh and exciting so that others will be inspired to believe in you and venture out on their own faith walk.

February 13

Visiting my dad

"In My Father's house are many mansions; if it were not so, I would have told you. I go to prepare a place for you. And if I go and prepare a place for you, I will come again and receive you to Myself; that where I am, there you may be also."

John 14:2-3 (NKJV)

When my brother and I traveled to Washington, D.C. in 1950 to see our dad, we were both excited about the destination because neither of us had ever been very far from home. But for me, the greatest thrill came from knowing I was going to see the father who had been absent from my life for seven years. Except for brief visits to Indiana once a year, he hadn't been part of our life. The trip was a huge occasion for me!

As much as we look forward to our home in heaven, the most thrilling part of that destination is that we will at last be with our Lord and Savior. I had a few pictures of my earthly father so I knew what he looked like. I don't have one of my Heavenly Father, but I know I will recognize him because he has told me all about himself in his Word. He'll embrace me and tell me how much he loves me. All I will be able to do is thank Him over and over again for his amazing love and gift of grace.

Loving Father, thank you for your unconditional love.

FEBRUARY

February 14

Valentine's Day

"See what great love the Father has lavished on us, that we should be called children of God! And that is what we are! The reason the world does not know us is that it did not know Him."

I John 3:1 (NKJV)

Valentine's Day is a special day, celebrated by couples in love, children and families that are close. But what about the lonely, and the grieving who have lost someone precious to them? What about the homeless, those imprisoned (real or in prisons of their own making) and those suffering from depression or mental illness? Do they ever feel loved? They may not have anyone to tell them how much they're loved or how special they are. There is someone who loves them more than they could ever imagine. Maybe they've forgotten about him or perhaps they've never met him, but his love could change their life.

Even when we're in the depths of despair or grief, God showers us with an unconditional love that's not based on how we look, what we've accomplished or even how we've behaved. He demonstrates his love every day, not just on Valentine's Day. All he wants from us is to receive him and believe that he died for us to show that unbelievable love. Our Lord's love will never leave us or fade. That is a real valentine gift!

Lord, teach me to recognize opportunities you place in my path. Help me have courage to tell lonely and lost people that God can fill their empty hearts with love and bring comfort and peace to their soul.

February 15

Lost and found

"Count on it -- there's more joy in heaven over one sinner's rescued life than over the ninety-nine good people in no need of rescue."

Luke 15:10 (MSG)

We had decided to visit the mall during an annual evening sale. Tyler, who was around four years old, often went with me when I shopped. On this occasion I had him carry an inflated balloon so I could see where he was in case we were separated. As a rule he stayed right with me, but this time he wandered out of my sight. While we were in one of the department stores I noticed he had wandered away. I hurried to the door than opened into the mall in case he went that direction, but no Tyler! I was starting to panic when I heard an announcement on the intercom about a little tow-headed boy that had lost his mamaw. He was safe in the cosmetic department, being cared for by one of the clerks; I was filled with relief and joy when I saw him.

Jesus told the parable of the shepherd who left the ninety-nine in the wilderness and went to search for the one that was lost. When the lost sheep was found, he celebrated with great joy. How joyful God feels when one of his lost children is found and brought into his kingdom of grace. There is a celebration in heaven, for all of his children are precious to Him and he's not willing that any should perish.

Lord, help me to point those who are lost to your safe haven. Let me be an instrument of light that you can use in a dark and dying world.

February 16

Friends

"O Lord, you have examined my heart and know everything about me. Search me, O God, and know my heart; test me and know my anxious thoughts."

Psalm 139:1, 23 (NLT)

"I want to know Christ and experience the mighty power that raised him from the dead. I want to suffer in his death, so that one way or another I will experience the resurrection from the dead!"

Philippians 3:10-11 (NLT)

Over the years I've made many friends, some of whom I grew to love as though they were family. Being a friend involves getting to know each other on a deep, personal level. You know true friends will not be judgmental about you. They'll often be a sounding board and are there for you when you need them. They grieve when you face a loss and rejoice when you have victory. These friendships develop because time is spent together, sharing and listening to each other. I am also acquainted with a lot of people and a list of my "acquaintances" could go into the hundreds. These are the people that you know socially, or casually. You converse with them in a general way but never go deep enough to know them in a personal way.

Our Lord desires a deep personal relationship with us. He already knows us intimately, but often we haven't made the effort to know him. He longs to be more than a casual acquaintance. We were created to share with him the same kind of trust and fellowship that we have with our closest friend. It takes time spent in prayer and meditation to reach the point where we feel this kind of closeness with our Lord.

Father, thank you for the gift of friends.

February 17

What I am today

"Then Moses said to God, 'Indeed, when I come to the children of Israel, and say to them, "The God of your fathers has sent me to you", and they say to me, "What is His name?" what shall I say to them?' And God said to Moses, 'I AM WHO I AM.' And He said, 'Thus you shall say to the children of Israel, "I AM" has sent me to you.'"

Exodus 3:13-14 (NKJV)

When we say "I am", we usually follow it with a description of how we are in that moment. What "I am" today reflects my mood and may change from day to day. As I write this today, "I am" content, ready to have a normal day. Before we left home in December for our trip to Florida I would have said, "I am so stressed!" Some days I am excited, some days I am anxious; other days I am frustrated or upset. My moods don't change dramatically, but they are influenced by what is going on around me. Therefore, what "I am" only defines me at that moment.

God doesn't change from one day to the next. He remains the same today, tomorrow and forever. We can depend on him to be constant, the same today as he was in the days of Moses. That's why he said to Moses: "Tell them 'I AM'" when Moses asked God how he should answer the children of Israel if they asked Moses who sent him. "I AM" is present tense now just as it was present tense for Moses. "I AM" is eternal and never changes!

Lord, in a world that's always changing, thank you for being I AM.

February 18

Snuggling my babies

"He tends his flock like a shepherd; he gathers the lambs in his arms and carries them close to his heart; he gently leads them who have young."

Isaiah 40:11 (NIV)

When our babies were small, my favorite place to carry them was snuggled in my arms close to my heart. I loved feeling the warmth of their body and hearing the soft breathing. I knew they were relying completely on me to meet all their needs. I was their protector and sustainer. Even when they were crying, holding them close and speaking softly to them seemed to calm them. As a mother, I wanted my babies to know they were always safe and loved. Holding them near my heart established a bond that continued to grow over the years.

Our Lord carries us close to his heart just as a mother does. His greatest desire is for us to feel his love and care. He reassures us and soothes our hearts when we're hurting and holds us near when we're afraid. He calls out gently when we wander away and guides us back to the safety of his forgiving arms.

I may occasionally lose sight of the comfort and love he has for me, but I know he is always there for me, just as I was for my babies.

Thank you Father for the comfort you offer me that only a father can give.

February 19

Dating Jack

"But our citizenship is in heaven. And we eagerly await a Savior from there, the Lord Jesus Christ."

Philippians 3:20 (NIV)

At the time Jack and I began dating, he was living about 200 miles away so we didn't get to see each other very often. When he would come though, I would clean the house and then sit by the window to watch for him. I was excited about his visit but I didn't want to appear overly anxious, so I would wait discreetly behind a curtain.

Waiting for special guests is exciting, but knowing our Lord will be coming for us someday should fill us with joyful anticipation. Now that I'm older and realize that time is drawing closer, I think about it more often. However, I'm not going to hide myself behind the curtain like I did with Jack. I'll be at the door eager to show him how glad I am to see him. I want Jesus to know how much I love him and how my heart is filled with joy at his arrival. Since I don't know when that time will be, I'm working on keeping my spiritual house in order.

Lord, I am so grateful that you sent Jack into my life. I am amazed that you had this planned even when we were children.

February 20

Follow-up surveys

"The Kingdom of God is not a matter of what we eat or drink, but of living a life of goodness and peace and joy in the Holy Spirit. So then, let us aim for harmony in the church and try to build each other up."

Romans 14:17, 19 (NLT)

When we've had a service call for a repair on an appliance, the company often calls with a follow-up survey on the experience we had with the repairman. I'll be asked a series of questions on how I rate different aspects of the repairman's job and the quality of his work. When they say "on a scale of 1-10, did he address the problem to your satisfaction?" I find it difficult to answer in a way that's fair to the repairman and yet is completely honest about my opinion.

It's even harder for me to rate a job I think I have to do. On a scale of 1-10, how important is it really? It's even more difficult to rate how well I did. When the children were growing up, I always felt like the house had to be cleaned on Friday and I rarely let anything interfere with that routine. How much valuable time with my children was sacrificed because I was focused on a clean house? Some of the things that I do should only rate a 2 or 3 and really aren't important at all. However, when I feel led by God to serve him, that needs a rating of 9 or 10. It's tempting to do the easy, less important things first and then use the excuse, "I don't have enough time" to get out of "putting first things first."

Lord, help me to keep you at the center of my being, no matter how much trivial, unimportant stuff tries to crowd you out. My desire is to walk with you every moment of my day.

February 21

I'm not a morning person

"But each day the Lord pours his unfailing love upon me, and through each night I sing his songs, praying to God who gives me life."

Psalm 42:8 (NLT)

I'm not a morning person! Jack tells everyone that it takes me all morning to come alive after I get up. I enjoy the daylight hours but I am not "Miss Susie Sunshine" when I first get up; Jack, however, is up at the crack of dawn raring to go. Somehow we've managed to function well in spite of this difference.

I do love the nights when we have time to kick back and relax. God knew we would need the darkness of night to shut out the distractions that hold our attention. The night gives me an opportunity to have an uninterrupted conversation with my Lord. I'm thankful for the darkness that offers a restful night of sleep.

God created the sun, moon and stars. In the daytime you see his handiwork and that is awesome, but at night you can look into the depths of space and see its vastness. There's something peaceful about seeing the moon and stars, knowing that God is up there beyond what is visible to our eyes; we only see the edge of it.

In the beginning God separated the day from night and put the sun, moon and stars there to light them - and he said it was good. I am thankful he provided both of them.

Father, thank you for mornings and nights, for both of them bring blessings every day.

February 22

A mother's love

"But from everlasting to everlasting the Lord's love is with those who fear him, and his righteousness with their children's children---."

Psalm 103:17 (NIV)

There's no way to measure the depth of love a mother has for her child. Her love begins the moment she realizes she is going to bear a child and that love takes a giant leap the minute she lays eyes on her baby. It doesn't matter if you bore the child or adopted; the love is immediate and boundless. We have a built in sensor that locks in on our children and it doesn't shut off when your child grows up and leaves home. We nurture, protect and guide our children, trying to meet their every need.

As adults, our children have times when they'll face hurts, disappointments and illnesses and we can't do anything to change it. Our instinct tells us we need to share their burden. Even when we can't help them, we're often consumed with worry and concern.

We've learned how important it is to place ourselves in God's care, but it's more difficult to bring our children into his safekeeping and leave them there. As moms, we think nobody can love them as much as we do, but God loves our children more than we could ever imagine. We need to lift our children up to God daily in our prayers and then trust him to work in their lives.

You are a Father who knows exactly what each child needs. Thank you for mothers who love their children with love that only you understand. Watch over the children that don't receive that kind of love.

February 23

Boiled peanuts

"Take everything the Master has set out for you, well-made weapons of the best material, and put them to good use, so you will be able to stand up to everything the Devil throws your way. This is no afternoon athletic contest that we'll walk away and forget about in a couple of hours. This is for keeps, a life-or-death fight to the finish against the Devil and all his angels."

Ephesians 6:10-12 (MSG)

My dad liked boiled peanuts which came in a can and looked wet. I never could bring myself to try one. I'd rather have them coated with chocolate. The boiled ones always looked as though someone sucked the chocolate coating off and, to me at least, the coating was the best part. However, the chocolate on the outside is full of empty calories.

Satan comes along to tempt us with things which seem to be attractive and innocent. But what he offers is disguised so you only see the part that looks good. In fact, when we're taken in by his bait, we find it leaves a bitter, lingering aftertaste. Like the chocolate coating on a peanut, his bait is coated with empty promises. If we seek our Lord's guidance we'll be able to recognize and avoid Satan's traps.

This is a daily war with Satan whose bait comes in many forms. It may be lust, greed and always wanting more, but it also comes in the form of worry, thinking you're too busy to study God's Word, not taking time to pray, missing worship or any other activity that keep you from spending time with God.

Lord, give me wisdom and discernment today so I won't be drawn into the ways of the world.

FEBRUARY

February 24

Chloe's locked in

"For the law of the Spirit of life in Christ Jesus has made me free from the law of sin and death."

Romans 8:2 (NKJV)

Every summer my son Steve and his family come for a visit from Pittsburgh. They stay in the front bedroom because it has its own bath. Occasionally when the weather is humid the bathroom door sticks making it difficult to open it from the inside. A few years ago, when their children Jessie, Brooke and Chloe were about 8, 11 and 13, respectively, we were sitting in the family room visiting one evening when we heard a persistent knocking. We thought someone was at the front door, so Jessie ran to see who it was. In a few minutes she returned with Chloe, who had been politely knocking on the bathroom door, unable to get out without help.

Jesus, our Savior, came to free us from the locked door of our sins. On our own we would have been imprisoned in those sins for all eternity, but his saving grace opened the door to forgiveness and freed us to join his family. However, we have to open the door and invite him in.

Loving Father, I thank you for knocking on the door of my heart.

February 25

Hitting the delete button

"You were dead because of your sins and because your sinful nature was not yet cut away. Then God made you alive with Christ, for he forgave all our sins."

Colossians 2:13 (NLT)

I do a lot of work on the computer. When I'm finished with the project or I don't need it anymore, I'll hit the delete button. It's out of my sight which makes me think it's gone. However, what I thought I deleted is still stored in the hard drive.

My memory is like that. Down in the corners and crevices of my memory, all of my past experiences lay waiting for a chance to resurface. I can convince myself that I've forgotten mistakes and disappointments from the past, then all of the sudden they pop up on the screen of my mind and I have to hit the delete button again, hoping they'll be gone for good this time.

I'm so thankful that God only had to delete my sins once - then they're gone completely. If God had been using a computer when I came to him for forgiveness, the screen would have been full of my offenses. Then the moment I said, "I believe" and accepted his grace, he would have hit the delete button and the screen would be white as snow. I would have worried that they were still stored in that computer somewhere. But, my sins aren't buried in a computer. They are gone permanently! I will forever praise God for his amazing grace!

Father, thank you that I can now stand in your presence knowing that my Savior's blood washed me clean.

February 26

Crumbling marriage

"The Lord is good. A strong refuge when trouble comes. He is close to those who trust in him."

Nahum 1:7 (NLT)

There was a period of time while my children were young, when problems began to crack the foundation of our marriage. I felt like I was in a pit of quicksand and no one could help me. It was one of the loneliest, most helpless times I've ever faced in my life. I knew I needed to reach out to God, but I didn't know how. What I didn't realize was - God was there anyway, and he led me through a long dark tunnel until we reached the solid ground on the other side of Heartache Valley.

We can become so overwhelmed with the problems and heartaches we're facing that we fail to feel God's presence. He is always there, gently moving us forward until we're able to stand firm in our faith again. He wants us to believe in his presence even when we can't feel it. Friends can encourage you and maybe even walk with you but no one can offer you what your Lord can! All we need to do is whisper his name and his gentle touch lifts us up and gives us comfort. The soothing balm of his love eases our pain and restores our peace, leading us back to solid ground...

Father, I will never be able to thank you enough for carrying me through the valley of hurt and fear I faced.

February 27

Blessings #1

"The Lord will give strength to His people; the Lord will bless His people with peace."

Psalm 29:11 (NKJV)

I used to equate blessings with a good job, a nice home, having my health and enough money to do extra things. It didn't occur to me that I knew strong, committed Christians who didn't seem to be "blessed" with what I considered important. Their faith and love for the Lord was built on more than counting their "material blessings." I am thankful for what we have but I'm not sure I should consider them blessings. Even nonbelievers have good things happen to them. The Bible tells us that the sun shines on the righteous as well as the unrighteousness.

The suffering we endure during our trials produces the kind of blessing that cannot be measured by the world. Nonbelievers don't understand peace, for they cannot attain it. They can't comprehend hope, for they see nothing beyond this life. They never get to experience the kind of love our Savior has bestowed on us. They could have all of these and more, but they have chosen to chase after what the world offers.

The real blessings we have are internal, provided abundantly through the Holy Spirit. They won't fade or disappear like the ones the world offers. The trials we endure produce the kind of blessings that will lift us into a deeper, more personal relationship with our Lord and Savior.

Father, you always know just what I need and you provide it at just the right time.

February 28

In a fog

"In view of all this, make every effort to respond to God's promises. Supplement your faith with a generous provision of moral excellence, and moral excellence with knowledge, and knowledge with self-control, and self-control with patient endurance, and patient endurance with godliness, and godliness with brotherly affection, and brotherly affection with love for everyone."

II Peter 1:5-7, 9 (NLT)

Even in "sunny Florida" it can become foggy; occasionally that fog develops without warning. Often drivers are not prepared and drive into dangerous conditions before they realize it. The fog has been known to become so thick that drivers are unable to see the tail lights in front of them until it's too late, which has resulted in major pile ups, especially when speed is involved. When Jack sees fog developing, he slows down, but many don't.

In our Christian walk, we are tempted to be distracted by the world, caught up in what we see on TV, what we read in the paper, and what our friends and neighbors are saying. As a result we may become critical, resentful and occasionally even angry over things we can't control. We can even be drawn back into old sins for which we had been forgiven. When these things happen to us, we begin traveling our faith journey in a fog, in danger of stumbling or falling. If we see traces of fog in our walk, we need to reach out and grab the hand of our Lord so he can guide us back to a clear path.

Lord, I trust you even when I can't see the road ahead. You are my guide and protector.

February 29

Too much on my plate

"Then Jesus said, 'Come to me all of you who are weary and carry heavy burdens, and I will give you rest. Take my yoke upon you. Let me teach you, because I am humble and gentle at heart, and you will find rest for your souls. For my yoke is easy to bear, and the burden I give you is light.'"

Matthew 11:28- 30 (NLT)

"I can't believe I did that!" I exclaimed as I looked in dismay at the can of freshly opened peas I had just dumped into the garbage. It had been a busy day, and my mind was swirling with all that still needed to be done. Creamed peas had been on the menu for supper and now I would have to find another vegetable to serve. It seemed as though time was becoming an elusive element in my daily life as I struggled to keep up and my mind wasn't always on what I was doing.

"I've got a lot on my plate" is the phrase we use when we feel overwhelmed by circumstances and responsibilities. Jesus has offered us help when we are stressed and running on empty. He's not asking you to share *his* burden; he's telling you he will lighten *yours* and give you true rest.

We think we have to carry the whole load ourselves and we neglect to go to him before we start our day. When the children were still at home, I felt responsible for meeting their every need. Usually I was doing it without going to my Lord for guidance and strength for the day. How much more peaceful our days would be if we just gave them to God in the first place.

God, you created time. When my days are too full, help me pause for a moment so I'll recognize your blessing in the smile of a friend or the burst of sunshine through the clouds.

March

*He leads me beside
the still waters*

*Father, in your care my waters
are stilled, for you bring
calmness and serenity
to my life.*

March 1

I'll do it myself

"Cast your cares on The Lord and he will sustain you; he will never let the righteous be shaken."

Psalm 55:22 (NIV)

When we return home from an RV trip, Jack always tells me to pile the things that need to be unloaded on the bed and by the door, and he will carry them in later. Then he usually has to deal with cutting grass, picking up sticks or raking leaves. Since I want it done now, I'll start carrying it in. By the time I finish, I'm exhausted. On a couple of occasions, because I wasn't willing to wait, I developed muscle spasms in my back from the lifting and carrying. I pay a price for not being patient and waiting for Jack's help.

When we're carrying a burden too big for us to handle, our Lord stands ready to pick it up for us. He offers to carry it, but if you're like me, you'll pick it back up when you feel as though he isn't responding fast enough. Then we wonder why we struggle with worry and stress.

It is hard to put that big bundle of my "stuff" at his feet and walk away from it. I keep looking back to see if it's still there. I'm a slow learner but I'm working on it.

Lord Jesus, you told me you would take my burden, but sometimes I'm too stubborn to relinquish it. Help me learn to rest in your promise.

MARCH

March 2

Long-lost cousins

"This is the day that the Lord has made. We will rejoice and be glad in it."

Psalm 118:24 (NLT)

As we walked through the front door, a feeling of excitement permeated the air. Scattered around the room were the cousins I had longed to know for nearly half a century. I'd heard about them, seen a few pictures and had contact with one of them, but because of broken family ties long ago, I had never been offered the opportunity to know them as family.

Last year, through the vast resources of Facebook, I was able to track down one of them, and the news spread quickly through their family. At that point we began trying to schedule a time when we could meet together. We were finally able to set a date. Jack and I had decided to "seize the moment," for we are not promised tomorrow and, as the song goes, "we may never pass this way again." I am so grateful that God gave me the opportunity. There were six cousins, all who had their own story. As we shared information and memories, a bond developed among us that cannot be broken. We shared a Thanksgiving meal on a Saturday (in March) but it was appropriate for the occasion. The greatest blessing was learning that we shared a love for our Heavenly Father. It's amazing - that weekend my family grew by eleven people and I praise God for all of it!

God, you never cease to amaze me with the joyful blessing you bring to me. Thank you for the amazing encounter with cousins who have enriched my life beyond description.

March 3
Florida temperatures

"He only is my rock and my salvation; He is my defense; I shall not be greatly moved..."

Psalm 62:2 (NKJV)

"Unless your faith is firm, I cannot make you stand firm."

Isaiah 7:9 (NLT)

Usually winters in Florida will be mild with an occasional cold snap. However in 2010 the temperature remained low for an extended length of time, dipping into the mid 20's for several nights in a row. We stay in an area known as "The Strawberry Capital of the World." Farmers were spraying water on their crops at night to keep them from freezing. As a result, the water table in that area was drastically reduced and in a very short time sinkholes began to develop. A few properties developed sinkholes which swallowed up their yards or claimed part of a house. Many neighborhoods were considered unsafe because the ground is sandy and porous, with no bedrock beneath.

When we become a Christian we have a solid rock to build our faith on. If we cave in to fear and doubt, our foundation is weakened and we run the risk of falling into a sinkhole of despair and hopelessness. The good news is, we built our faith on a foundation that will never fail - we must continue to build on it until we can stand strong.

Father, thank you for providing a solid foundation for my walk with you.

MARCH

March 4

Telephones

"He calls his own sheep by name and leads them out. When he gets them all out, he leads them and they follow because they are familiar with his voice. They won't follow a stranger's voice but will scatter because they aren't used to it."

John 10:3-5 (MSG)

I will forever be grateful that Alexander Graham Bell invented the telephone. I love this tool which allows me to have conversations with friends and family when we can't be together. Every week I'll get calls from one and sometimes all of my children. They don't have to identify themselves for, when I hear their voices, I recognize them immediately. I look forward to their calls and the opportunity to share news with each of them.

God longs for times of conversation with us. He recognizes our voice when we call out to him. We don't have to say, "Hi God, this is 'so-and-so,'" for the moment our mind begins to focus on him, he knows who is there.

I'm learning to recognize his Spirit stirring in me, directing me in how I should walk and act. There is no greater blessing offered to us than having a Father like that. He knows our voice, our heart, and he loves us beyond measure, even when we're not listening to him.

Gracious Father, thank you for being there when I call out to you. Remind me to come to you for your wise counsel so I don't act on impulse.

March 5

A crushed rose

"I'm not saying that I have this all together, that I have it made. But I am well on my way, reaching out for Christ, who has so wondrously reached out for me. Friends, don't get me wrong. By no means do I count myself an expert in all of this, but I've got my eye on the goal, where God is beckoning us onward – to Jesus. I'm off and running and I'm not turning back."

Philippians 3:13-14 (MSG)

It has been said that a crushed rose produces the most fragrance. Some of the most dynamic Christians I know are the ones who have overcome the most heartache in their lives. The brokenness they have experienced produced a spirit that demonstrates God's love and encourages others.

Having faced many major trials of my own, I have learned to "get over it." Otherwise I would have been mired down in the muck of anger and bitterness. There were a few times I stopped to linger in that pit, but I found it a very uncomfortable place to be. An unforgiving spirit becomes a ball and chain locked onto your heart. When you learn how to forgive, that weight you're carrying will fall away and you are free again.

We are capable of overcoming our anger and we can forgive through the power of the Holy Spirit. When we have victory, we become a sweet fragrance to God.

Faithful Father, thank you for being with me through my trials. Even though I sometimes felt overwhelmed, you were always there to help me navigate the turbulent waves of doubt and insecurity. Let my victories bring glory to you.

March 6

I forgot something

"But the Holy Spirit produces this kind of fruit in our lives: love, joy, peace, patience, kindness, goodness, faithfulness, gentleness and self-control. There is no law against these things."

Galatians 5:22 (NLT)

Each time Jack and I get ready to leave on a trip or even for the day, I'll try to lay everything I think we may need on the kitchen table or counter where I'll be sure to see it. Sometimes I'll make a list of the things and check them off as we load them. There have been occasions, however, when we'll get on the road and one of us will remember something we forgot. If it's not that important we'll go on without it, but it can cause frustration and delays.

There are even more important things we need to take with us anytime we go out the door. We have the fruits of the Spirit which reflect our walk with The Lord. If we encounter an aggressive driver who cuts us off, we need to display SELF-CONTROL. We can show KINDNESS toward the homeless man on the corner asking for help. We can extend LOVE by offering to help load groceries in the car for a young mother with small children. Letting someone with fewer items go before you in the checkout lane displays GOODNESS. Showing PATIENCE with a waitress who gets your order wrong is another way.

I'm trying to make a mental list of these fruits so I don't forget any of them at home or when I go out the door. They need to be part of my life all day - every day.

Father of all gifts, teach me to embrace the gifts of the spirit so they become a natural part of who I am.

March 7

Feeling the music

"My heart is confident in you, O God; no wonder I can sing your praises with all my heart!"

Psalm 108:1 (NLT)

"Shout joyfully to the Lord, all the earth; break forth in song, rejoice, and sing praises."

Psalm 98:4 (NKJV)

Some of the most spiritually moving elements of worship are the music and hymns we sing. If it's a song with a beat, I am unable to stand still for I feel the rhythm in my innermost being and I have to move. Even when I'm sitting, I find myself tapping my feet and bobbing my head. The music lifts my soul to a higher level of joy. God planned for music to be part of our worship.

As a youth, David played the harp in the fields while he tended the sheep. His music reflected his deepest emotional feelings and gave him strength, comfort and joy during his long, lonely hours. The words he penned in the psalms reflect every type of feeling we experience and are the source for many of our songs today.

Music comforts the grieving, soothes the troubled soul, gives expression to love and fills the worshipper with joy and hope. I can study God's Word without music but I cannot worship fully without it.

God of music, help me recognize your voice in the melody of a dirge as well as songs of joy. Draw me closer to you through each note.

March 8

Spring cleaning

"In a wealthy home some utensils are made of gold and silver, and some are made of wood and clay. The expensive utensils are used for special occasions, and the cheap ones are for everyday use. If you keep yourselves pure, you will be a special utensil for honorable use. Your life will be clean and you will be ready for the Master to use you for every good work."

II Timothy 2:20-21 (NLT)

One of my favorite memories of childhood is helping Grandma with spring cleaning. After heating with a coal furnace all winter, her house needed freshening up. Rugs were carried out, hung on the clothes line and beaten with a big wire paddle. Lace curtains were washed and stretched onto a wooden frame to dry. Wool clothes were hung on the clothes line to air out. My favorite part was cleaning the wallpaper with a product similar to play dough. We would start at the top and work our way down the wall. It was exciting to see clean paper reappear.

Our hearts and minds need a good clean-up now and then as well. We should toss out the negative thoughts and clean up our attitudes, for they pick up dirt and grime of worldly views. We need to rinse away our doubts and worries by allowing the Holy Spirit to strengthen and renew our faith. Let all that keeps you from a joyful walk with your Savior be tossed in the trash and flushed down the drain as you give yourself a good spring soul-cleaning.

Lord, I long to come before you, uncontaminated with anger, doubt, greed or anything else that prevents our fellowship. Help me rid myself of thoughts or actions that are not in your will.

March 9

A pile of drapes

"Then I let it all out; I said, 'I'll make a clean breast of my failures to God.' Suddenly, the pressure was gone - my guilt dissolved, my sin disappeared."

Psalm 32:5 (MSG)

As I walked through the living room, I noticed the drapes lying in a pile on the floor by the picture window. When I questioned my children about it, Debbie who was six years old, said "Steve did it" So he was promptly disciplined. I found out later the culprit was Debbie who occasionally had trouble accepting responsibility for her actions. I learned to do more investigating before punishing any of them.

Some adults are quick to blame an unhappy childhood, a dysfunctional family environment or peer pressure for their poor decisions and criminal behavior. They don't want to take responsibility for how their life has turned out. The family we're raised in and the kind of values we learn while growing, do color our view of life, but each of us has to make our own choices. If our choice is to pattern our life after bad examples, we can only blame ourselves. We are responsible for our own decisions, good or bad.

Owning up to the mistakes we make is a sign of spiritual maturity. When we admit our failures we're able to overcome them and move on. The Holy Spirit can't change us until we recognize our weaknesses, seek his guidance and follow his leading. Taking ownership of our bad decisions isn't easy, but when we do, we've taken a huge step forward.

Lord, teach me to recognize and confess my sins and failures, for much of the time, I need a prod from your Holy Spirit.

March 10

In a race

"For we are God's masterpiece. He has created us anew in Christ Jesus, so we can do the good things he planned for us long ago."

Ephesians 2:10 (NLT)

We have two nephews and one grandson who have participated in races and marathons. I've never been in a race but I understand there's a lot of excitement and a big rush of adrenaline as they cross the finish line. All through their run they have one goal in mind and that is to complete the race. That involves pushing themselves to the limit so they'll give it their best effort.

In our faith walk, we are sometimes guilty of thinking salvation is equivalent to crossing the finish line. We have victory over our sins, but in reality our race has just begun. Resting on our salvation is like starting the race and then letting God pull you down your faith journey in a wagon. He's doing all the work and you're not giving anything of yourself on the way. You'll get to your destination but you'll have missed so many opportunities on the way. Our rewards come from using our gifts to further his kingdom.

We're given grace to start us on this race, equipped with the Holy Spirit and a generous gift of talent so we can serve our Lord. These works don't save us, but they're our part in the race we are running.

Father of hope, bathe me with perseverance for my life often seems to be on hold. Give me a glimpse of the finish line so I will continue my race.

March 11

New growth

"As long as the earth remains, there will be planting and harvest, cold and heat, summer and winter, day and night."

Genesis 8:22 (NLT)

By the time we return home from Florida in the spring the trees are adorned with new growth, grass is sprinkled with green, birds are chirping merrily and the flowering trees along the creek behind our house are arrayed in colors of pink and white. It's easy, though, to become so involved in getting the RV unloaded and the house in order that we miss what God has displayed as a "welcome home" gift. If we're not observant enough, the awesome sights and sounds of spring soon fade and we'll have missed this blessing.

What our loving Father does at the end of a long, harsh winter is give us a glimpse of the hope we have in eternity. He shows us the beauty of spring - newness unmatched by anything man could create. The changing seasons provide us with their own elements of unique splendor and God's unlimited blessings.

Let us not become so focused on what we have to do every day that we miss the opulent beauty of his creation. Look up from that path you're on and see his glory.

Father, thank you for the blessings that accompany the incomparable beauty of spring.

March 12

Pleas for help

"If you see your enemy hungry, go buy him lunch; if he's thirsty, bring him a drink. Your generosity will surprise him with goodness, and God will look after you."
Proverbs 25:21 (MSG)

For thirteen years I worked as a secretary at a small church in Louisville, Kentucky. My office faced the outside door and quite often the homeless and people living "on the edge" would come looking for help. A couple of them were regulars, always asking to see the pastor. Some requests were sincere and some were just to feed a habit or addiction, but most had a rehearsed approach. I learned pretty quickly to field the requests and shield the minister from interruptions. It's easy to become skeptical of all pleas for help, for you don't know who you can believe.

On one occasion, a man came into the office just asking for enough money to buy a pack of cigarettes. He said "I know I shouldn't smoke but I just can't give it up." I appreciated his honesty and managed to come up with enough change to give him what he needed.

Since that time in my life, God has laid on my heart a need to respond when I'm approached for help. It's not my place to question how it will be used or if they deserve the help. Only God can judge their motive. My responsibility is to serve with open hands - not expecting anything in return. When we feel a tug of compassion, we should respond and let God handle the results.

God you are the provider of everything we need. Thank you for sending people when I needed help. Teach me to reach out willingly to others in need.

March 13

Wait 'til Daddy gets home

"See what great love the Father has lavished on us, that we should be called children of God! And that is what we are! The reason the world does not know us is that it did not know him."

I John 3:1 (NIV)

"Endure hardship as discipline; God is treating you as his children. For what children are not disciplined by their father?"

Hebrews 12:7 (NIV)

Occasionally my children gave me a hard time and my patience would be stretched to the breaking point. I would tell them, "Wait until your dad gets home!" However, my children and I both knew that was an empty threat. Mike could never bring himself to deal out punishment so I became the disciplinarian.

As a child, my perception of God as a father was more of a policeman who sat on a big chair, watching every move I made. I thought there was a set of rules I had to follow so I was obedient, not because I loved him and wanted to please him, but because of fear of the consequences of disobedience.

When we do stray out of God's will, he corrects us to steer us back just as our earthly fathers do, but he does it as a loving father not a harsh disciplinarian. He longs for us to be safely back under the shelter of his wings.

Merciful God, forgive me when I step out of your will.

March 14

Our wedding

"Delight yourself in the Lord, and He will give you the desires of your heart. Commit your way to The Lord, trust also in Him, and He shall bring it to pass."

Psalm 37:4-5 (NKJV)

Almost twenty years ago Jack and I joined our lives together in a marriage that launched me into the happiest season of my life. It was a blessing neither one of us dreamed possible. Who would have imagined that the two little children living next door to each other in 1st and 2nd grade would eventually be linked together in marriage?

Our wedding brought together two wounded hearts that had endured a lot of pain and disappointment. It made our mothers, who had witnessed their children facing so much hurt and pain, very happy. The icing on that very special occasion was having Leigh, our childhood friend and playmate, serve as our best man. Since we each had families of our own, we were blessed to have children and grandchildren involved in the ceremony.

Leading up to that special day were years of seeking God's will for my life. He had to lead me to a new trust level so I could open up my heart enough to love again. Overcoming hurts from the past doesn't happen overnight, but with honest and open prayer, you can have victory.

Father of love, thank you for bringing so much happiness to us and to our families through our marriage.

March 15

What are we wearing today?

"Above all, clothe yourselves with love, which binds us all together in perfect harmony."

Colossians 3:14 (NLT)

On Sunday mornings Jack usually asks me, "What are we wearing today?" He knows I want our outfits to be coordinated. We both like to look our best when we're going to be in our Lord's house. Actually, I care about how I look anytime I go out in public, so I'll spend a good bit of time getting ready, including coordinating the colors. Since I have to use a cane now, I try to make sure it goes with my outfit, which is a source of amusement to some.

Looking good on the outside is important to us, but God is more concerned with our heart. How can we demonstrate our faith if we go out, perfectly dressed and made up, yet wearing a bad attitude, intolerance and other characteristics that don't show love? If we're Christians, how can we reflect God without his love shining through us?

Others may briefly notice our physical appearance, but will only be drawn to us by the love we display. That's all they'll remember in the long run.

Lord, help me learn to focus on demonstrating Godly character and not be so hung up on my outward appearance.

MARCH

March 16

Laughter

"Sarah said, 'God has brought me laughter, and everyone who hear about this will laugh with me.'"

Genesis 21:6 (NIV)

"We were filled with laughter and we sang for joy. And the other nations said, "What amazing things the Lord has done for them."

Psalm 126:2 (NLT)

"Blessed are you who weep now, for you shall laugh."

Luke 6:21 (NKJV)

Nothing is quite as infectious as laughter, especially the kind that wells up within you and erupts in a burst of guffaws. One evening, when our son Steve was eight or nine years old, we were watching an episode of the Syd Caesar Show. Steve got tickled and was soon rolling on the floor, convulsed in laughter. The rest of us were caught up in the fun of it and soon laughing, more at seeing Steve than with the show. There have been times when I've laughed so hard my side would hurt and tears would roll down my cheeks. I love hearing my granddaughter, Jessie, burst out in giggles. I always wanted a giggle like hers, but it's a gift not everyone is given.

Laughter can lift a heavy heart. It can display joy or diffuse a tense situation. When we're able to find humor in our lives, we have achieved a major balance to offset the turmoil and unrest we see in the world around us.

Father, thank you for the gift of laughter, for it brightens my dark days and lightens my load.

March 17

Come as you are

"Jesus followed up, 'Yes. For there was once a man who threw a great dinner party and invited many. When it was time for dinner, he sent out his servant to the invited guests, saying, "Come on in, the food's on the table." They all began to beg off, one after another making excuses. The servant went back and told the master what had happened. He was outraged and told the servant, "Quickly, get into the city streets and alleys. Collect all who look like they need a square meal, all the misfits and homeless and wretched you can lay your hands on, and bring them here."'

Luke 14:16-17, 21 (MSG)

While we were raising our children, it was popular to host a "Come as You Are" party. The gathering would be casual with last minute invitations and instructions to wear whatever you had on at that moment. Half the fun of the event was seeing how everyone dressed.

Some people say they won't accept the Lord until they can clean up their life. They're under the mistaken idea they have to be better before God will accept them. Our Lord doesn't tell us to come to him all cleaned up. He wants us to come just as we are: broken, sinful and hurting children, and he will clean us with his amazing grace. We can't do it on our own. Only through the cleansing blood of our Savior Jesus Christ will we ever be acceptable in God's presence. The sad reality is that many people think they're fine just cleaning themselves up without God's help, so they choose to ignore his invitation.

Gracious Father, thank you for welcoming me into your family, and washing me clean even though I was stained and dirty with sin.

MARCH

March 18

Commitments

"God affirms us, making us a sure thing in Christ, putting his Yes within us. By his Spirit he has stamped us with his eternal pledge - a sure beginning of what he is destined to complete."

II Corinthians 1:21-22 (MSG)

A number of years ago my granddaughter, Morganne, and her boyfriend, Peter, were getting serious in their relationship. They'd been dating for several years. Her parents (my daughter and son-in-law) asked Peter to join the family on a trip to Disney World. Unbeknownst to Morganne, he had asked her dad for permission to propose on the trip. He shared later that he didn't know what he would do if she turned him down, and feared he might have to find another way home. Peter proposed in front of the castle, and Morganne did say "yes".

Some people will say yes when asked to make a commitment and then go back on their word. Because of our human nature, we're often cautious about committing to a firm "yes", more comfortable with saying "I'll see how I feel about it later" or "let me think about it."

Our Lord never goes back on his word. When we said yes to his offer of salvation, he said YES to our eternity with him. We may waffle now and then with our commitment but God is faithful even when we're not.

Lord, I want to be a person others can count on, but you know I sometimes fail. Help me learn to stay true to commitments I make even when it's inconvenient.

March 19

Someone's watching

"The Lord is my strength and my shield; my heart trusts in him and he helps me. My heart leaps for joy, and with my song I praise him."

Psalms 28:7 (NIV)

We don't realize the influence our life has on others. I have three friends, Waneta, Shannon and BoBo, whose courage enabled each of them to move past the storms they endured and live in victory and joy. Their common denominator is their faith in Jesus who strengthens them.

Waneta's teenage daughter was killed in an accident caused by a drunk driver. Later she accidently lost an eye while working on storm windows. She's faced two major changes in her life but maintains a positive attitude, never complaining or harboring bitterness.

Shannon was severely injured in a couple of accidents that left her unable to walk or accomplish all that she had hoped. She exercises faithfully at the gym, assisted by her dad, who prods her to "keep on keeping on." Shannon is so loving, and always smiling and singing. Her life is not what she had hoped for but God has led her through the valleys.

BoBo lost her husband, a son-in-law and a daughter-in-law within three years of each other. Because of her declining health she has given up all independence, yet she always displays a positive, cheerful attitude. If asked how she is doing, her response is "I am doing fine." Her strong faith and commitment keep her involved in church.

Father, thank you for the blessing of friends who display patience and perseverance in overcoming challenges in their lives. Help me learn from their victories.

March 20

Having a dad

"Therefore do not worry, saying "What shall we eat?" or "What shall we drink?" or "What shall we wear?" For after all these things the Gentiles seek. For your heavenly Father knows that you need all these things. But seek first the kingdom of God and His righteousness, and all these things shall be added to you."

Matthew 6:31-33 (NKJV)

I grew up without my dad around so I lacked the benefits of having an active father in my life. His military service kept him away from home at first, but after years of separation my parents' marriage also failed, a common military casualty. A father's role is not only to provide for our physical needs when we're children, but also to comfort, encourage and establish firm guidelines to keep us on the right path. I have a great deal of respect for single moms who have the responsibility of parenting by themselves, but they cannot replace what a dad gives to a child. My mother did the best she could, but my brother and I both lacked the influence and security only our dad could have brought.

God fills the father role in our lives when we become believers and develop a relationship with him. He promises to supply all our needs, to comfort us when we're hurting, to calm us and give us peace when we struggle with worries and he's preparing a new home for us in heaven. He corrects us when we stray off course and gives us firm guidelines to keep us on the right path. He gave us the Bible, detailing his love and plans for us within it, and fills us with his Spirit so we can be victorious. We're his beloved children and he is our eternal Father.

Father God, you are the loving father I never had in my life. Thank you for showing me an unconditional love that has filled my life with joy and given me hope.

March 21

Growing our gift

"Blessed is the man who trusts in the Lord, and whose hope is in the Lord. For he shall be like a tree planted by the waters, which spreads out its roots by the river, and will not fear when heat comes; but its leaf will be green, and will not be anxious in the year of the drought, nor will cease from yielding fruit."

Jeremiah 17:7-8 (NKJV)

Several years ago a friend gave us money to plant a tree in our yard in memory of my mother. For the first couple of years, Jack made sure the tree was supported with ropes until it established a root system. Every year we have a number of significant storms bringing down trees that aren't healthy or have a shallow root system, but our tree is strong and healthy and thriving.

We're like trees in God's garden of grace. When we're first planted, we need support from other Christians until we grow our roots of faith. God waters us with his Word and Spirit and as our roots grow deeper, we're able to withstand the storms that come into our life.

I'm so grateful for friends who encouraged me and walked along side me when I was a "newly-planted" believer. Now I'm strong enough to reach out and help others grow in their faith.

Loving Father, thank you for the friends who supported me while my faith was taking root, your Son who shines in my life and the living water that refreshes my soul.

MARCH

March 22

Learning to pray

"Be anxious for nothing, but in everything by prayer and supplication, with thanksgiving, let your requests be made known to God, and the peace of God which surpasses understanding, will guard your hearts and minds through Christ Jesus,"

Philippians 4:6-7 (NKJV)

Since becoming a Christian I have worked on learning how to pray effectively. I've heard lots of sermons on prayer, some saying to pray over and over - like the man in the parable who pesters his friend until he grants his request for bread. Others suggest we should pray once with faith and then rest on the promise that God hears and will answer. I still don't have a definitive answer, but in reflecting on prayers that I've offered up, it seems as though many that were high on my concern list were answered without my begging. If I bring my request to God and leave it there, just trusting that he will answer it the way he deems best, I am able to continue my journey in peace; and peace, after all, is what we need the most.

God never promised to answer all our prayers the way we want. His plan for our life doesn't include everything we have on our agenda, nor does it eliminate the trials we endure. I don't understand why some prayers are answered and some aren't, especially when they involve healing, but God has a reason. His desire is for us to grow in our faith and rest in the eternal hope we have through Christ Jesus our Savior.

Lord, help me trust in your answers to my prayers even when they weren't the way I had hoped. I want to accept that your way is the best.

March 23

Riding a bike

"But those who wait upon God get fresh strength. They spread their wings and soar like eagles. They run and don't get tired, they walk and don't lag behind."

Isaiah 40:31 (MSG)

"Whatever I have, wherever I am, I can make it through anything in the One who makes me who I am."

Philippians 4:12-13 (MSG)

For a few years I was able ride my bike with Jack when we went camping. Once in a while we had to pedal up a hill. Not being a seasoned biker, I would start up the incline and then have to dismount and walk the bike the rest of the way. Jack would slow down to stay with me, or walk his bike alongside so I wouldn't be alone. I enjoyed riding but always dreaded hills.

Sometimes we may feel like our life has become one long climb up a hill. There may be too many demands on our time or we simply try to pack too much into each day. Whatever the reason, it seems as though we're trudging up an endless hill with no end in sight. We don't always have a choice in some of what we have on our plate, but our Savior Jesus promises to walk beside us, giving us strength and sharing our burdens. All we have to do is reach out and grab his hand. With his help, the hill levels out and we can walk confidently again with renewed energy and strength.

Lord, sometimes I feel like all I'm doing is climbing up an incline, and I grow weary. Give me a vision of the top so I won't become discouraged.

MARCH

March 24

Saving stuff

"Search me O God, and know my heart; try me and know my anxieties; and see if there is any wicked way in me, and lead me in the way everlasting."

Psalm 130:23-24 (NKJV)

Jack is a 'saver" so consequently our garage is filled with things he 'might need someday." Some of the stuff stored out there dates back twenty or more years. If we're expecting company he closes the garage door so no one will see how messy it is. A few times he's cleaned it up a little and has actually tossed out or given away a few things, but for the most part, the garage is off-limits to all but a few. When I ask about it, his standard answer is "One of these days I'm going to clean this place up."

We're like that with our hearts. There are areas we don't want others to see: little secrets, hidden sins or habits that we find hard to change. We keep them hidden to everyone but ourselves. We *think* we're hiding them from God, too, by closing the door to that part of our heart and not allowing him access. Until we're ready to open every room in our heart to his presence, we cannot be fully transformed into the person he created us to be. The power of his Spirit in us is the only way we'll be able to clean up the mess we're hiding.

Lord, help me to grant you access to all of me, even the areas I'm clinging to, so that I can be completely filled with your presence.

March 25

Visiting churches

"We wait in hope for the Lord; he is our help and our shield. In him our hearts rejoice, for we trust in his holy name."

Psalm 33:21-22 (NIV)

In our travels, we've visited many churches from different denominations. Several of our friends come from other faith backgrounds and in our blended family there are various denominations represented. Early in my faith journey, I tended to judge the ones who worshipped differently than me; however, as I matured in my understanding I realized that the way we worship isn't set in stone. As long as we have accepted Christ Jesus as our Savior and try to live a life pleasing to him, the rest isn't that important.

We won't always agree on traditional or contemporary music, the structure of the service, how others dress or any of the other issues that divide Christians. We all worship in our own individual ways and I don't think God is concerned with the details, only with the sincerity of our heart.

Lord, help me embrace other believers in love, even if we don't agree on how we worship. Enable me to accept changes in my own faith community with a positive attitude. I want my whole focus to be on you and not on myself and what I want.

March 26

Addresses

"This is how we know we're living steadily and deeply in him, and he in us: He's given us life from his life, from his very own Spirit. Everyone who confesses that Jesus is God's Son participates continually in an intimate relationship with God."

I John 4:13, 15 (MSG)

Addresses are an important part of our connection with other people. If you don't have a valid address, no one can find you and you won't be able to receive mail. One of the details we have to deal with when we travel south for the winter is filling out a change of address form so mail can be forwarded. However, we have to get the correct form, because there is a temporary one and a permanent one. If we turn in the wrong form it creates multiple problems,. as we found out the first year.

If you ask people what God's address is, how do you think they will answer? Heaven? Actually, he has billions of addresses, for he resides in the heart of every believer. If we need to get in touch with our Lord, it's not necessary to use a phone, text, send an email or mail a note. We don't have to wait to know if he received our message because it doesn't go through processing, sorting and delivery like our mail. He lives within us and receives immediately every thought and prayer that we offer.

Father, it's difficult to wrap my head around the knowledge that you dwell within me. You have chosen to abide in me, even though my life doesn't qualify for a temple status. Thank you for this incomprehensible blessing.

March 27

Waste not

"Look to the Lord and his strength; seek his face always. Remember the wonders he has done, his miracles, and the judgments he pronounced."

I Chronicles 16:11-12 (NIV)

"Waste not, want not." That's a saying I have come to appreciate during the past couple of years. When I began this journey in writing two years ago, I only had a dozen or so ideas. I knew the only way I could accomplish my goal was to put my trust in the Spirit's leading. Through the process, I've learned to listen and observe more intently, to take notes, and I'm becoming adept at looking for the right scripture in a Bible concordance. I'm amazed at how one little statement or word can give me an idea; I carry a small notebook with me all the time so I can write them down, not wasting any idea that comes to mind by trusting it to memory alone. Combing through those notes and writing about my experiences and how God's Word speaks to them resulted in "Remind Me Today".

All our life experiences are stored in our memory. Now and then something we see or hear will bring an episode to the surface of our thought. In the Bible, God addresses everything we'll experience in our life and how to deal with it. When we read the Bible, the Holy Spirit allows strength, guidance, encouragement and comfort to come to the surface and help us, no matter what we face in life.

Father, words cannot fully express the gratitude I feel for the way you have led me through this journey of writing. May the words I have written encourage and strengthen those who read them.

March 28

Selfies

"Not unto us, O Lord, not unto us, but to Your name give glory."

Psalm 115:1 (NKJV)

One of the newest words in our vocabulary is "selfie" meaning a picture you take of yourself with your cell phone and then post on social media. At first I didn't realize there was a name for all the posted pictures people were taking of themselves. Sometimes the pictures are flattering and sometimes they're not. We are tempted to showcase ourselves because that's what the world does, showing our good side as well as our flaws. A few people catalogue their daily activities on Facebook starting in the morning until they go to bed at night.

Does what we're sharing with the world reflect our Heavenly Father? Is it bringing glory to him, or is it bringing attention to us? Many of the younger generation have developed a "selfie lifestyle". We need to show them that life isn't just about ourselves, but about demonstrating God's love through the way we love and treat others.

Lord, help me to focus on you and not to showcase myself by trying to impress the world. May what I do and say be a reflection of your love and mercy.

March 29

Going home

"God is a safe place to hide, ready to help when we need Him."

Psalm 46:1 (MSG)

By the end of March we're ready to head home to Indiana. As much as we enjoy our time in Florida, we begin longing for our home up North in the spring. However, once we arrive, we have a lot to do. My biggest chore is unloading the RV. Jack always tells me to pile it up by the door and he will carry it in, but I like to bring in one load at a time and put it away before tackling another one. If everything is brought in all at one time, I can become overwhelmed and frustrated.

We're tempted to think we have to do it all when we deal with our problems, worries and little trials we face in our lives. If we would simply tackle them one at a time, trusting God for guidance, they would be manageable. But, if we consider the pile of concerns and problems our responsibility instead of trusting him, we become discouraged and negative.

I need to look at my pile of "stuff" envisioning my Lord standing in the midst of it, reminding me to pick up one task or trial at a time and he will help me take care of it.

Lord, I have struggled for years thinking it was my responsibility to come up with solutions for problems. Teach me how to lay them at your feet and leave them there.

March 30

Thistles on the path

"May integrity and uprighteousness protect me, because my hope, Lord is in you."

Psalm 25:21 (NIV)

"Wise choices will watch over you. Understanding will keep you safe. Wisdom will save you from evil people, from those whose words are twisted. These men turn from the right way to walk down dark paths."

Proverbs 2:11-13 (NLT)

One morning we walked down the creek behind our house and up a hill on our way to a restaurant about a block away. As we were climbing up the hill, we noticed a patch of thistles but thought we could skirt around them. By the time we got to the top, we were covered with the sticky, prickly things that clung tenaciously to our clothes. I attempted to pick mine off, but some had penetrated the fabric and were nearly impossible to remove.

We live in a world that has its patches of sin everywhere. If we're not diligent about what we watch on TV and in the movies, where we go and who we allow to influence us, we will have those pesky, clingy ideas permeating our minds and hearts. Once imbedded, they're extremely difficult to erase. I've heard it said "Once a thought or image enters your mind, it's there forever." Our eyes and ears are the channels through which these evil thistles gain entrance to our heart. The only way to protect ourselves is to avoid anything that puts us at risk.

Father, Satan is an expert at lying and deceiving. Help me reinforce my defense with your truth so I can stand strong and resist his bait.

March 31

Granny's hearing

"After he has gathered his own flock, he walks ahead of them, and they follow him because they know his voice. "I am the good shepherd. The good shepherd sacrifices his life for the sheep."

John 10:4, 14 (NLT)

As she got older, my mother-in-law often smiled and nodded her head when we talked to her. It became obvious that she was having difficulty hearing what we said and didn't want to ask us to repeat it. I thought it amusing at the time because sometimes she didn't understand what she was affirming. Now it is becoming a reality for me as it does for many others as they age. Too much background noise keeps us from hearing voices clearly. The diminished ability to hear isn't our choice but simply happens over time.

Our Lord talks to us through our spiritual ears. Unlike our physical hearing though, we make a choice whether or not we hear him. Often we're so caught up in the noise of this world that we can't hear him. He doesn't speak loudly or shout to get our attention but communicates in a still, small voice. When we stop to focus our hearts and mind on him, we hear his gentle voice drawing us closer. Jesus promised us that he would always be there waiting but we have to take the time to listen.

Lord, help me to slow down today and listen as you call out to me. Keep me from getting so caught up in the noise around me that I don't hear you.

April

He restores my soul.

*Father, thank you for showing me
that I need to repent
so I can walk in fellowship
with you again.*

April 1

Pretending

"We can say with confidence and a clear conscience that we have lived with a God-given holiness and sincerity in all our dealings. We have depended on God's grace, not on our own human wisdom. That is how we've conducted ourselves, before the world and especially toward you."

II Corinthians 1:12 (NLT)

One of the mainstays of play time as a child was pretending. We didn't have gadgets and electronic games to entertain us so we had to be creative. If I was playing house, building something with blocks, sculpting a structure in the sand or reading, I used my imagination or pretended I was somebody else. When my two boys played cops and robbers or acted out an adult activity, my youngest son would say "plank like I'm the cop" instead of "play like." Mr. Rogers focused on make believe and his show encouraged creative thinking. An important part of learning is thinking outside yourself.

However, as adults we need to discover who we really are and grow beyond pretending or play acting. If we spend our whole life putting on an act, we'll never discover that real person inside of us. God created something worthy and excellent in each of us that is designed to be used for his glory. The only way to discover that child of God in you is to peel off the artificial layers that you have accumulated over the years. The real you is the one God can use and has much more value than the pretend person you have become.

Father, I have the mind and body that you designed just for me. Help me be content with who I am, yet not so content that I don't use what I have for your glory.

APRIL

April 2

A narrow ledge

"You make known to me the path of life; you will fill me with joy in your presence, with eternal pleasures at your right hand."

Psalm 16:11 (NIV)

"For we live by believing, and not by seeing."

II Corinthians 5:7 (NLT)

One fall while camping in Turkey Run State Park in West Central Indiana, we took a hike on a trail rated "moderate". The signs along the trail were confusing, and at one point we headed the wrong direction by mistake. The path led us to a narrow ledge along a cliff overlooking a creek. By then it was too late to turn back, so I crept cautiously along the ledge. There wasn't anything to hang on to, and I was pretty nervous. At the end of the ledge we descended to a creek that we had to traverse by stepping on small, slippery rocks. Both of us successfully navigated the ledge and crossed the creek without mishap.

We're navigating a path in our faith journey and if we're not watchful, we'll make a wrong turn and head into dangerous territory. We have the Holy Spirit guiding us, but if we're too busy looking around at what the world is offering we may wander away from him. When we finally reach the point where we no longer sense our Lord's presence, his Spirit convicts us and draws us back to the protection of his wings.

God, you have been faithful to guide me along narrow ledges, around boulders in my path and through the barren wasteland. Your unending care for me brings me to my knees every day.

April 3

Losing a baby

"But now that he is dead; why should I go on fasting? Can I bring him back again? I will go to him, but he will not return to me."

II Samuel 12:23 (NIV)

David penned those encouraging words for us after he and Bathsheba lost their child, for he had God's promise that he and his son would someday be reunited.

In 1957, when our first child was about thirteen months old, I had a miscarriage. Although it was upsetting, having a little daughter to love and care for helped us accept the loss, and we ended up having two more healthy babies. When our son Steve and his wife suffered the same loss, they ultimately chose to adopt three wonderful girls from China. Then, in 2002, my grandson Tyler and his wife lost their first baby. God later blessed them with two precious children. There are times when all of us think about those babies that we never got to see or hold. I wonder sometimes if those three children living in heaven realize they're related.

Isn't it wonderful that we have God's assurance we'll see them someday? He says we will recognize them! We have his promise of that reunion because we're his children. It is comforting to know that our unborn babies escaped the trials and disappointments of this world and went straight into the loving arms of Jesus. Maybe they'll be standing at the Pearly Gates waiting for us to come home.

Father, I know in my heart that I will embrace the children lost by me and my family when I get to heaven. Thank you for sparing them the hurts and trials of this life and placing them in the care of my Savior.

April 4

Where is God?

"He created each of us by Christ Jesus to join him in the work he does, the good work he has gotten ready for us to do, work we had better be doing."

Ephesians 2:10 (MSG)

When people watch the news about disasters on TV or see all the pain and trouble in our world, they often say "Where was God? Why doesn't He do something?" As believers, we sometimes wonder why he allows so much suffering, even though we believe that our God is in control. However, the Bible tells us that we have the responsibility to reach out and help others in his name.

I've faced some nearly overwhelming problems and heartaches in my life and always had faithful friends who stepped up to the plate and stood with me. They've mopped up water, shoveled snow, brought meals, loaned me cars, sent me cards, visited me in the hospital, sat with me in the funeral home, cried with me and prayed for me. Complete strangers have also come to my rescue; that's God working! We're the hands and feet that demonstrate God's love to an unbelieving world as well as to our friends and family. We are to be his "angels unaware", to friends, family, even strangers as God directs.

Lord, help me to be sensitive to the needs of others, whether physical or spiritual. May I always respond to those who are hurting in a way that brings honor to you.

April 5

Feeling alone

"For you have been called to live in freedom, my brothers and sisters. But don't use your freedom to satisfy your sinful nature. Instead, use your freedom to serve one another in love. For the whole law can be summed up in this one command: "Love your neighbor as yourself."

Galatians 5:13-14 (NLT)

For several years we visited Jack's cousin while she still lived in her home in Florida. Because of increasing dementia, she was eventually placed in a secure facility and we continued to make an occasional visit. No one else had been there to see her or even bothered to call and check on her. It seemed as though nobody even cared. She had no church family, no close relatives in the area and apparently no friends. Though the people who worked there provided her physical needs, she felt alone and isolated.

We need to show compassion to the shut-ins. Many people are homebound or in nursing homes and have no one close to them who will visit. Their days are long and lonely. We don't take time to think about how empty our life would be if we didn't have family and friends to love and spend time with.

There may come a time when we, or someone we care about, will be home bound and lonely. We'll have our hope, but we'll still need the fellowship of others. Reach out to bring a little happiness to some lonely person today.

Father, bless those who extend comfort and care with visits to hospitals, nursing homes and shut-ins. Teach me the value of showing compassion on those who need it the most.

April 6

Waiting

"Wait patiently for the Lord. Be brave and courageous. Yes, wait patiently for the Lord."

Psalm 27:14 (NIV)

Waiting is hard for me. If I'm in a long line at the grocery, I'll be looking around for a shorter one. If we're stuck in traffic because of construction or an accident I can feel my stress level rise. During times when we're expecting important mail, I anxiously check the mailbox. Sometimes on Sunday morning the paper is late getting here and Jack might make two or three trips to the paper box looking for it. Because of the today's culture, we're used to having everything instantaneous: news, emails, fast food. We've lost our ability to be patient and wait for anything.

We have the spirit of God living within us and He is the supreme example of patience. For thousands of years he has waited for his chosen people to recognize their Messiah, and yet he's still patient with them. He waited for each of us to accept his offer of forgiveness and grace - and he still waits for us to make him Lord in our life. His patience is beyond my understanding.

Lord of patience, waiting is hard for me. When I'm impatient, remind me how long you waited for me. I want to sit in your waiting room and use the time to draw closer to you.

April 7

Taking a taste

"Oh taste and see that the Lord is good; blessed is the one who takes refuge in him."

Psalm 34:8 (NIV)

I've learned through years of cooking that tasting is the best way to make sure what I'm preparing turns out the way I hope. I prefer food with a lot of flavor so I often alter recipes by add more seasoning or spices, making it necessary to try a bite before I serve it. Sometimes grocery stores will offer taste samples of their featured items, hoping you will purchase them. Tasting is an important part of determining whether you like certain foods.

God's love and grace have to be tasted before we can know how wonderful they are. Unlike the food we prepare, his grace doesn't need anything added to it. It is perfect just the way he prepared it. One little bite of his incredible love and care for us will create an appetite for more. Pretty soon we're feasting on his word. You can be filled, but you never get enough.

Father, thank you for the Word which offers me a taste of your love and goodness. Infuse me with a hunger that can only be filled by you.

April 8

Under a magnifying glass

"Love never gives up. Love cares more for others than for self. Love doesn't want what it doesn't have. Love doesn't strut, doesn't have a swelled head, doesn't force itself on others, isn't always "me first," doesn't fly off the handle, doesn't keep score of the sins of others, doesn't revel when others grovel, takes pleasure in the flowering of truth, puts up with anything, trusts God always, always looks for the best, never looks back, but keeps going to the end."

I Corinthians 13:7 (MSG)

Lately I'm finding I need my magnifying glass to read extra small print or look at little pictures, and it helps being able to slide my fingers out on the screen of the iPad to enlarge the image. But enlarging a picture often distorts and blurs it, making it more difficult to make out small details.

Sometimes we use a magnifying glass to look at someone with whom we've had a problem. All we see are flaws and faults which are enlarged as we examine them. Consequently, we fail to notice the good qualities.

I'm learning to focus on the good in all people. I've never met anyone who didn't have some good in them. If you have an irregular person in your life, find something positive in them, however small it may seem, and tell them how much you appreciate it. When you focus on the good, the negative will grow smaller and smaller in your eyes - no longer under your magnifying glass.

Father, I have my own flaws. Forgive me when I focus on the faults of others and help me show them love and acceptance.

April 9
Gifts are not loans

"So, humble yourselves under God's strong hand, and in his own good time he will lift you up. You can throw the whole weight of your anxieties upon him, for you are his personal concern."

I Peter 5:6-7 (Phillips)

"He that did not hesitate to spare his own Son but gave him up for us all – can we not trust such a God to give us, with him, everything else that we can need?"

Romans 8:32 (Phillips)

Over the years I've received and also given many gifts. As the giver of a gift, I would never dream of asking for it back.

God gave us the gift of salvation when we accepted Jesus as our Savior, and he will never take that gift away from us. With that gift comes the promise that he hears and answers our prayers, and God never breaks a promise.

I give my concerns and worries to my Lord every day but sometimes I'm guilty of taking them back again when the answer or relief doesn't come quickly enough. .

The creek pictured on the front of this book is in our back yard and, like any creek, it occasionally rises past its banks. We have only had water damage from the creek one time and God was faithful to walk with us through the stress of that. Yet, even though I trust him, when we get a big storm and the creek rises, I'm tempted to worry as if I had never experienced his faithfulness. I hope someday I'll learn to leave it at his feet for he is always faithful.

Father, I don't understand why I worry about things that I have no control over. Remind me every day how faithful you have always been.

April 10

Lost dreams

"He knows the way that I take; when He has tested me I shall come forth as gold."

Job 23:10 (NKJV)

Twenty-eight years ago my youngest son was in the ministry, a fulfilled dream that he had spent five years preparing for. He was married, had a baby girl and a bright future as a minister. During a fall revival at his little church, the world he had worked so hard for suddenly fell apart. His wife took their five-month-old daughter and their car and walked out on him, filing for divorce, and because of the divorce he lost his dream of being a minister. Emotionally, he was lost; physically, he was homeless. For over a year, he stayed with one friend or another until he finally came home to live with me.

If you ask him how he survived, he will tell you "one step at a time." When your whole life crumbles down around you and you lose everything you held dear, you find out what you're made of. He sacrificed time and money so he could remain part of his daughter's life, but God was still working; now he has a grandson who brings great joy to his life. Several years after the divorce, he married a Christian woman and is now very happy.

Recovery from devastating, life-changing events may take years. Finding peace again doesn't erase the loss you endured, but in your healing, you're able to look at the pain objectively and see how God held you through the painful journey. He restores your joy and brings new blessings.

Father of hope, bathe me with perseverance when everything I've worked for seems to be slipping out of my grasp. Give me a glimpse of the finish line so I can continue my race with hope.

April 11

Congested traffic

"Let the morning bring me word of your unfailing love, for I have put my trust in you. Show me the way I should go, for to you I entrust my life."

Psalm 143:8 (NIV)

As we drove north on our way home from Florida, we encountered several miles of congested traffic. For half an hour or so we would creep along for ten or twelve feet, stop for a few seconds, then move another few feet. Neither one of us minded because we weren't in a hurry, but it would have been frustrating if we had needed to be at an appointment. Jack spent the time checking the map while I watched the traffic, telling him when he could inch forward.

Sometimes our days can go along at a comfortable pace and then we'll get unexpected interruptions. We may start one project and then have to stop to take care of something else. That happens a lot when you're raising a family. You can plan your day, but there's no guarantee that it will work the way you thought.

We don't plan our traveling down to the minute because we've learned to allow extra time for unexpected delays like road construction, detours or accidents. Life is more peaceful when we're flexible and make room for the unexpected delays that inevitably occur from time to time.

Lord, when I take on too much and then have interruptions, help me maintain a patient spirit so I react with a loving heart.

April 12

Grocery stores

"Give me enough food to live on, neither too much nor too little. If I'm too full, I might get independent, saying, "God? Who needs him?" If I'm poor, I might steal and dishonor the name of my God."

Proverbs 30:8-9 (MSG)

When we're traveling, one of our favorite activities is visiting grocery stores, especially the ones we've never been in before. I'm usually looking for items to use in a recipe or an upcoming meal. When there's a choice in size for a particular item, a lot of times Jack will suggest we get the bigger one because it's more economical, but since storage is an issue in the RV, I prefer to get a couple of the smaller sizes. Both of us like to be prepared so we tend to stock up unnecessarily.

In The Lord's Prayer, we ask God to "give us this day our daily bread." He didn't tell us to fill our pantries in case he didn't get around to providing what we need. I guess I like the security of having plenty on hand, but then, I'm trusting in my own resources instead of depending on God to honor my faith.

We need to go to him each morning, asking him to provide whatever we need for the day, natural or spiritual. He wants us to think ahead and plan for tomorrow, but allow him to lead us. We live in a "gimme more" culture that elevates possessions to a whole new level and if we're not careful, we can be drawn into that mindset.

Lord, help me have a faith that will believe you are faithful when I offer up my day to you. I want to trust that you will provide what I need.

April 13

Our lilac bush

"I am the vine, and my Father is the gardener. He cuts off every branch that bears no fruit, while every branch that does bear fruit he prunes so that it will be even more fruitful. You are already clean because of the word I have spoken to you. Remain in me as I also remain in you. No branch can bear fruit by itself; it must remain in the vine. Neither can you bear fruit unless you remain in me."

John 15:1-4 (NIV)

When we first bought our house there was a straggly lilac bush by the creek in the back yard. It had a few blooms in the spring but the bush had been neglected and was not healthy. A couple of years ago Jack threatened to cut it down. When I protested, he decided to prune it, cutting it back so much I was afraid it wouldn't make it. This summer, to our surprise, the bush was beautifully shaped and filled with lovely, fragrant lilac blooms.

God prunes us when we develop habits and attitudes that limit the spiritual fruit in our lives. If we've gotten out of balance in our walk, focusing too much on the world and ourselves, he allows us to struggle for a while, until we get our eyes back on him. God's pruning shears can be found in his Word. If we read and obey his Word, the Spirit convicts us and helps us cut out what hampers the growth of fruit in our life. Pruning isn't pleasant, but in the end it produces abundant fruit that brings glory to our Father in Heaven.

Savior Jesus, I was planted in you when I believed. Thank you for keeping me watered and nourished with your word and pruning me when I grow the wrong kind of fruit.

APRIL

April 14

Prayer slips

"You can be sure of this: The Lord set apart the godly for himself, the Lord will answer when I call to him."

Psalm 4:3 (NLT)

"Open up before God, keep nothing back; he'll do whatever needs to be done;"

Psalm 37:5 (MSG)

Prayer is an essential part of an intimate walk with God. It keeps you focused and strengthens you. I don't go into a "prayer closet" but have short conversations with him throughout the day.

I faced an uncertain future after the death of my husband in 1983. There were many unknowns stretched out in front of me. Eight months after he died, my daughter remarried and she and my grandson moved out. For the first time in my life I was going to be alone, at least in making decisions.

I wrote six different prayer concerns on little slips of paper and randomly tucked them in my Bible. Once in a while I would run across a slip and if the prayer had been answered I'd note it on the paper. God was faithful and all those concerns were met, the last one being – "someone to share my life with." A few of them took years but God's timing is always just right. I recently got that Bible out and retrieved those little prayer requests, which I'm keeping to remind me of God's faithfulness.

If you use a prayer journal or write your prayers down on paper, it's amazing to look back and see how your prayers are answered - perhaps not the way you planned, but always in the best way.

I thank you Father, for hearing and answering my prayers.

April 15

Heading home

"Yes, we are fully confident, and we would rather be away from these earthly bodies, for then we will be at home with The Lord."

II Corinthians 5:8 (NLT)

Jack and I both love traveling south for the winter. We look forward to escaping the cold and snow of Indiana and enjoy sharing fellowship with friends we've made in Florida. By living in an RV for four months, we get a break from keeping up the house and yard. However, after about three months, we have a longing to be "back home again in Indiana". Even though we're blessed to have very special friends in Florida, memories of fun times and warmer weather, there's still no place like home. Home is where we've been planted - where we have our roots.

We're just visiting here on earth for a season. We fellowship, make friends, perhaps raise a family, work, play, have struggles, laugh and occasionally cry and many of us suffer pain and loss. It's all part of life. But as we grow older, we begin to long for home. Home is where our Savior lives, where our roots are, and where many of our loved ones and friends are waiting eagerly for our arrival. I purchased my ticket for that trip when I accepted My Savior, Jesus, but only he knows the date it will be redeemed.

While I'm waiting for that trip, I'll continue to enjoy my time here and celebrate the hope I have.

Father, help me keep my heart focused on the home that awaits me so I won't get caught up in the troubles and temptations of this earthly home.

April 16

A forgotten commitment

"Each time he said, "My grace is all you need. My power works best in weakness." So now I am glad to boast about my weaknesses, so that the power of Christ can work through me."

II Corinthians 12:9 (NLT)

In the mid 1970's, I was president of the Women's Fellowship one year at our church in Clarksville. That spring the church camp director decided to spruce up the girl's dorm, and put out a plea to the churches for new curtains. I suggested that my circle might be interested in making them. In the hustle and bustle of spring, I pushed it to the back burner and consequently forgot about it. The day before camp was to begin, the camp director called to see if the curtains were ready. I was embarrassed and ashamed that I had let them down; it was a painful lesson to learn. I know God desires better from me.

Jack occasionally asks me to do something on the computer, and I'll tell him to put it on the desk and I'll do it "a little later". It may be quite a while before I get around it. When he has a job to do, he generally does it immediately. On the other hand, I am sometimes a procrastinator. We are both working on accepting our differences and being more patient.

As Christians, our integrity should be reflecting that of our Lord's. We should take very seriously our pledges to help or contribute for he always keeps his Word and never breaks a promise.

Lord, teach me to take my commitments seriously when I volunteer to help others. How can I mirror a faithful God if I'm not dependable?

April 17

Movie sets

"But all of us who are Christians have no veil on our faces, but reflect like mirrors the glory of the Lord. We are transfigured by the Spirit of the Lord in ever increasing splendor into his own image."

II Corinthians 3:18 (Phillips)

I've never been on a movie set, but I'm sure that much of the scenery we see on the screen looks real, but is actually only a facade. If we were present during the filming, we'd find there's nothing behind the front of the set, and some of the magic of the movie would be lost.

Unfortunately, many people claim to be Christians but are only putting on a front. They don't have God's Spirit directing their life. Sometimes they've even fooled themselves into believing they're OK. But if you notice behavior and language that aren't consistent with Christian values, you realize it's only a facade. There's nothing real behind what they're displaying. Just belonging to a church or attending sporadically doesn't make you a Christian. Faith becomes more than a front by accepting Jesus as your Savior and immersing yourself into that faith, realizing that you have received God's grace as a gift, not by anything you have done or could ever do. Walking in that faith is what brings reality to it.

If we're going to be our Lord's ambassadors to a lost and dying world, we must have depth to our character. What we say, how we treat others and our compassion for people that are different than us, says much about our commitment to our Savior Jesus Christ.

Teacher Father, help me learn humility and compassion in my relationships with others.

April 18

Good Friday

"By this time it was about noon, and darkness fell across the whole land until three o'clock. The light from the sun was gone. And suddenly, the curtain in the sanctuary of the Temple was torn down the middle. Then Jesus shouted, 'Father, I entrust my spirit into your hands!' And with those words he breathed his last."

Luke 23:44-46 (NLT)

"The angel said to the women, "Do not be afraid, for I know that you are looking for Jesus, who was crucified. He is not here; he has risen, just as he said. Come and see the place where he lay.'"

Matthew 28:5-6 (NIV)

It's been said that you can't buy or put a price on things that are the most meaningful and important in life. But the gift of salvation did come with a price, and it was paid for with the blood of our Savior Jesus Christ.

As I meditate on the sacrifice Jesus made for me - for all of us - I am overcome with love and gratitude. I will never completely know or understand the pain, agony and rejection he felt, nor comprehend the depth of his love for me.

Many people view the crucifixion as an ugly picture displaying the cruelty of the Roman soldiers, but we know Jesus chose to give his life as a sacrifice. Because he arose, we have a hope that will sustain us through anything we will ever face. He fills us with his presence, sustains us with strength, offers us peace and gives us joy. The hope he gives us is ours for all eternity.

Eternal Father, Thank you for the gift you offered through the sacrifice of our Savior, Jesus Christ.

April 19

That's just the way I am

"But if God himself has taken up residence in your life, you can hardly be thinking more of yourself than of him. Anyone, of course, who has not welcomed this invisible but clearly present God, the Spirit of Christ, won't know what we're talking about.

But for you who welcomed him, in whom he dwells - even though you still experience all the limitations of sin - you, yourself experience life on God's terms...When God lives and breathes in you (and he does as surely as he did in Jesus), you are delivered from that dead life. With his Spirit living in you, your body will be as alive as Christ's!"

Romans 8:9, 11 (MSG)

All of us have little flaws in our behavior that have taken root and developed over the years. If I am criticized or corrected, I am tempted to get defensive, not necessarily vocalizing it, but inwardly getting a resentful attitude. I've heard people justify an angry outburst saying, "I can't help it, that's just the way I am." We don't have to settle for a half-filled heart. God wants us to open it completely to him.

We have the Holy Spirit living within us and he is the one enabling us to overcome issues that keep us from enjoying a peaceful heart. If we cave into these old, destructive feelings, we're choosing to ignore what the Spirit offers, but when we tap into the power he makes available to us, we're able to develop peaceful and productive lives.

Father, teach me to tap into the resources you offer your children through your Holy Spirit. On my own, I have no strength to battle sin, but through your Spirit I can have victory.

April 20

Reading

"For we are looking all the time not at the visible things but at the invisible. The visible things are transitory; it is the invisible things that are really permanent."

II Corinthians 4:18 (Phillips)

Reading was one of my favorite pastimes as a child. Through the stories, woven into the print in a book, I was able to escape into the land of make-believe, a world of perfect families and adventures that I could never experience personally. Not only did I have a love of reading, but the hours I spent devouring those stories were times I could escape the unhappiness I was feeling each time my dad left us to return to his service in the Navy, and when he ultimately left us permanently. Books offered me a glimpse of the way I thought life should be. The best part of every story was the ending, for it seemed as though they always "lived happily ever after."

We know, however, life isn't perfect. We face circumstances that can't be changed with the stroke of a pen on paper. We can't solve the mystery of why "bad stuff" happens. We won't have a prince that will come to carry us off into the sunset.

Most of what I read as a child was unattainable in real life. There is good news, though. The Bible is filled with mysteries, adventures, love stories, battles and victories. Best of all, as his children we're guaranteed that we'll "live happily ever after" when we finish our final chapter. It's a perfect book with a perfect ending. The dragon will be slain and we'll be with the Prince of Peace forever! Praise His Holy Name!

Father of all good and truth, thank you for your Word. Help me immerse myself in the strength and wisdom that can only be found in the writings of your faithful servants.

April 21

It's boiling over

"The Lord is my light and my salvation, whom shall I fear? The Lord is the strength of my life, of whom shall I be afraid?"

Psalm 27:1 (NKJV)

"For God has not given us a spirit of fear and timidity, but of power, love and self-discipline."

II Timothy 1:7 (NLT)

"There is no fear in love. But perfect love drives out fear, because fear has to do with punishment. The one who fears is not made perfect in love"

I John 4:18 (NIV)

I was only nineteen when I first married and had very little experience with cooking. Most of my culinary skills were learned from trial and error. One very important thing I did discover was that you can't fill a pan with water and dump in a whole box of rice, macaroni or spaghetti. By the time it has cooked, there isn't room for anything else. In fact, it will probably spill over the top of the pan and mess up the stove.

Giving in to fear is like the macaroni cooking in the water. It takes over your heart and mind, filling them so full there isn't room left for peace and joy. The fear will spill over into every part of your life and make you miserable. In God's Word, we are told over and over to "fear not." I did manage to become a fairly accomplished cook, but I'm still learning how to conquer all my fears and leave ample room for his blessings to cook up a pot full of joy in my heart.

Lord, free my heart from any fear that threatens to overtake me today.

April 22

Artists

"Yet you, Lord, are our Father. We are the clay, you are the potter; we are all the work of your hand."

Isaiah 64:8 (NIV)

Several of our friends are gifted artists and one such artist is a camping neighbor at our RV park in Florida. Every winter she spends countless hours working on and perfecting her artwork. One March a group of artists from the park had a display of their work in the clubhouse to showcase their paintings. As we walked around admiring their work and chatting with them, you could see the pride on their faces, saying, without words, "I painted that!" God had given them the talent and they used it to create something beautiful.

God created each one of us in a different way. All of us are beautiful in his sight. Some of us are tall, some short, some skinny, and others not so much. Only identical twins will look exactly alike, yet they have differences as well. No matter what we look like, we are loved unconditionally. He fashioned each of his children just the way he wanted and I imagine he looks down on each one with a smile and says "I made that!"

Father of all creation, forgive me when I complain about my body and my abilities. Remind me that I was designed in a special way so I could be used as your instrument.

April 23

Falling down the steps

"If God hadn't been there for me, I never would have made it. The minute I said, "I'm slipping, I'm falling" your love, God, took hold and held me fast."

Psalm 94:18-19 (MSG)

When I was around two, I loved playing with my grandpa. One of the things we liked to do was throw a little ball up and down the stairs. I would stand on the landing and throw the ball down to him. He would then toss it up to me. In my excitement, on one occasion, I slipped off the top step and came tumbling down with the ball. I don't recall the fall, but I do remember clearly that he picked me up, dried my tears and held me on his lap. There was security in being comforted by someone who loved me. My grandma wouldn't let us play that game again.

God offers us comfort when we fall or fail in our faith journey. I've slipped and fallen many times in my Christian walk. God has always been there to pick me up and comfort me. He binds up my broken spirit and sooths my troubled heart. If I have fallen because of something I did, he forgives me. In the process, I learn not to go that way again. Experience is a great teacher.

Father of comfort, thank you for being there when I have a broken heart, a faltering faith or become crippled by feelings of rejection. You always bring peace and healing to my soul.

April 24

Putting people in categories

"Every time you cross my mind, I break out in exclamations of thanks to God. Each exclamation is a trigger to prayer. I find myself praying for you with a glad heart."

Philippians 1:3-4 (MSG)

Our society is big on grouping people according to their age. Consequently, the younger and older people aren't always comfortable around each other and sometimes have trouble communicating. We can, however, step out of our comfort zone, reaching across the aisle, so to speak, to meet those who are of a different generation. We were there at one time ourselves, or will be someday, and all of us have something we can share with each other.

Our Church Camper's Club offered the opportunity to bridge that gap. Since the ages of the campers ranged from toddlers to seniors, there were multiple opportunities to develop friendships with many people with whom you would have had little contact at church. Camping in a close-knit group encourages bonding. Sitting around campfires in the evening, sharing meals and worshipping together all contribute to a closeness that only a camper can understand.

Even if you don't have camping experiences, you can forge into new territories and bridge new horizons by reaching out to other age groups. Each generation has special blessings that can enrich someone else's life.

Lord of all, thank you for the opportunities you provide to connect with all ages of my brothers and sisters. Endue me with a heart that desires to bridge the gap so I'll better understand that we are all family, even when we look and talk differently.

April 25

Love you!

"...for I have always been mindful of your unfailing love and have lived in reliance on your faithfulness."

Psalm 26:3 (NIV)

"But the eyes of The Lord are on those who fear him, on those whose hope is in his unfailing love."

Psalm 33:18 (NIV)

"For the Lord is good and his love endures forever; his faithfulness continues through all generations."

Psalm 100:5 (NIV)

Every week I have phone conversations with one or more of my children, discussing everything from family to world events. I treasure these phone calls and look forward to them. Some are short and some last an hour, but they're all important to me. The call is always finished with a "love you" and "love you, too." Even though we are confident of their love, it is comforting to hear it expressed audibly.

The Bible reassures us over and over of God's love for us. Almost every psalm makes reference of his love. I have felt and experienced God's love in my life and in my prayer time; I feel his peaceful affirmation of it. I think hearing me finish my prayer with "I love you" pleases him. Don't let the list of people and situations you're praying about become so long that you neglect to tell your Lord how much you love him.

Lord, forgive me for neglecting to express my love for you. You demonstrate your love in countless ways every day and yet I don't always express my love for you. Until we talk next time, I love you.

April 26

Lunch Bunch

"But when you pray, go into your own room, shut your door and pray to your Father privately. Your Father who sees all private things will reward you."

Matthew 6:6 (Phillips)

Once a month, I join a group of friends from church for lunch and some "girl time" at a local restaurant. We call ourselves "The Lunch Bunch." It's a time of fellowship, sharing, laughter and good food. I'm especially close to a couple of them and occasionally we share personal struggles and encourage one another. I'm especially thankful to have a few special friendships that allow for open and transparent conversations without judgment.

However, there are some things I only share with my Lord. He knows me inside and out. I can go to him with something that I'm struggling with and know he won't judge me nor condemn me. He gives me peace when I'm wrestling with guilt, fills me with joy when I'm hurting and showers me with hope when my heart is overcome by fear. My friends can often console me and let me know they care, but no one else can give me what God offers. He is there for me 24/7, no matter where I am or what I'm doing. All I have to say is, "I need you, God."

Father, thank you for being patient when I grumble and complain. You are always there even when my mood is low. I will forever need your listening ear and wise counsel.

April 27

Being baptized

"The godly are showered with blessings;..."

"We have happy memories of the godly,..."

"The words of the godly are a life-giving fountain;..."

"The words of the godly encourage many,..."

"... the hopes of the godly will be granted."

"The hopes of the godly result in happiness,..."

"The godly will never be disturbed..."

"The mouth of the godly person gives wise advice..."

Excerpts from Proverbs 10:6-31 (NLT)

I was baptized on an Easter morning when I was twelve years old and, though I had some idea of what that meant, I carried the gift of salvation, still unopened, for years. It would be another 23 years before I actually opened that gift to see what it contained. As I began to grow in my faith, I still had the insecure feeling that I might do or say something that would cause me to lose what I had received. I didn't completely understand God's grace. I was hearing from well-meaning Christians who believed that salvation required certain behavior: modest dress (no slacks in church), attending every service, etc. None of us really understood what that "amazing grace" really meant.

What a joy it has been to finally come to the realization that salvation is based on belief and not on behavior. I am not able to walk a perfect walk, nor will I ever be, but God has declared me righteous. I know God loves me unconditionally and that makes me want to please Him. Accepting this truth has made my faith walk exciting as I watch how God works in my life.

Lord, thank you that accepting your saving grace was all I needed to be welcomed into the family.

April 28

Hiding behind mom

"For you died to this life, and your real life is hidden with Christ in God."

Colossians 3:3 (NIV)

"They called to the mountains and the rocks, 'Fall on us and hide us from the face of him who sits on the throne and from the wrath of the Lamb!'"

Revelation 6:16 (NIV)

I occasionally took my preschool children for a walk in our neighborhood. If I stopped to talk to a neighbor, my boys would often hide behind me. My daughter wasn't intimidated by people she didn't know but the boys were more shy. They seemed to feel more secure if I stood between them and the person I was talking to.

We serve a Holy and perfect God who cannot look upon sin. If I were an unbeliever, I would be terrified to be in his presence.

However, as his forgiven children, we are hidden in Christ. God no longer sees our sin - He sees only the Lamb, Jesus Christ, and we are protected by standing behind him. Our sins, failures and bad attitudes are no longer visible. God only sees us through our pure and holy Savior's righteousness.

Precious Jesus, thank you for standing in front of me as the perfect Lamb of God. I am grateful to be in your shadow.

April 29

Remind me

"The Friend, the Holy Spirit whom the Father will send at my request, will make everything plain to you. He will remind you of all the things I have told you."

John 14:26 (MSG)

"Remind me that I have an appointment in the morning,." Jack said as he headed for bed. Sometimes he has so much on his mind that a scheduled appointment gets bumped completely out of his memory. He depends on me to remind him.

That's the reason I make a list every morning; I also need reminders of the tasks that need to be taken care of. I feel like I've had a really good day when everything has been crossed off the list by evening.

Sometimes, what we put at the top of our "To Do list" isn't what others think should be our highest priority, and sometimes our priorities *are* out of order. Jack might forget an appointment but remember a chore that he wants to deal with. I might remember to go pick up some things at the grocery but forget to iron the white shirt he needs the next morning.

What we plan for each day may seem important to us and ends up taking precedence over time spent meditating and talking with our Lord. As I reflected on what was on my lists, I realized that time with him was one thing I didn't write down. I need to be reminded every day of how much I am loved by my Lord and what he's done and continues to do for me. His Spirit reminds us if we'll just listen, but he won't interrupt our schedule when we've pushed him clear out of our mind.

Lord as I plan my day, remind me that it isn't my will but yours that I need to put first on my list.

April 30

Praising our children

"Your words have supported those who stumbled, you have strengthened faltering knees;"

Job 4:4 (NLT)

"Encourage those who are timid. Take tender care of those who are weak. Be patient with everyone."

I Thessalonians 5:14 (NLT)

When my children were in school and participating in various activities, I tried to commend them on the good job they were doing. I'm sorry now that I didn't encourage them as often as I should have. A word of appreciation does wonders for their self-confidence. It creates a desire to try even harder. However, when you criticize or put down their effort, they become discouraged and ready to give up. Pleasing a parent or a spouse is important to everyone.

The words we speak leave a larger fingerprint than we give them credit for. The words we store in our mind and recall are either the most harsh and demeaning or the ones that lift our spirit and give us encouragement. All the rest are lost or forgotten over time.

Consider carefully how you form your words and the manner in which you express them, for they have a bigger impact than you realize.

Lord God, I know it's too late to take back the hurtful words I have already spoken. Please forgive me and help me learn to speak in ways that encourage and uplift others instead.

A Forgotten Memory

It floated to the surface
of my mind
like a dead fish in the pond.

I picked it up
wondering why this memory
I thought I had discarded
had resurfaced again.

Somehow that forgotten hurt,
attached by a cord of bitterness,
remained intact through the years.

Why today?
I wasn't expecting it!

I didn't want to revisit it again,
but now I had no choice.

So I examined it
then let it slip quietly back
into the depths of my heart.

There it will stay hidden
until some other unforeseen moment.

May

He leads me in the paths of righteousness for his name's sake.

Precious Father, thank you for leading me on the path that draws me closer to you.

May 1

A new direction

"Every time I think of you, I give thanks to my God. Whenever I pray, I make my requests for all of you with joy... I pray your love will overflow more and more, and that you will keep on growing in knowledge and understanding. For I want you to understand what really matters, so that you may live pure and blameless lives until the day of Christ's return. May you always be filled with the fruit of your salvation - the righteous character produced in your life by Jesus Christ - for this will bring much glory and praise to God."

Philippians 1:3-4, 9-11 (NLT)

1988 was a year of big adjustments for me. I had survived the loss of my husband five years earlier, entered the work force and begun to feel like the ground was steady under my feet. Then my children all decided to relocate. No longer would I see my grandchildren on a regular basis. Visits would be fewer and conversations would be on the phone.

Letting go of your children when they are grown is difficult. We have a job to do while they are in our care but the time comes when they're ready to travel their own path. We know in our mind that time will come, but in our heart it's not as easy as we thought. What we can do is let them know how much we love them and that our prayers go out for them every day. Now we need to place them in God's hands. Send them off with this scripture: *"He who has begun a good work in you will complete it until the day of Jesus Christ."* (Philippians 1:6). The faith journey we led them on will now become theirs and they have a Heavenly Father to lead them forward.

Father, you led me through the years of raising my children. Now keep them in your watch care.

May 2

Jack's Illness

"The world's a huge stockpile of God-wonders and God-thoughts. Nothing and no one comes close to you! I start talking about you, telling what I know, and quickly run out of words. Neither numbers nor words account for you."

Psalm 40:5 (MSG)

When we got home from Florida one spring, Jack came down with what we thought was the flu. I nursed him along, trying to get him to eat, pleading with him to go to the doctor and researching his symptoms on the internet. Every day we hoped for improvement but finally realized it was time to get help and went to the emergency room. I was ready to put him in the hands of people who knew what to do. After he was admitted to the hospital, I was finally able to relax. He was in the care of experts. The burden was off my shoulders.

Through the ups and downs in my Christian walk, I've attempted to handle many trials by myself. However I've learned one very important truth. When I feel responsible for the outcome of all my problems my stress level only increases.

Taking your burdens to the One who knows just what to do, our Great Physician, removes that load you're carrying. He's the expert in every issue you face and will comfort you, restore peace, calm your spirit and guarantee what he does is exactly what needs to be done. Whatever the outcome of any trial, he will supply what you need to have victory.

Lord, when I encounter trials in my life, help me remember that you already have the solution. I take comfort in having you in charge and I'm resting in your love.

May 3

A new container of coffee

"Be imitators of God, therefore, as dearly loved children and live a life of love, just as Christ loved us and gave himself up as a fragrant offering and sacrifice to God."

Ephesians 5:12 (NIV)

I love opening a brand new container of coffee. Breathing in that first hint of the freshly opened coffee evokes feeling of anticipation. Even people who don't care for coffee often enjoy the aroma wafting out of the coffee container. The fragrance reminds me of my mornings when I pour that first cup of coffee and settle into the recliner with my devotion book and Bible. From where I sit I can see the morning opening up as I meditate on God's goodness, celebrate his love for me and think about my upcoming day.

I've begun asking God to guide me through the day and give me strength to deal with whatever comes along. I haven't always taken time to do that and it's amazing what a difference it's making, for my days become his days as I breathe in the fragrance of my Lord's love and let it follow me through each activity.

Father, fill me with joyful anticipation as I wait to see how you work in my life today.

May 4

Daylight savings

"I am GOD - yes, I AM. I haven't changed."

Malachi 3:6 (MSG)

A few years ago, Daylight Savings Time was made official in most of Indiana. Having lived in the "Kentuckiana" area for nearly 45 years, I was already accustomed to adjusting clocks twice a year and enjoyed having the extra daylight in the summer evenings. I know that change in time creates hardship for a lot of people. Change isn't easy. It seems as though we'll just get adjusted to something and then it begins to change.

Learning to be flexible has enabled me to adjust to the changes in my life. Friends come and go, families move away, loved ones die, finances are altered, health deteriorates; when these things happen we're forced to rearrange our lives. Some changes will be good and some will hurt deeply - nothing in this life is guaranteed to stay the same.

EXCEPT our Lord and Savior! He has always been the same and he will never change. That's why he's The Great I AM. He's the one constant in my life that I can always depend on; the same yesterday, today and forever. He is my Savior, Redeemer, Creator, the Spirit that lives within me and the King of my eternity. With that hope to strengthen me, I can accept any changes that I face in my life.

Father, I know changes are inevitable and I'll continue to face them in the future. Help me adjust to them through the power and strength of your Spirit.

May 5

What's in a name?

"Take a census of the whole Israelite community by their clan and families, listing every man by name, one by one."

Exodus 1:2 (NIV)

"...for I bear your name, Lord God Almighty."

Jeremiah 15:18 (NIV)

What's in a name? "A rose by any other name would still smell the same," is an old saying. But names are important. Every expectant parent puts a lot of thought into the name their child will wear for the rest of his or her life.

When I meet someone new, the first thing we'll do is exchange names, which becomes our "label" after we are acquainted. Without a name to go by, I'll often draw a blank if someone asks about my new acquaintance, but if her name is mentioned, an image of her comes to my mind. Once, in Florida, I wanted to say something to the choir director's wife, whom I hadn't met. I couldn't catch up with her so I called out, "Hey, David Shenning's wife." She paused, turned around, smiled and said "My name is Debbie." Now when I hear the name Debbie, three people in my life come to mind. God felt names were important enough to place long lists of them in the Bible.

The most important name I have is "Child of God". That's the one that I'll wear through all eternity, the one that carries the most benefits and the one that connects me to my Heavenly Father.

You are truly my Father, and I treasure the name "Child of God" more than any other name I will ever wear.

May 6

Awestruck

"He provided redemption for his people; he ordained his covenant forever - holy and awesome is his name."

Psalm 111:9 (NIV)

Have you ever been awestruck by anything? I've had couple of experiences that nearly blew me away. When I first visited Niagara Falls, seeing the thundering water cascading over the falls took my breath away; I was hypnotized by the power and beauty of it. The first time I viewed the Grand Canyon, its walls were arrayed in a palette of reds and golds that could have only been created by a God who loves beauty. I just wanted to stand there and drink it all in. However, I'm noticing that I'm not as easily awestruck as I once was. Having seen so much in my life, it takes something off-the-charts to put me in awe.

The disciples lost their sense of awe in their journey with Jesus. He had performed so many miracles in their presence that they began overlooking their significance. Consequently, when they were handed the responsibility of feeding the four thousand, it never occurred to them to expect a miracle. They faltered in their faith. *"The disciples responded, "What do you expect us to do about it? Buy food out here in the desert?"* Mark 8:4 (MSG)

Our Father demonstrates his amazing love for us every day by gently guiding us over the obstacles in our path, steering us through unknown, sometimes frightening circumstances and always shining a light of hope in front of us

Lord, the depth of your love is more than I can even imagine, and I am awestruck by what you sacrificed so I could become your child. I love you more than my words can express.

May 7

National Day of Prayer

"…..if my people who are called by My name will humble themselves and pray and seek My face and turn from their wicked ways, then I will hear from heaven and will forgive their sin and heal their land."

II Chronicles 7:14 (NKJV)

Each year in May our nation observes the National Day of Prayer. Though many Christians do take time to attend a local service, most believers probably don't even stop to offer up a prayer on behalf of our country and its leaders.

Our beloved nation is rapidly slipping from the Christian base on which it was founded into a mix of worldly ideas and values that drift further and further from what we, as believers, hold sacred and essential for our future.

Christians complain, protest and write letters, but neglect the most effective weapon we have at our disposal. As much as we'd like to cause change in our land, we are fighting a battle we can't win unless we use the weapon of prayer. You see, we are not just fighting a political battle. It has been ramped up to a battle for the souls of mankind. We can only have victory through the power of prayer. Humble yourself before him and ask for deliverance.

Lord, I love my country, but I'm seeing it decline almost daily. I'm praying for your intervention and deliverance from the evil that is trying to overtake us as a Christian nation. I have no power on my own, so strengthen me in my witness that I might let others see the hope that only you can offer them.

May 8

Mothers

"Her children respect and bless her; her husband joins in with words of praise. Charm can mislead and beauty soon fades. The woman to be admired and praised is the woman who lives in the Fear of God."

Proverbs 31:28, 30 (MSG)

Mother's Day is drawing near and many of us are reflecting on our mom and how she shaped and influenced our life. My mother was a single parent for most of my growing up years. She had to get a job to help support us. Although she was away from home much of the time, she was able to instill strong Christian values in her children. She was emotionally strong and resilient which taught me how to cope with my own trials. Because of her influence, I held fast to a struggling marriage. Late in her life, she "adopted" a granddaughter in her church, inspiring me to organize "The Grandparent Connection" in my own church. My "adopted" grandchild's mother then became an "adopted grandma" to someone else's children, so the ministry my mother began is still being carried on.

My scope of influence on the lives of my children has diminished, so I pray they will focus on the good I tried to accomplish and forget the times I was less than what I should have been.

We don't get a "do-over" so prayerfully consider how you're guiding your children. When we're in the midst of raising them we don't think about the legacy we're leaving, but what you do now will be passed on to future generations.

Father, thank you for giving me a godly mother who demonstrated her faith in the way she lived so I would have an example to follow.

May 9

Stepmothers

"Don't just pretend to love others. Really love them... Love each other with genuine affection, and take delight in honoring each other."

Romans 12:9-10 (NLT)

As we approach Mother's Day, I can't ignore the role stepmothers play in our lives as well. I have walked in the shoes of both a stepchild and a stepmother. Neither path is an easy one but when you approach your challenges with acceptance, the relationship grows into love. The blessings will flow abundantly.

As a 13-year-old, I became an unwilling stepchild and was harboring a lot of anger and some fear the first time my brother and I met our stepmother, Elsie. I was determined to dislike her, but, she reached out to me in love and always made me feel special. Elsie was caring and I loved her, not as a substitute mother, but as a friend and confidant.

In 1998, I took on the role of stepmother to two very special people. Finding my way in that role has taken time and I've made a few mistakes in that journey, but I love them and their families. Although I can't share in their old memories, we are making new ones each time we get together.

In both of these roles, I had to learn acceptance which led to a deep, bonding love. Many times I was forced out of my comfort zone and stretched to new levels of unselfish love. As a result I've been blessed beyond measure.

Lord, thank you for the stepmothers that bring unconditional love into blended families.

May 10

A pinched nerve

"He heals the broken-hearted and binds up their wounds."

Psalm 147:3 (NKJV)

"As a mother comforts her child, so will I comfort you;"

Isaiah 66:13 (NIV)

Several years ago I developed a pinched nerve in my back which caused me a lot of pain in my hands, shoulders and neck. My doctor prescribed prednisone to give me some relief. It was amazing! The day after I began taking it, the pain was gone and I spent the whole day buying and planting flowers and working around the yard. After having suffered through several weeks of pain, it was a wonderful relief. The prednisone didn't remove the problem, it only took away the pain, and that relief was only temporary

When we're faced with painful trials in our life, we have access to an even better pain-killer. The Lord surrounds us with His peace and comfort, soothing our wounds and calming our broken spirits. He doesn't remove the trial, but he offers us everything we need to deal with it. The good news is, unlike the prednisone, his help doesn't have a time limit and doesn't need a prescription.

Father, you offer the soothing antiseptic that calms and heals all my hurts and disappointments.

May 11

Unfolding news

"And so there will be strange signs in the sun, moon and stars. And here on earth the nations will be in turmoil, perplexed by the roaring seas and strange tides. Watch out! Don't let your hearts be dulled by carousing and drunkenness, and by the worries of this life. Don't let that day catch you unaware, like a trap. For that day will come upon everyone living on earth. Keep alert at all times. And pray that you might be strong enough to escape the coming horrors and stand before the Son of Man."

Luke 21:25, 34-36 (NLT)

Often "unfolding news" isn't encouraging. People are being persecuted and slaughtered in the Middle East; there's unrest, unstable weather and threatening disease everywhere - things I really don't like to hear about and yet I'm drawn to the TV like a magnet. God's Word warns us these things will occur. We are told to watch for signs and we're seeing them all around us. There've always been wars, storms and unrest in the world, but some of what's happening now is more threatening to God's children. Our values and beliefs are under attack and we're ridiculed and ostracized if we stand up for the truth in God's Word. Many Christians are feeling as though they are under attack personally and have trials descending from all directions.

Don't give up! Stand strong in God's promises. Satan knows his time is short and he's ramped up his battle to defeat us. Remember always, *"He who is in you is greater than he who is in the world."* (1 John 4:4) Keep oil in your lamp, stand on the Rock and watch for the coming of our Lord. Maybe today!

Lord of all eternity, help me focus on the hope I have. I long to go home; but until I do, use me as your hands and feet.

May 12

Tornadoes

"For you have been a shelter for me, a strong tower from the enemy."

Psalm 61:3 (NKJV))

"He shall cover you with His feathers, and under His wings you shall take refuge; His truth shall be your shield and buckler."

Psalm 91:4 (NKJV)

In the Midwest, we are acutely aware that a tornado could develop quickly, especially in the spring. Therefore, many of us make plans for a place of safety in the event we have a tornado warning. In the fall of 2013, Jack and I retreated to the basement when warnings came over the TV. As it turned out, all we lost was our electricity, but many lost their homes and possessions.

A year before that, my daughter-in-law's parents sought refuge in a relative's underground shelter during a devastating tornado that ripped through Henryville, Indiana. Their relative had enough foresight to bury a pod in the ground to be used for a shelter. Knowing where you can go for safety and protection could mean the difference between life and death,

Storms come and go in our life, often without much warning. We have One to whom we can run for shelter. He will cover us with his wings so we're not tossed about by the winds of adversity or hit by the flying darts of Satan's attacks. He protects us from the raging waters of fear which threaten to wash over us. Best of all, you have that shelter with you, no matter where you are.

Protecting Father, thank you for the shelter of your wings.

May 13

Jack's recovery

"We've been surrounded and battered by troubles, but we're not demoralized; we're not sure what to do, but we know that God knows what to do; we've been spiritually terrorized, but God hasn't left our side; we've been thrown down, but not broken."

II Corinthians 4:8-9 (MSG)

"Right now, therefore, every time we get the chance, let us work for the benefit of all, starting with the people closest to us in the community of faith."

Galatians 6:10 (MSG)

A couple of years ago while Jack struggled with some health issues, I was focused on taking care of him and trying to keep up with other responsibilities. Even though friends were praying for both of us, it began to wear on me and I felt lonely and isolated. As that loneliness enveloped me, I called a friend whose husband is dealing with a lot of physical challenges. As we shared our stories, she told to me how lonely she often felt.

As I reflected on her story and the feelings I had experienced, I began to see how God was working. I always sympathized with friends who were caretakers, but never really comprehended the depth of their sacrifice. I only had a small taste of that bitter trial but it taught me that God uses everything we go through to grow us into a vessel that he can use. Now when I pray for caregivers my heart is burdened in a new way, and when I reach out to comfort and encourage them I'm better equipped to understand their pain.

Healing Father, give me a compassionate heart so I will more fully share the pain and grief of those around me.

May 14

Weeding the tomato bed

"Surrounded then as we are by these serried ranks of witnesses, let us strip off everything that hinders us, as well as the sin which dogs our feet, and let us run the race that we have to run with patience, our eyes fixed on Jesus, the source and the goal of our faith."

Hebrews 12:1-2a (Phillips)

One warm summer morning I spent time pulling weeds and grass out of the tomato bed. It had rained the night before and the ground was soft and a little damp which made pulling the weeds easier. As I finished the job and stood up to walk back to the porch, my shoes felt very heavy. Looking down, I noticed they had picked up a thick layer of loose, damp dirt, so I had to remove my shoes before I could walk.

Do you ever notice when we're in the hustle and bustle of daily living, we pick up the sticky mud of worldly views and attitudes. Before we realize it, we're burdened down with our own complaints, frustrations, greed and empty pursuits. They stick to our heart and mind and slow down the spiritual journey we're on.

I couldn't shake the mud off my shoes. I had to beat them against each other to dislodge it. We have to shake off the influences of the world before we can walk unhindered with renewed hope in our Lord and Savior, Jesus Christ.

Lord, help me keep my mind free of worldly attitudes and empty pursuits. Let me keep my heart open so your guidance will keep me focused on you.

May 15

Unsigned degree

"The future for me holds the crown of righteousness which God, the true judge, will give to me in that day – and not, of course, only to me but to all those who have loved what they have seen of him."

II Timothy 4:8 (Phillips)

When my son Jeff graduated from Bible College he received his degree at the ceremony, but it was unsigned because he still owed the school about $50. After he paid the amount owed, they signed the degree and he was officially a graduate. No diploma or degree was issued until all the work was completed and all the fees he owed the school were paid in full.

I am so thankful that Jesus has paid my full debt and I don't owe anything. It was a gift. No amount of work I do or money I pay could ever satisfy what I owe. My Savior Jesus, in his mercy, paid it for me. I can walk in faith, confident that my "diploma" is waiting for me when I "graduate" and God will present it to me.

Savior Jesus, I will be forever thankful that you paid my debt for me.

May 16

Weaknesses

"'My grace is enough; it's all you need. My strength comes into its own in your weakness.' Once I heard that, I was glad to let it happen. I quit focusing on the handicap and began appreciating the gift. It was a case of Christ's strength moving in on my weakness. Now I take limitations in stride and with good cheer...I just let Christ take over! And so, the weaker I get, the stronger I become."

II Corinthians 12:9-10 (MSG)

Most of us have some kind of weakness, and learning to live with it can be challenging at times. If we try to conceal it, we lose opportunities to encourage others.

When I learned my hip couldn't be repaired, I had to make a choice. Using a cane was an adjustment but I decided to put a "smiley face" on my handicap. My fashionable canes draw attention and open up many conversations giving me an opportunity to show others that, even though I wouldn't have chosen this route, I have accepted it as part of who I am. I now notice others who also depend on walkers and canes and I love encouraging them.

No matter what our weakness is we can show others how to live a life of joy and victory through the amazing strength God has given us. As the older generation, we can display joy, even in our infirmities, and show those coming after us they need not fear their senior years. Whatever they may face in the future, they have God's promise to provide the strength they need.

Lord, help me stay positive no matter what my future holds so I will be an encouragement to others in their physical and personal struggles.

May 17

Irregular people

"I'm telling you to love your enemies. Let them bring out the best in you, not the worst. When someone gives you a hard time, respond with the energies of prayer, for then you are working out of your true selves, your God-created selves. This is what God does. He gives his best - to everyone regardless; the good and bad, the nice and nasty. If all you do is love the lovable, do you expect a bonus? Anybody can do that--------Live generously and graciously toward others, the way God lives toward you."

Matthew 5:44-46, 48 (MSG)

Several years ago I read a book called *"Irregular People"*, written by Joyce Landorf, which helped me understand my responsibilities in challenging relationships. All of us encounter those who Joyce refers to as "irregular people" in our lives. It might be a co-worker, neighbor or perhaps even a relative who just seems to rub you the wrong way. As hard as we try to get along with them, more often than not, we end up frustrated and sometimes angry. I've dealt with a few of these people in my life and, in retrospect, I'm sure I didn't always handle the conflicts in a way that pleased God.

Loving others the way God wants isn't always easy. Most of the people I know are easy to get along with and love, but once in a while I'll encounter someone who seems to push the wrong button. Maybe God has presented me with a chance to stretch my spiritual patience muscle and develop my capacity to show his love through my acceptance.

Father, help me respect the ideas and opinions of others, even when I don't agree with them. May I learn to disagree in a loving way.

May 18

Love is.....

"Love each other with genuine affection" and take delight in honoring each other."

Romans 12:10 (NLT)

"Love is patient and kind. Love is not jealous or boastful or proud or rude. It does not demand its own way. It is not irritable, and keeps no record of being wronged. It does not rejoice about injustice, but rejoices whenever the truth wins out. Love never gives up, never loses faith, is always hopeful, and endures through every circumstance."

I Corinthians 13:4-7 (NLT)

I've been guilty of speaking unkindly or having an unforgiving spirit if I've been hurt. A few years ago there was a popular saying that began with "Love is." When you really do care about someone, you try hard to do things that please them whether it's a family member or a friend. That love encompasses: being there to encourage or comfort them, spending time with them, praying for them, being patient and not having to say you're sorry. Many times though we take that relationship for granted and grow careless in the way we treat them. We're careful to treat casual acquaintances and strangers with courtesy and yet don't extend the same respect toward those closest to us?

Our Savior Jesus was patient and gentle with Peter, even when he acted impulsively; Jesus showed love for Judas, even knowing what lay ahead. He commands us to love in the same way and with his help we can.

Father, teach me to love the way Jesus did. In the heat of the moment, it's so easy to get caught up in emotions. Help me learn to love more fully.

May 19

Times have changed

"Be on your guard; stand firm in the faith; be courageous; be strong."

I Corinthians 16:13 (NIV)

Every day in the news we see more cases of shootings, more crime, riots and unrest around the world. As a result of the violence in our country, many of the places we used to visit freely without concern for our safety now have security guards at the door. Jack and I had to go through security to visit the Air and Space Museum in D.C. a few years ago and were turned away from the military base in San Diego where Jack was once stationed.

As disturbing as all of this is, we have to accept the reality that life has changed. It may never return to what we once knew as normal and we really can't do anything about it.

We can, however, do something about what we allow into our hearts and minds. I've learned that fear, worry, anger, an unforgiving spirit, arguments, foolish talk and negative thinking are all under my control. God's Word tells me that I can set up a guard in my life to protect me from these intruders which threaten my state of mind and rob me of peace.

As far as what is reported in the news, I'm saddened by the increasing evil in our world, but I'm resting securely in the hope I have in my Savior Jesus Christ. He has a plan and I will not fear! In the meantime, I have a security guard in my heart.

Lord, it would be nice to have a filter on my mind so nothing sinful could enter, but then I would have no responsibility. Help choose wisely what I look at, listen to or talk about.

May 20

New gym equipment

"May our Lord Jesus Christ himself and God our Father who loved us and by his grace gave us eternal encouragement and good hope, encourage your hearts and strengthen you in every good deed and word."

II Thessalonians 2:16-17 (NIV)

Sometimes at the gym I'll see someone working out on a machine that I've never tried before and I'll give it a whirl. The next couple of days I'll pay for my efforts with sore, stiff muscles. However, if I continue to use the machine my soreness diminishes and the muscles are strengthened. My body benefits from each new exercise I add to my workout.

I've had opportunities to serve the Lord that were new for me. I decided to try them and for a while I would be uncomfortable with unfamiliar responsibilities. They would stretch my faith and trust in God's provisions. With time, though, the strength of my faith increased and my acts of service would become fulfilling and joyful. It seemed as though my overall trust in God grew through each new step of faith.

Don't be afraid to try new adventures in serving him. You will grow in trust, for he promises to lead you and supply what you need to serve in an exciting new way.

Father, you give me opportunities to serve and sometimes I am afraid to even try. Infuse me with faith so I will trust in your provisions.

May 21

Curb appeal

"You paid careful attention to the way we lived among you and determined to live that way yourselves. In imitating us, you imitated the Master. The word has gotten around. Your lives are echoing the Master's Word, not only in the provinces but all over the place. The news of your faith has gotten out. We don't even have to say anything anymore -- you're the message!"

I Thessalonians 1:5, 7-8 (MSG)

One of the most important elements of marketing a house is curb appeal. If the house appears run down or unkempt, perspective buyers are less likely to be interested. Their decision to contact the realtor hangs on the first impression.

Does our faith walk have "curb appeal" for those around us who are not Christians? There've been times that I haven't displayed a loving attitude towards others. Maybe I was impatient with poor service at a restaurant, showed frustration when waiting in a long line or ignored people who genuinely need a handout. If I'm to be effective as a witness for my Lord, I have to be showing love the way he would.

Our faith walk is what creates an interest in those around us. That often involves stepping out of our comfort zone to connect with others. Praying before our meal when eating out, showing patience with poor service or disruptive children in a restaurant, letting someone else go before you in line or reaching out to a person in need are small ways we can display God's love.

Father, remind me to demonstrate your love as I interact with others. Let me reflect the love you show me in my walk today.

May 22

In the shadow of the cross

"Because you are my help, I sing in the shadow of your wings. I cling to you; your right hand upholds me."

Psalms 63:7, 8 (NIV)

What I love most about the dawning of spring is when earth is adorned with a canopy of green. Summer heat soon follows on its heels, but God created trees to offer shade where we can escape the unrelenting discomfort of summer and bask in the coolness provided by a green umbrella of relief and protection.

Before I accepted the forgiving grace of our Lord and Savior, I stood in the glaring heat of judgment. I can rejoice, though, for I have relief and shelter as I stand in the shade of the cross, which is like the wings of God giving me refuge.

Our Savior presented us with that incredible gift by taking our sins to the cross. After we accept his forgiving grace we stand in God's protecting shadow and find rest.

Loving God, you show me newness every day, through the breaking of dawn, the chirping of a bird, the bud of a new flower, the freshly-brewed cup of coffee. Thank you for each brand new morning when I can refresh and renew my spirit.

May 23

Blue days

"Forget the former things! Do not dwell on the past. See, I am doing a new thing! Now it springs up; do you not perceive it? I am making a way in the wilderness and streams in the wasteland.

Isaiah 43:18-19 (NIV)

Every now and then I'll have a blue day. For some reason days like that give birth to memories of the poor decisions I've made in my life. I end up wallowing in guilt and regret over past actions. Knowing I could have used more wisdom and patience in my behavior makes my mood even darker. I begin to feel as though I'm wandering in a desert of despair. If I was given the same set of choices to make with the same limited wisdom and maturity, I'd probably make the same mistakes again.

God tells us not to look back. How amazing! He's forgotten all those misguided decisions from my past. So now I have to make another choice - whether to dwell on all my poor decisions or to focus on what my Savior has given me. Through his grace I've been given an unblemished past and the indwelling Holy Spirit to help me make wiser choices now and in the future. Therefore I will praise my Lord and my day will be transformed from blue to shining gold.

Father, you have forgotten all my mistakes. Teach me to rest in your presence each day without dragging along the baggage from my past.

May 24

Memorial Day

"Jesus said to her, 'I am the resurrection and the life. The one who believes in me will live, even though they die, and whoever lives by believing in me will never die.'"

John 11:25-26 (NIV)

Every year, Jack and I go to a couple of cemeteries to put flowers on two graves for Memorial Day. One of them is a family friend who served in the army. The other is my mother's grave. The friend's cemetery is well maintained; all we have to do is take the old flowers down and hang the new ones. My mother's grave is in our home town; she is buried in one of the oldest sections of the cemetery. The maintenance crew there is only able to run the mower between the headstones. We go equipped with a broom, grass clippers, wire and a new basket of flowers. When we're finished, it stands out from the surrounding graves. It tells anyone who passes by "someone is remembering me and cares about my grave." We can't tell those who have gone home how much we loved them and miss them, but we can honor them in other ways.

On Memorial Day, we remember those who influenced and guided us throughout our life. They may not have served in the military but many, like my mother, were left at home to take care of their families when the spouse went off to war. They deserve our respect and honor too.

In our remembering, we have God's assurance that we'll see them again when we celebrate our homecoming with our reunited family and friends.

Thank you Lord, Jesus for giving me the gift of eternal life. I am joyfully anticipating the homecoming when I join those who have gone before me.

May 25

A new knee

"Create in me a clean heart, O God, and renew a steadfast spirit within me."

Psalm 51:10 (NKJV)

For years I endured knee pain until I reached the point when I could no longer do things I enjoyed. I finally gave in to having a knee replacement which, after it healed, eliminated the pain and made life enjoyable again. Different parts of our body will inevitably wear out or become diseased and modern technology affords us the opportunity to have them replaced. Knees, hips, kidneys or almost any other part of us can now be successfully transplanted or replaced, which gives people a better quality of life.

Heart surgeons can replace a heart that no longer functions well enough to sustain life, but recipients will often remain on a waiting list for a long time waiting for a donor. If they are lucky enough to get a heart transplant, it will come from someone who lost their own life.

God is the only one who can give us a new spiritual heart. When we realize how broken and sinful our hearts are, we can turn to our Lord in repentance and he lovingly replaces it, along with a new spirit. There's no waiting list for our new heart, which will beat with renewed joy and hope in our Savior Jesus Christ who willingly gave his life so we could have a new and righteous one.

Father, my spiritual self wants to be holy but my earthly body sometimes gets in the way. Help me stand strong against caving into desires that are harmful to my relationship with you.

May 26

I can't hear you

"Are you listening to me? Really listening?"

Matthew 11:15 (MSG)

"Whoever belongs to God hears what God says."

John 8:47a (NIV)

Jack and I sometimes accuse each other of not talking loud enough. Age has taken a toll on our hearing. Consequently neither one of us hears as well as we used to. If we're in a crowd of people, it's even more difficult because the sounds we are trying to hear are swallowed up in the background noises.

We can hear God's voice even when the sounds of the world are swirling around trying to distract us. We have spiritual ears that aren't affected by aging or deafness. Psalm 95:7 says *"Today, if you will hear His voice, do not harden your hearts as in the rebellion."* Even the deaf are able to hear God speaking to them. Someday, if I'm no longer able to listen to the voices of family and friends, I will still hear my Lord.

It is our responsibility to listen for his voice for he is the One that guides us through turbulent waters. True wisdom comes to us through the inner voice of the Spirit who directs our path.

Eternal Father, help me keep listening for your voice amidst the noise of the world that threatens to distract me.

May 27

There was a time...

"Keep vigilant watch over your heart; that's where life starts. Don't talk out of both sides of your mouth...Keep your eyes straight ahead...Watch your step...Look neither right nor left."

Proverbs 4:23-27 (MSG)

There was a time when doors, windows and cars could be left unlocked. Even bikes could be left outside, unattended, and no one would steal them. Occasionally someone would be burglarized but even that didn't happen very often.

Today things are very different. Everything must be locked up and secure. Even the neighborhoods once considered immune to crime have become open game.

Once upon a time, our hearts and minds weren't bombarded with all the temptations that currently saturate the TV, movies, magazines and internet. Oh, we had our weak moments when our defenses were down and temptations would gain a foothold, but today we have to be on guard constantly.

God in His sovereignty didn't equip us with a lock to keep the bad stuff out but he did provide us with the tools to make our hearts secure. They are all available to us in his Word but we have to put them to use. We're responsible for guarding our hearts against intruders trying to undermine our faith and rob us of the joy we have through our Savior, Jesus Christ.

Father, the world doesn't consider purity or walking in faith as relevant anymore. Enable me to stand strong even when I suffer ridicule or persecution for my beliefs.

May 28

Weddings

"Love is patient and kind. Love is not jealous or boastful or proud or rude. It does not demand its own way. It is not irritable, and it keeps no record of being wronged. It does not rejoice about injustice but rejoices whenever the truth wins out. Love never gives up, never loses faith, is always hopeful, and endures through every circumstance."

I Corinthians 13:3-7 (NLT)

In the spring many couples are making their wedding plans and dreaming of the life they will soon be spending together. They're in love and imagining their lives will be filled with bliss and unbroken harmony.

A Godly marriage begins like a newly-planted tree which will grow strong and mighty when properly nourished and cared for. Through the process of growth, it survives storms because it is securely anchored by cords in the ground. Its branches offer a place of refuge for birds and squirrels

A good marriage thrives because the two people who made a commitment were willing to invest time and work to make it strong. They learned how to stand strong in the storms of life that sometimes blew around them. They watered and nourished it with love and forgiveness. Their roots grew deep through trusting in the Lord. The Godly couple that works at making their home a place of refuge and peace will become an example and inspiration to others.

All knowing Father, you knew your children would need the love and commitment found in a marriage. Thank you for the Godly husband you brought into my life.

May 29

A big yellow magnet

"Come close to God and he will come close to you. Realize you have sinned and get your hands clean again. Realize that you have been disloyal and get yours hearts made true once more."

James 4:8 (Phillips)

When my grandson was little he had a large yellow magnet shaped like a horseshoe. It had a separate red bar with its own magnet that attached to the base. The bar had one positive end and one negative end. The positive end clamped the bar tightly to the horseshoe and the negative end would not, actually pushing it away. It was fascinating to see how differently they reacted to each other.

When we accept Jesus as our Savior, we are drawn to him like a magnet. Once that connection is made, we are safely attached to him like the positive end of the magnet. How comforting to know that, even if the connection is briefly broken by our sin, his love and forgiveness draws us back and holds us securely once more.

Those who choose not to believe and accept his saving grace are like the negative end of the magnet. There's no connection so they have no hope. They are pushed away by their unbelief.

Father, like a magnet, your love draws me to your feet in wonder and worship.

May 30

Every experience tells a story

"Show me how you work, God; school me in your ways. Guide me in your truth and teach me, for you are God my Savior, and my hope is in you all day long."

Psalm 25:4-5 (NIV)

Throughout my journey in writing, I've tapped into personal experiences and those I shared with family as I gathered material for my devotions. In the process, I've discovered that everything that happens in life has a story to tell. It's not something you think about at the time you're in the middle of it, but in retrospect, you see it unfold in the way God worked in your life, even when you didn't feel his presence.

In reflection, I realize that things have always worked out in the best way for me during the times I faced seemingly insurmountable challenges. It wasn't always the way I had planned, but it was the plan God had for me. God's plan was always better, for it developed my faith and put my feet on a secure path. I'm so thankful God choreographed my journey, for if it had been in my control I would have crashed and burned long ago.

Lord, thank you for leading me through the mountaintops and valleys of my life. Help me to be strong while I'm learning the valuable lessons you are teaching me. You are the light on my path.

May 31

Consistent prayer

"In peace I will lie down and sleep, for you alone, Lord, make me dwell in safety."

Psalm 4:8 (NIV)

My prayer life isn't always consistent. When a friend shares a need or I have one of my own, I'll pause to offer up a short prayer. We have mealtime prayers, also community prayers in Bible Study and in small group gatherings, but most of my praying is done when I go to bed at night. Everything is quiet and dark so there aren't distractions. However, when I've had an especially busy day, I'll struggle to stay awake long enough to finish. That used to frustrate me and I would feel guilty. Lately I've thought about this and have decided that perhaps God isn't disappointed in me. I imagine he's pleased that the last words I speak before drifting off are part of my conversation with him. I'm working on making God the first one that comes to my mind when I wake up in the morning, thanking him for a good night's sleep, a brand new day and asking for guidance in my activities.

Putting ourselves in touch with the Master and resting in his fellowship before falling asleep brings peace to our hearts and erases the concerns we are tempted to carry to bed. There's not enough room in the bed for peace and concern at the same time so choose peace as your bedfellow.

Faithful Father, help me remember that our relationship is a personal one.

June

Yea though I walk through the valley of the shadow of death . . .

Lord, I know you are there in the midst of my suffering and pain, even when I can't feel your presence.

June 1

Facing death

"Who can live and not see death, or who can escape the power of the grave?"

Psalm 89:48 (NIV)

"God blesses those who mourn, for they will be comforted."

Matthew 5:4 (NLT)

There are few things in life that affect us as much as the sudden death of someone you love. Everyone has to face losing family and friends. Sometimes we're prepared emotionally but often we're not.

In the winter of 1961, I received a letter from my stepmother, Elsie, informing me that my dad had been admitted to the hospital for tests on his lungs. He had been under the weather and coughing a lot. The doctors were going to check him for emphysema and lung cancer. Until I received that letter, I hadn't been aware he was sick. I received a phone call from Elsie at 6:30 a.m. the next day informing me that my dad had died. I wasn't prepared emotionally for that devastating news. My dad was only 52 and I had a life time of unfulfilled experiences with him and many unanswered questions. That was probably the most difficult death I have ever faced.

Times lost can never be retrieved. As I estimate it, the total time I spent with my dad after he left for war, was less than 4 months. I was angry at my dad, angry at God and struggled with a profound grief for months. But God in his mercy brought joy back into my life. Some things we may never know or understand, but somehow we accept what life brings and move on to a new and brighter day.

Father of comfort and strength, thank you for filling in the empty places left by an absent dad. You supplied what I needed and led me to a relationship with you that exceeds more than I ever dreamed I would have.

June 2

Driving in a fog

"Send me your light and your faithful care, let them lead me; let them bring me to your holy mountain, to the place where you dwell."

Psalm 43:3 (NIV)

One evening, in the 1970's, my friend June and I were driving home from a women's gathering where she had given a talk. As we drove along the dark country roads, it began to get foggy. The farther we drove, the foggier it became, finally becoming so dense that I had my nose against the windshield trying to see the road ahead. Nothing seemed to help - running the windshield wipers, opening the windows and turning on the headlights. It was scary but also comical - two women driving cautiously along a dark, foggy road, one with her nose against windshield, the other gripping the steering wheel and fussing about the ordeal. We arrived home safely, but it was an experience I won't forget.

The road we travel in this life sometimes becomes fogged up with the troubles and pains we endure. We can't see where we're going and start to fear what's ahead, so we try everything we can think of to shed some light up the road. Worries cloud our mind, panic sets in and soon we slow down to a crawl in our faith walk.

God is the light that helps us get up and start forward again. We still may not see what lies ahead, but his light shines on each step we take. We can continue our journey without fear, confident that he will guide us safely home.

Loving Father, I thank you that you walk ahead of me each step of the way, leading me through the darkness and fog of the storms.

June 3

An empty reserve tank

"He gives power to the weak, and to those who have no might He increases strength. But those who wait on the Lord shall renew their strength, they shall mount up with wings like eagles, they shall run and not be weary, they shall walk and not faint."

Isaiah 40:29, 31 (NKJV)

Sometime situations will interrupt our life and nearly empty the reserves of our physical or emotional strength. About three times a year our life becomes so full of the physical demands that I nearly reach a point of exhaustion. The most challenging annual task is setting up the courtyard and porch outside our home in late spring. It involves carrying items to the front of the house, buying and planting the flowers and climbing up and down a step stool to hang the curtains and bamboo blinds on the porch. Using my cane, which offers me support and stability, isn't an option when I'm carrying something or climbing up on a stool.

Our Lord offers us a source of strength that we can tap into when we have none left of our own. If we serve in any area of ministry, he enables us to do things that wouldn't be possible without his help. I've often wondered how Abraham managed to keep going at his advanced age. Moses was a senior citizen by the time he led the Israelites through the wilderness. God gave them the strength they needed and he will supply ours too. My cane gives me support physically but God promises so much more than that. He says we will fly like eagles on the strength that he offers us.

Lord, you are my strength. Help me recognize my weaknesses so I will depend on your power to fill my empty tank.

June 4

Wasted food

"When the people had eaten their fill, he said to his disciples, "Gather the leftovers so nothing is wasted." They went to work and filled twelve large baskets with leftovers from the five barley loaves."

John 6:13 (MSG)

We have become a society of waste. In our homes the waste results from buying more than we need. Jack and I both grew up during a time when much of the food was rationed. My mother and grandma only bought what they needed and they were careful to use all of it. We were expected to clean off our plates before being excused from the table. Jack still cannot stand to leave any food on his plate, but I've mostly broken that habit.

I've seen a lot of perfectly good food tossed in the trash because someone took more than they needed. We live in a culture of excess: more clothes, more gadgets, more toys, more food. We've managed to teach the upcoming generation that you can never have too much, no matter what it is.

When Jesus fed the five thousand, he instructed the disciples to gather what remained and those "leftovers" filled twelve baskets. God cares what we do with our abundance. If we're discarding possessions or food because we're bored with them or full, then we're being wasteful, and I don't think that pleases God. Our challenge is to shed the habit of excess and share our abundance with those less fortunate.

Lord, teach me to be content with just enough to meet my needs.

June 5

Going to the park

"Step out of the traffic! Take a long, loving look at me, your High God. Above politics, above everything. Jacob-wrestling God fights for us. God-of-Angel-Armies protects us."

Psalm 46:10-11 (MSG)

In the town where I grew up, there was a big park located about 3/4 of a mile from my home. That became my favorite destination in the summer. My friends and I often rode our bikes to the park in the afternoons where we could visit a mini zoo, go to the swimming pool and enjoy a playground that included a very tall slide, swings, a see-saw and two merry-go-rounds. When there were enough of us, some would get on the merry-go-round and a couple others would start pushing. Once it began to spin no one could get on or off until it slowed down.

When our mind is so busy with things we're planning, our worries, temptations and all the stuff we see and hear, it becomes like the merry-go-round, which needed our help to keep it going. Our too-full schedules and cluttered minds are that way because of our efforts, and we lose our sense of calm and peace. The Holy Spirit is waiting patiently for us to slow down enough for him to step in and restore peace in our heart. Peace is most cherished when it is restored after a battle, and there is a battle going on for the control of our hearts and minds.

Father, help me to slow my life down to a pace that makes room for you to join me in the journey.

June 6

Answered prayer

"Teach me your way, Lord, that I may rely on your faithfulness; give me an undivided heart, that I may fear your name. I will praise you, Lord my God, with all my heart; I will glorify your name forever."

Psalm 86:11-12 (NIV)

Recently I was thinking about my prayer life over the years. A few of my prayers were answered immediately, but most took longer than I hoped. There were a couple of prayer requests I nearly gave up on before God answered and many of them weren't answered the way I'd planned. Sometimes I struggled with that. I'll admit that when I began, my prayers consisted primarily of requests. The petitions were mostly for others, but I was doing all the talking and not listening to what God was teaching me.

God's responses to our prayers often will change circumstances and answers can occasionally be miraculous. However, as I think about my years of prayers and how they sometimes changed the course of my life or that of someone else, I began to realize that prayer had changed *me* the most. I learned hard and sometimes painful lessons as God dealt with me on this journey. He sees the whole picture while I see only what's in front of me.

Through this process I've learned to shift my focus from my petitions to developing a trust in my Lord and what he is doing in my life. I am so grateful that the answers he gives are the ones that build my faith and prepare me for whatever may come in the future.

Lord, help me grow through the lessons I've learned from my prayers, no matter how you answered them.

June 7

Feeling used

"For it is God who is at work within you, giving you the will and the power to achieve his purpose. Do all you have to do without grumbling or arguing, so that you may be God's children, blameless, sincere and wholesome, living in a warped and diseased world, and shining there like lights in a dark place. For you hold in your hands the very word of life."

Philippians 2:12-15 (Phillips)

I've heard people say resentfully, "I felt like I was being used" when they realized someone had taken advantage of them. I've had that feeling a few times myself. I love helping others but I prefer it to be something I volunteer for or have been asked about rather than forced or manipulated into doing. No one likes to feel used.

I do want to be used by God, though. There've been occasions in the past when God used me in ways that took me out of my comfort zone. I'm someone who likes things neat, orderly and calm. A few times, God has interrupted my calm and ordered environment and replaced it with chaotic circumstances that nearly pushed my patience and tolerance to the limit. Through those times, I learned to love in spite of the uncomfortable challenges I faced.

If we desire to be useful to God, we have to allow ourselves to be led into new and diverse experiences. We're to be like clay in his hands and he will mold us into a vessel that can be used for his glory.

Lord, equip me with the patience and endurance I need when I step into new and different areas of service and sacrifice.

June 8

Mockingbirds

"Listen to my instructions and be wise; do not disregard it."

Proverbs 8:33 (NIV)

"Don't let anyone capture you with empty philosophies and high-sounding nonsense that come from human thinking and from the spiritual powers of this world rather than Christ."

Colossians 2:8 (NLT)

One evening Jack and I were sitting on my daughter's front porch in Kentucky. They live in the country, close to a horse farm where the hills are rolling and beautiful. We were enjoying the view and listening to the birds chirping when we heard one bird warbling with several different trills. I told Jack it was a mockingbird mimicking other birds' songs. They're able to imitate a number of different bird trills and are fascinating to hear.

With all the chatter around us: news, talk shows and even some religions, we hear deceiving messages constantly. Satan is a master at mimicking God's message, trying to fool us into believing him. He uses fear, greed, discontent, doubt or any other way he can to fool us into thinking we're hearing God's message.

The Bible holds words of wisdom about anything we will ever face. If we're not familiar with God's word, we're easily led astray. Like the bird's trills we heard on my daughter's porch, the deceiver's message sounds authentic, but the one sending it is nothing but a mocking bird.

Lord, help me to walk so close to you that I recognize the call of false gods. You alone offer the music of true hope.

June 9

Our cherry tree

"I am the vine itself; you are the branches. It is the man who shares my life and whose life I share who proves fruitful. For the plain fact is that apart from me you can do nothing at all."

John 15:5 (Phillips)

We used to have a cherry tree in our backyard. Even though the tree was old, it provided enough cherries each year for us to freeze several bags and still have a lot left to share with friends. The cherries that were too high for us to reach gave the birds a tasty treat as well. One summer during a storm, about 1/3 of the tree blew down with the fallen limbs partly connected. We picked an abundant crop of cherries that summer because the limbs still had some life in them. The tree lasted several more years and continued to give us fruit until Jack finally had to cut it down.

When you're a tree in God's garden you produce fruit even as you grow older. Many seniors think they don't have anything left to offer. As long as you're alive and stay connected to God, the source of your strength, he can use you. If you'll pray about where he wants to use you, his Spirit will give you direction.

Lord, help me to stay focused on you and not myself. As long as I have breath in me, I want to bear fruit. Help me to recognize areas where I can serve, and help me keep my determination to be used by you.

June 10

Aggravation

"Let us not grow tired of doing good, for, unless we throw in our hand, the ultimate harvest is assured."

Galatians 6:9 (Phillips)

"The man who patiently endures the temptations and trials that come to him is the truly happy man, for once his testing is complete he will receive the crown of life which the Lord has promised to all who love him."

James 1:12 (Phillips)

In the 1960's there was a popular board game called Aggravation. The object of the game was to move your four little wood discs onto the board and safely to the finish called home. Once your players were home, no one could send them back. However, while you were moving them around the board, someone else could land on the space you occupied and send you back to the start. It was possible to get almost home and be sent back. That's why it was called Aggravation. It was fun but could be very frustrating.

In traveling from the starting place of my faith journey to my eternal home I've had setbacks. I'd be making good progress and growing and then some trial or temptation set me back. I would feel like I'd lost ground and had to start over. Those challenges still jump on my space and set me back, although I've managed to "stay on the board" longer each time. I know one of these days I'll be in that "safe place" called home and I won't have to cope with the "aggravations" any more.

Gracious Father, guide me as I plan my days. Equip me with wisdom so I won't have setbacks and lose touch with you.

June 11

Allergies

"See, God has come to save me. I will trust in him and not be afraid. The Lord God is my strength and my song, he has given me victory."

Isaiah 12:2 (NLT)

For those of us who suffer with allergies, spring and early summer are difficult seasons. Even though this is my favorite time of the year, there's a lot of pollen floating around which causes problems for me. Lately a lot of people who never were troubled with allergies before have begun to suffer as well. All the fresh beauty of new growth comes with a cost. The only way to escape is to isolate ourselves in the house with all the doors and windows shut. I can also lessen symptoms by taking an antihistamine for relief.

I also think I've developed an allergic reaction to all the stuff the world throws at us. We've reached a time on this earth when the spread of new ideas and endless opinions that largely contradict our core beliefs causes a reaction in our minds and hearts. We can become disturbed, angry and anxious. It isn't possible to be isolated from the world we live in, but we can become immune to its effect by protecting ourselves. The only successful solution to these attacks on our peace is to be immersed in the Word and in prayer. This will bring relief to your troubled mind and comfort your anxious heart. With the help of the Holy Spirit, we can live with these attacks without suffering the effects.

Lord, comfort my anxious heart with your soothing balm of peace so I won't be affected by the world around me.

June 12

Hate

"But I say to all of you who will listen; love your enemies, do good to those who hate you, bless those who curse you, and pray for those who treat you badly."

Luke 6:27-28 (Phillips)

"Hate" is a powerful word used to express strong feelings about something or someone. The Webster definition is: to feel extreme enmity or dislike. Sometimes we use the word loosely, not actually harboring the strong emotion that the word implies. I might say "I hate getting up in the morning" or "I hate going to the gym" when in reality, it's simply hard for me to get excited about it. Usually when I've felt hate toward someone, the feeling left when I actually got to know and understand them. The real danger in that emotion is that it takes root in your heart and can spread, affecting those around you. I do hate conflict, whether it's in the home, in church or among friends.

I researched how the word "hate" is used in the Bible and discovered that we are told to hate actions such as: sin, evil, wickedness, wrongdoing, bloodshed. We are instructed to love our enemies and do good to them. So often, we end up hating the wrong things and embracing the things that God hates. As believers filled with the Holy Spirit, we are equipped with the power to turn our emotions around and love the way God loves. It's not always easy, but we can learn to direct our feelings of "hate" to the actions that are a result of sin, and not the person caught up in the sin.

Father, help me distinguish between the sin and the person committing it. Enable me to love as you have loved me.

June 13

Healing

"The sacrifice you desire is a broken spirit. You will not reject a broken and repentant heart."

Psalm 51:17 (NLT)

Our prayer chains are filled with requests for healing. My own prayer life is usually saturated with pleas for God's healing touch on those I've lifted up. Oftentimes God has answered with mercy and compassion, restoring health to many. Physical healing is, therefore, high on our list when we offer up our petitions.

Even more important is the healing of a heart that is far from God. The world is filled with people whose hearts are sick and in desperate need of a Savior. Until they realize their condition, they won't seek help from the Great Physician. They have a heart disease called unbelief that will lead to eternal death. All of us know people who suffer with this condition and they should be at the top of our prayer list. Until their heart is broken, they cannot be healed.

Father, touch the hearts of those who have never recognized their need for the Savior who will heal their brokenness. Open their eyes to your love and grace.

June 14

Visiting D.C.

"One day, however, no one else was around when he went in to do his work. She came and grabbed his cloak, demanding, "Come on, sleep with me!" Joseph tore himself away, but he left his cloak in her hand as he ran from the house."

Genesis 39:11, 12 (NLT)

"The highway of the upright avoids evil; those who guard their ways preserve their lives."

Proverbs 16:17 (NIV)

When we were teenagers, my brother and I would visit our dad in Washington, DC., enjoying some of the sights during our stay. One day when we were headed toward the Smithsonian, we unknowingly walked into a swarm of gnats that we hadn't noticed. We tried to get away from them but they seemed to be following us. We tried swatting them but nothing was helping. In desperation, we began to run and managed to escape them.

Sometimes we may not see the danger in a situation we've become involved in where temptation rears its ugly head. We assume we're immune because we're Christian, so we try to walk through it without realizing how it affects us. Like the swarm of gnats that followed my brother and me, temptation will not leave you, so you have to flee (run) from it. Your temptation may be immorality, gambling, acquiring more "stuff" or anything you know is a weakness with you. Turn away from it and run to God for help, for you cannot conquer temptation without him.

Father, I need your strength and wisdom every day to conquer temptation.

June 15

Wheels

"The Lord is my light and my salvation - whom shall I fear? The Lord is the stronghold of my life - of whom shall I be afraid?"

Psalm 27:1 (NIV)

As a child I loved riding my tricycle and later a bicycle I was given by my grandma. Pedaling along the road with the breeze gently blowing in my face gave me a sense of freedom. Experiencing the joy of riding was only possible because of wheels. Without them, we wouldn't have the mobility we take for granted. As important as they are, however, they would be worthless without a hub. That vital element connects the wheel to the frame, allows it to spin and keeps it from getting out of line, bending, wobbling and eventually collapsing. The hub is a center around which other things revolve or from which they radiate; a focus of activity or authority or importance.

Our lives are like a wheel. There'll be a main focus in all of us. Without God as our hub, our lives cannot roll along without struggling, bending this way and that and perhaps coming apart in a heap of defeat and failure. Most people put something or someone else at the center of their focus and they end up feeling empty and void of real purpose. Their hub has no lasting strength or power and will soon disappoint or desert them. Our life can never have real balance until we put God in the center. He alone is our hub, a stronghold who removes fear, gives us direction, helps us over the rough spots in our journey and leads us safely to our destination.

Lord, no matter what is going on in my life, I want to keep you front and center. Help me stay focused on you in every decision, every trial, every victory, every moment of my life. I need you as my hub.

June 16

Small jobs

"And so, brother of mine, stand firm! Let nothing move you as you busy yourselves in the Lord's work. Be sure that nothing you do for him is ever lost or wasted."

I Corinthians 15:58 (Phillips)

Sometimes I have days filled with small jobs and I feel as though nothing important was accomplished. I didn't do anything significant enough to even be noticed by anyone. Occasionally I worry that others might think I wasted my time. However, the small tasks we do, almost without thinking about them, are the very things that keep the home running smoothly.

There are a lot of small almost invisible labors of love done by people behind the scenes in our churches. We give accolades to the minister, the musicians and those involved in the worship service and yet that service could not happen without the many others who clean, print bulletins, work in the nursery, set up the computer, work the sound system and all the other things that take place behind the scenes.

No matter whether we're in the church building or out in the community, everything we do to serve our Lord is important. It might be helping a neighbor, buying groceries for the food pantry, sending a card to a shut-in, or anything else we do in his name for it is all helping to build his kingdom. These may seem like insignificant responsibilities, but God notices the small things we do and he considers them all important.

Father, help me to be more concerned with serving and less about being recognized for that service.

June 17

Good luck charms

"I pulled you in from all over the world, called you in from every dark corner of the earth, telling you, 'You're my servant, serving on my side. I've picked you, I haven't dropped you.' Don't panic, I'm with you. There's no need to fear for I'm your God. I'll give you strength. I'll help you. I'll hold you steady, keep a firm grip on you."

Isaiah 41:9-10 (MSG)

A lot of people carry a good luck charm in their car or on their person. There was even an athlete who said he had a pair of socks that brought him good luck. He claimed he wouldn't play unless he wore those "lucky" socks. These good luck charms could be anything from a rabbit's foot to some small treasure handed down from a loved one. The people trust the charm to protect them or help them succeed, and they don't feel secure if they don't have it with them.

Sometimes even Christians are tempted to shrink God down to a size they can carry with them. They'll say they have faith, but they choose to keep the Lord in their pocket and they only pull him out when they need him.

The God we serve cannot be contained. His power and majesty are beyond our wildest imagination. He created everything and he is everywhere. I know my Lord is there for me, no matter where I go or what I do, and he alone is all I need. I don't carry him, he carries me. I store his words in my heart to remind me of his faithfulness and love for me and that enables me to live in peace and security.

Father, I want to carry your love for me in my heart. Help me reflect it in my life so others will see it in my faith.

June 18

Walking on water

"Faith is the confidence that what we hope for will actually happen; it gives us assurance about things we cannot see."

Hebrews 11:1 (NLT)

In April of 2001 we put our house in Walton on the market. We found a house in Kokomo we liked and put an offer on it, contingent on selling our house in Walton. The home we were selling had been on the market for several weeks and no one was even looking at it. A few days before the contingency was to run out, someone else made an offer on the one we wanted to buy. With no activity on our house in Walton, we had to make a decision. Would we play it safe and give up on the house we wanted to buy or take the contingency off the plate and risk having two houses to pay for?

After praying about it, we felt like God was directing us to take the risk and "get out of the boat and walk on the water." A couple of days later we left for a wedding in Ohio, followed by a trip to Niagara Falls. We were to call our realtor after we arrived at Niagara Falls and we made the call with a lot of apprehension. The realtor told us that, after we left, several people looked at the Walton house and one made an offer. When we tried to have control nothing happened, but as soon as we gave it to God our house sold.

You can say you have faith, but until you're willing to exercise it, faith is a noun. Completely trusting God requires taking steps to test and confirm your faith. When you act in your faith it becomes a verb and he will step in and honor it.

Lord, sometimes it's really hard to take that first step "out of the boat." Give me courage when I hesitate in fear.

June 19

Raising obedient children

"Direct your children onto the right path, and when they are older, they will not leave it."

Proverbs 22:6 (NLT)

It's not an easy task to raise children in a way that teaches them how to become responsible adults. We, as parents, have aspirations for our children and try our best to encourage, instruct, discipline and love in the right way.

As a mom, I hoped for, but didn't always get obedience. I wanted them to experience life without distress or heartache but they all had their share of bumps in the road. There were times I was anxious about the choices they were making but, amazingly, they are all fine. They were imperfect children being raised by imperfect parents. They made mistakes and we made mistakes. However, whatever challenges we faced, we tried to handle them with love; our children, now parents themselves, are passing the lessons they learned on to their own children. If we did anything right, it was in pointing them toward Jesus. We couldn't make them believers, but each have accepted God's saving grace in their own time.

Lord, thank you for guiding me through the process of raising my family. May you continue to bless them as they bring up their own families.

June 20

Journaling

"And the words of The Lord are flawless, like silver purified in a crucible, like gold refined seven times."

Psalm 12:6 (NIV)

"Then the angel said to me, "Everything you have heard and seen is trustworthy and true. The Lord God, who inspires his prophets, has sent his angel to tell his servants what will happen soon."

Revelation 22:6 (NLT)

I have been journaling all of our trips since the summer of 2000. We enjoy looking through them occasionally as we reflect on some of our experiences. Now and then Jack and I will remember some things differently, and each one of us is convinced we're right. We can solve the disagreement by going to my journal, because what we did was recorded the day it occurred and therefore is accurate. When it's in writing, we believe it.

God's Word is our source of truth. The writers penned the words that were inspired by God. There's no question that they are valid and we can depend on their accuracy. God said his Word was true so I don't need any more proof. In my journaling, certain places we visited may be gone now, roads may have changed and what we remembered may not look the same anymore. God's Word has stood the test of time and will never fail or change!

Father, thank you for your Word, the hope it offers and the guidance it gives me for each day.

June 21

How long can you stay quiet?

"My soul, wait silently for God above, for my expectation is from Him."

Psalm 62:5 (NKJV)

My mother, brother and I were living with my grandma when I was eleven years old. The grandma of a playmate lived two doors up the street. When my friend was visiting we often played at her grandma's house where her aunt lived as well. One day when we were playing on the front porch, her aunt said, "Let's see which one of you can be quiet for ten minutes." I think we must have been chattering and giggling a lot. Well, I tried really hard. I don't remember which one of us talked first, but both of us always had a lot to say. I love having a good conversation and when I find a friend to share with, I'm in "seventh heaven." Several times a year I'll have a long lunch with a friend.

Waiting in silence is still something I struggle with. If I don't hear from my Lord pretty quickly, I'm tempted to start pestering. Sometimes we have to wait in silence for God's response. He doesn't operate on our time frame and waiting patiently is difficult. He may be waiting for us to let go and let him do what is best. It doesn't matter, because we have his promise that he will always be here with us. We can wait in peace, without fear, while our amazing God charts our path.

Father, help me learn to wait patiently while you continue to chart my path.

June 22

Word definitions

"In love he predestined us for adoption to sonship through Jesus Christ, in accordance with the pleasure and will - to the praise of his glorious grace, which he has freely given us in the One he loves. When you believed, you were marked in him with a seal, the promised Holy Spirit, who is a deposit guaranteeing our inheritance until the redemption of those who are God's possession - in the praise of his glory."

Ephesians 1:4-6, 13-14 (NIV)

I love looking up words to read their definitions and how they should be used. John 3:16 says *"For God so loved the world that he sent his only begotten son, that whoever believes in Him should not perish but have everlasting life."* That sentence has four verbs which indicate action. Two of them are actions God already took and two of them require our response.

God LOVED us so much that he SENT. How amazing - He loved us even before we acted on his love. Now for that love to have completion in us, we have to act. When we BELIEVE in God's son, Jesus, we will HAVE eternal life. That one sentence contains the Gospel message in a nutshell, four little words that exemplify our eternity.

Lord, your Word fills me with joy and hope.

June 23

A song in my head

"Oh what a miserable person I am! Who will free me from this life that is dominated by sin and death? Thank God! The answer is Jesus Christ our Lord. So you see how it is: In my mind I really want to obey God's law, but because of my sinful nature I am a slave to sin...... So now there is no condemnation for those who belong to Christ Jesus. And because you belong to him, the power of the life-giving spirit has freed you from the power of sin that leads to death."

Romans 7:24, 8:2 (NLT)

Do you ever get a song in your head that just won't go away? I have that happen every now and then. It's usually not even a favorite song and I have never figured out what makes it roost in my mind and refuse to leave. I've tried replacing it with another song, and think I've won the battle when, suddenly, there it is again filling up my mind. It leaves when it's ready!

Sin is like a squatter that takes up residence in your heart. You don't like having it there but it's difficult to get rid of it once it has taken up lodging. Why would it want to leave when we feed it and make it comfortable? The only way to evict it is to replace it with the Holy Spirit who supplies us with the power to kick out the sin. Then you can put up a "No Vacancy" sign since all the rooms in your heart are occupied.

Lord, you're the landlord of my heart but sometimes I allow visitors in that stake out a claim and are difficult to evict. Help me empty the rooms of my heart so they can be filled with your Spirit.

June 24

Reflecting

"...what is your life? You are a mist that appears for a little while, then vanishes."

James 4:14 (NIV)

"Our days on earth are like grass; like wildflowers, we bloom and die. The wind blows, and we are gone - as though we had never been here."

Psalms 103:15, 16 (NLT)

I sat quietly in my chair, looking out the window as the sunlight grazed my face. Seeing, yet *not* seeing, memories rushed through my mind like the tumbling waters of a mountain stream cascading madly down the hill. I tried to stop the flow and catch a time long past but it could not be contained. Memory after memory raced by but wouldn't linger long enough for me to examine it. Now and then one of them splashed against a rock and bathed my heart. How did so much pass so quickly? I pondered all that had gone downstream only allowing me a glimpse of its beauty and power. And I was in awe, yet frustrated. But that stream that originates in my life continues to spring forth providing more memories for me to ponder some other morning.

Loving Father, you have blessed me with memories that enrich my life. May your Spirit walk with me as I continue filling my memory bank.

June 25

Visiting cemeteries

"I could see no Temple in the city, for the Lord, the Almighty God, and the Lamb are themselves its Temple. The city has no need for the light of sun or moon, for the splendor of God fills it with light, and its radiance is the Lamb. The nations will walk by its light, and the kings of the earth will bring their glory into it. The city's gates shall stand open day after day – and there will be no night there. Into the city they will bring the splendors and honors of the nations. But nothing unclean, no one who deals in filthiness and lies, shall ever at any time enter it – only those whose names are written in the Lamb's book of life."

Revelation 21:22-27 (Phillips)

The year I researched our genealogy, we spent some time visiting two very old cemeteries in Lafayette, Indiana where several of my ancestors are buried. The graves are 100 to 150 years old and the limestone headstones were impossible to read, having been worn off by weather through the years. I was unable to find any of the names I was searching for. It was as though their names had been erased from this earth and few people even know they ever lived. However, many of them have their names written in the Lamb's Book of Life and those entries will never be erased. Someday, instead of looking at headstones, I hope to meet them in person. What a joy that will be!

Father, thank you that my name is written in your Book of Life. Even if those who come after me never find a record of my life on earth, you know me and that's all that matters.

June 26

If momma ain't happy....

"A gentle response defuses anger, but a sharp tongue kindles a temper fire. Kind words heal and help, cutting words wound and maim."

Proverbs 15:1, 4 (MSG)

Whether they like to admit it or not, mothers and wives have a lot of control over the mood in the home. It has been said "If momma ain't happy, ain't nobody happy!" That doesn't mean they have to get their own way, but it does mean they have the ability to establish a peaceful environment for the family. If our initial response to a growing conflict is to respond with uncontrolled emotions, we add fuel to an already turbulent scene. Pretty soon everyone's in a bad mood and the home becomes a battleground. We have the responsibility to set the tone in our home.

There will be disagreements in a home, between a husband and wife, and especially among the children. Wives and mothers hold the key to restoring peace. A soft answer can defuse an explosive situation and avoid hurt feelings and anger. This has been a hard lesson for me to learn, but I have gotten better. If I pause for a few seconds and ask for God's help, I am less likely to react in an uncontrolled, emotional way.

Lord, help me to demonstrate patience and forgiveness when I'm in a conflict with someone I love. Give me the strength I need to display your grace.

June 27

Grandma's treasures

"When you believed, you were marked in him with a Seal, the promised "Holy Spirit," who is a deposit guaranteeing our inheritance until the redemption of those who are God's possession - to the praise of his glory."

Ephesians 1:13-14 (NIV)

As a child, I was fascinated by treasures passed down to my grandma from her mother. Among them was a dress, a couple of dolls and a tiny handmade set of doll furniture, stored in its own little handmade box. Occasionally I was allowed to look at them and hold them carefully, until my grandma would return them to a cabinet out of my reach. After I grew up and had a family, my mother passed them on to me. Every family heirloom she gave me came with instructions to "take care of it." Many of the items she left me have been passed on to my own children and they are special reminders of our ancestors.

God has promised us an inheritance. Unlike the ones handed down from my mother, our inheritance from God is safely held in our future home. We don't have to be concerned about it being broken or misplaced for it's in our Lord's safekeeping. I like to think each one of us will have our own, specifically designed with us in mind. We're not given a detailed description of what it is but since God has prepared it, we can be confident that it will be beyond our wildest dreams.

Giving Father, the inheritance I look forward to is waiting for me to claim someday. Thank you for making me your child.

June 28

Empty nest

"In my Father's house are many mansions, if it were not so I would have told you. I go to prepare a place for you. And if I go and prepare a place for you, I will come again and receive you to Myself, that where I am, there you may be also."

John 14:2-3 (NKJV)

After my children grew up and no longer lived at home, life was different - still good, but interests and responsibilities changed. My children were still on my mind a lot, but my time and thoughts began to fill with other activities and responsibilities.

Consequently, when they planned a trip home, it was an occasion to celebrate. I was excited about the prospect of spending time with them, just seeing their faces and sharing new experiences and old memories. I cleaned, cooked and got a room ready for them.

For most people in the world, envisioning God as a Father or parent is beyond their understanding. God loves his children even more than we can comprehend. He knows that someday we will be coming home. In fact he has the date for our arrival on his calendar. Even though those left behind, will feel the loss and emptiness when we leave, our Father will be celebrating because one of his children is finally coming, not for just a short visit, but to stay forever.

Loving Father, thank you for the gift of children and what they mean to parents. May your Spirit guide and protect all of them throughout their lives.

June 29

Complaining

"Do all you have to do without grumbling or arguing, so that you may be God's children, blameless, sincere and wholesome, living in a warped and diseased world, and shining there like lights in a dark place."

Philippians 2:14-15 (Phillips)

A few months after getting married in 1954, we moved to Southern Indiana where I got a job in Louisville, Kentucky. I was working in an office with four or five other women and a few of us went to lunch together nearly every day. At the time there seemed to be a lot of complaining from a couple of them. Normally I'm upbeat, but after a few months I found myself feeling negative as well. I began to notice what was happening and didn't like it. When you develop a habit of complaining it spills over into every corner of your life and rubs off on the others you spend time with.

As witnesses for our Lord, we have a responsibility to show a positive, loving attitude. Many believers become complainers, never taking the time to look for positive things to mention. When we criticize and complain we aren't reflecting God's love. Why would unbelievers want to become seekers if we, as Christians, spend so time much griping, especially if it's about something in own church? It affects us personally as well, for we end up with an unsettled spirit and lose our peace. We grew up with the saying, "If you can't say something nice, don't say anything at all," and that's an excellent rule to follow.

Father, help me to speak with words infused with joy and hope. Help me keep complaints and criticism out of my language.

June 30

What's in your hand?

"Then the Lord asked him, 'What is that in your hand?' 'A shepherd's staff,' Moses replied. 'Throw it on the ground,' the Lord told him. So Moses threw down the staff and it turned into a snake."

Exodus 4:2, 3 (NLT)

I had prayed for God to show me where I could be used, but wasn't getting any answer. One morning as I was meditating, the Spirit nudged me, saying "what's in your hand?" Since I'm always taking notes and making lists, it was a pen. I felt as though he wanted me to write, and I began the daily Facebook posts that eventually led to this book.

Over the years as I've written my poems, I learned to depend on God to inspire me with ideas. If I try to get ahead of him, I come up with nothing. My desire is to write about God's amazing love but I have to depend on him, for without his inspiration, I have nothing to offer. Several years ago, a good friend asked me to write a poem for her wedding bulletin. I agreed and tried to come up with ideas, but nothing was coming to me. One Wednesday, she said she needed it in a few days; I was frantic. She was counting on me and I had nothing. On my way to visit my daughter in Kentucky that Friday evening I began praying about it. Within a few minutes words were pouring in my mind like a flood. As soon as I arrived at my daughter's I asked for a pen and paper and wrote them down. God gave me the words but He was waiting for me to let him have control; I've included that poem for you, immediately following this devotion. I am still amazed at the way He works! What do you have in your hand that God wants to use? When you trust him with it, he will bless it!

Giving Father, you give each of us gifts to be used for your Kingdom. Thank you for my gift. Help me use it to glorify you.

The Marriage

His arm went gently around her,
as he helped her to her feet.
Then as she put her hand in his,
they exchanged a smile so sweet.

You might think that they're young lovers,
from the sparkle in their eyes.
Though their bodies are bent with age
they have a love that never dies.

As a young man he was tall and straight.
She was lithesome and sweet as a rose.
He knew he had found the girl of his dreams,
and mustered the courage to propose.

She accepted, of course, and they married
in the summer of thirty-two.
And each day their love grew stronger
through the trials and joys they knew.

She knew he wasn't a perfect man
often driving her to distraction.
And her little idiosyncrasies
sometimes brought his loud reaction.

But they never carried their anger
beyond the setting sun,
and they cherished each day God gave them
as though it were a prize they won.

They can look back with satisfaction
at a marriage they've worked hard to build.
God has blessed them in life's December.
All their dreams have been fulfilled.

July

*I will fear no evil,
for you are with me;*

Father, when I am afraid and
feel alone, help me trust in
your loving care.

July 1

Surviving turmoil

"Though the cherry trees don't blossom and the strawberries don't ripen, though the apples are worm-eaten and the wheat fields stunted, though the sheep pens are sheepless and the cattle barns empty, I'm singing joyful praise to God. I'm turning cartwheels of joy to my Savior God."

Habakkuk 3:17-19 (MSG)

During the past few years we've experienced a lot of turmoil, both among our circle of friends and family, and in our country. Friends have lost jobs, some had to move to other areas, families have struggled with relational problems and the moral standards we have always embraced are declining all around us. In addition to all that, the weather has been extreme in many areas around the world and we cannot listen to the news without hearing about another attack somewhere or a shooting in our own city. If we only look at what's happening, we'll soon become discouraged and not have the peace that God desires for us. We sometimes feel like God isn't watching.

In Habakkuk we are reminded that God works through all circumstances and we can praise him no matter what's happening. His purposes and plans are being unfolded before our eyes and everything is right on schedule. To coin a phrase: "How cool is that." What a blessing it is to know that God is in control!

Understanding Father, you know the uncertainties I face in life. Fill me with peace and safety when I feel surrounded by evil and sin.

July 2

A friend goes home

"So be careful how you live. Don't live like fools, but like those who are wise. Make the most of every opportunity in these evil days. Don't act thoughtlessly, but understand what the Lord wants you to do."

Ephesians 5:15-17 (NKJV)

Today I'm remembering a friend who died suddenly a few years ago and I'm reminded of how brief our time is on this earth. We tend to wish the time away, anxious for vacation, Fridays, getting through a difficult situation and all the other reasons that cause us to look at the time ahead instead of the time we are in right now. We check our watches or look at the clock to see if "it's almost over."

The time we spend in this temporary home is not even a speck of dust in the enormity of eternity and I'm realizing how much of my time I don't use wisely. Our life could be over in one brief moment and then we'll never have another chance to hold someone we love, to show compassion and forgiveness, to extend a helping hand or to share someone's burden. These are the things Christ did for us. He wants us to love like that. He set the example by forgiving those who crucified Him. He touched and held, fed, healed, comforted and as he was dying reached out to provide for his mother. If we want to live like Jesus, how can we not do likewise?

Lord, help me to live my life in a way that is a reflection of your love. May I treasure each moment that you give me and live it in a way that brings glory to you.

July 3

Our freedom

"It is for freedom that Christ has set us free. Stand firm, then, and do not let yourselves be burdened again by a yoke of slavery."

Galatians 5:1 (NIV)

"All glory to him who loves us and has freed us from our sins by shedding his blood for us."

Revelation 1:5 (NLT)

Tomorrow is Independence Day! Once a year, on July 4th, we celebrate the freedom we have as Americans and remember the courage of our forefathers who fought so hard to achieve it. One summer, as I worked on my genealogy, I discovered several ancestors who gave their lives to preserve that freedom. Many in our own generation still put themselves at risk and some have given their lives as we continue to fight for that freedom. In this life freedom is never guaranteed and we'll always have to guard it diligently.

Every day I rejoice because of the sacrifice Jesus Christ made to give us real freedom. If you've accepted his offer of Grace, that freedom will never be taken from you, no matter what happens around you. Now that's a reason to celebrate!

Sweet Jesus, thank you for the freedom you bought for me with your death and resurrection. Help me never take that or any other freedom for granted.

July 4

Rained-out fireworks

"But for you who revere my name, the sun of righteousness will rise with healing in its rays."

Malachi 4:2 (NIV)

The day was warm and sunny as we prepared the house for our annual small group 4th of July celebration. When we gathered on our back porch around 5:00 in the afternoon, clouds began to darken the sky and within an hour we were facing what turned out to be a "100-year-storm". There would be no fireworks in Kokomo that night! The lights flickered and the power finally went out completely. Our friends stayed for a little while, but finally gave up and headed home. Before that night was over, Kokomo had experienced one of the most significant rainfalls in their history. It brought stress and hardship to many in Kokomo and to us personally. We ended up with five feet of water in our finished basement. At the time I couldn't imagine anything good coming out of that unforeseen mess we faced.

However - (don't you love that word) - our basement had been finished with dark paneling and most of the furnishings were dark as well. We now had an opportunity to redo it in light, bright colors which would make the area so much more inviting.

Life will throw circumstances at you that are painful or you may be stuck in a job you don't enjoy. God gives a silver lining to everything we endure or experience, but we have to look for and expect it.

Father God, you always have silver linings behind the clouds of adversities I endure. Help me look for and recognize them.

July 5

Pray without ceasing

"Be happy in your faith at all times. Never stop praying. Be thankful, whatever the circumstances may be."

I Thessalonians 5:16-18 (Phillips)

Paul tells us to pray without ceasing. I've always had a struggle with that verse. I had a hard time devoting a few minutes of totally committed prayer each day, much less praying unceasingly. It has only been in the last few months that the verse has really opened up to me. It doesn't mean the quiet time you spend in devotion and prayer, your bedtime or rising-up prayers, or lifting up prayers when someone shares a burden with you. These important but real communications with God require a different attitude but, much of the time, our prayers are out of obedience, and not a desire to be in God's presence.

When I really began to immerse myself in the Word and the Holy Spirit opened up my understanding, I realized that the Lord was occupying more and more of my thoughts each day. Now he's in my thoughts when I go to bed at night and when I rise in the morning. Thoughts about him are sprinkled throughout my day, so he's never completely out of my mind. That's what Paul is referring to. We are to be so filled with the Holy Spirit that we will be enveloped with an unspeakable joy that cannot be described. Then you'll be in constant communication with your Lord; and *that* is praying without ceasing.

Gracious Father, thank you for being my one constant source of communication throughout every day.

July 6

Falling in love

"O Lord, You have searched me and know me. You know my sitting down and my rising up. You understand my thoughts afar off. You comprehend my path and my lying down and are acquainted with all my ways. For there is not a word on my tongue but behold, O Lord, You know it altogether. You have hedged me behind and before and laid Your hand upon me. Such knowledge is too wonderful for me. It is high. I cannot attain it."

Psalm 139:1-6 (NKJV)

When two people fall in love, they're just starting down the path of a deep relationship. The more time they spend together the closer they grow. At first they spend a lot of their time talking and as they become better acquainted they settle into a relaxed, comfortable relationship, confident in each other's love.

In my journey to know Jesus more intimately, I don't always approach him the same way. Some days I am exuberant and in a praising mood, talking to him off and on all day. Other days while I sit quietly in his presence, soaking up his love, a peace washes over me like a gently falling spring rain. Either way, I am keenly aware that the Spirit is stirring and leading me. There is no sweeter feeling than knowing you are secure in his love.

My prayer is that all who walk with Jesus can have this kind of relationship with him. After all, what he wants from us is to grow to love him as much as he already loves us.

Abba Father, as I walk my path today, fill me with the joy of your love.

July 7

I have no idea where we are!

"The Lord went ahead of them. He guided them during the day with a pillar of cloud, and he provided light at night with a pillar of fire. This allowed them to travel by day or by night."

Exodus 13:21-22 (NLT)

Sometimes when we're exploring the countryside in an unfamiliar area, Jack will announce, "I have no idea where we are." Fortunately we have a compass built into the truck enabling us to find our way back to a main road or someplace we recognize. It's amazing to me that it always points north, even when the sky is overcast. Ancient mariners could navigate the ocean and reach their destination by relying on a compass.

As believers we have a built in compass. The Holy Spirit directs us as we travel down the road of life. Even when we are following blindly through clouds of hurt and trials, or when we wander off, going on the wrong road, he points us in the right direction and leads us to our destination. In the exodus from Egypt the Holy Spirit guided the Israelites in a pillar of cloud by day and a pillar of fire by night. The Holy Spirit truly is our compass and guide and will be there in us to take us safely home someday.

Dear Father, your guidance keeps me pointed in the right direction every day. Thank you for being the compass in my life.

July 8

Chris's bike race

"Therefore we also, since we are surrounded by so great a cloud of witnesses, let us lay aside every weight and the sin which so easily ensnares us, and let us run with endurance the race that is set before us, looking unto Jesus, the author and finisher of our faith, who for the joy that was set before Him endured the cross, despising the shame, and has sat down at the right hand of the throne of God."

Hebrews 12:1, 2 (NKJV)

Our nephew, Chris, completed a world record-breaking bike race in 2013, culminating months of grueling discipline and training. He reached his goal by focusing on the prize of setting a new record. To train he rode daily, often taking his bike along on family vacations. During the race he had to push himself almost beyond his ability to endure, but he pressed on in spite of pain and, crossed the finish line in triumph. Friends and family went along to help and encourage him during his race.

In the book of Hebrews we're urged to persevere in the race that will bring us victory. We need to throw off anything in our run that slows us down or hinders us. Sin, apathy and other distractions can nearly cause us to give up. Sometimes the race pushes us to our limit, but with commitment and determination we will complete our race and receive our prize, a crown of righteousness. We're encouraged by others who run alongside us and by a cloud of witnesses who have already completed the race and received their crowns.

Loving Father, thank you for the encouragement of friends and the examples set by those who have already crossed the finish line in victory. Help me focus on the prize that awaits me.

July 9

Emily

"When I get really afraid I come to you in trust. I'm proud to praise God; fearless now, I trust in God......"

Psalm 56:3, 4 (MSG)

"Those who fear God get God's attention; they can depend on his strength."

Psalm 147:11 (MSG)

"Say to those with fearful hearts, "Be strong, and do not fear, for the Lord, your God is coming..."

Isaiah 35:4 (NLT)

Emily ran toward the slide, eager to have a new adventure but when she got there, it was bigger than she thought. She cautiously climbed the steps but when she was almost to the top, she became paralyzed with fear. "No, I can't!" she wailed. We tried to encourage her but she clung to the rail and wouldn't move. Suddenly her daddy swooped her up, placed her on the slide and held her hand. Within a few seconds she was safely down the slide with her feet planted firmly on the ground.

We are often wailing in fear when facing a challenge that is bigger than we expected, but our Father, just like Emily's daddy, is there to lift us up and carry us through to the other side.

Merciful Father, help me remember the many times you carried me before so I can face my future with faith.

July 10

Contagious

"I pray that God, the source of hope, will fill you completely with joy and peace because you trust in him. Then you will overflow with confident hope through the power of the Holy Spirit."

Romans 15:13 (NLT)

Contagious is defined as: communicable by contact, spreading from one to another. Quarantine is: to isolate from other persons so as to prevent passing on what you have.

When I was five years old I came down with whooping cough and then as a seven-year-old I had a bad case of measles. Both times my parents were given a "Quarantine" sign to put on the front door because I was contagious. I remember feelings of loneliness because, even as I was beginning to recover, my friends avoided me. If you are contagious you have something that can be caught by those who come in contact with you.

As believers we have something that others need to be infected with, so we need to be "Contagious Christians," as well-known Christian author and speaker Chuck Swindoll advised in his book "Contagious Christianity". Satan wants to put a "Quarantine" sign on us because he doesn't want the hope we have to be passed on to others. However, in order to be a "Contagious Christian" we have to display a spirit that sets us apart from "good people." The joy we have in our salvation needs to spill out in every area of our life drawing others to Jesus, the source of our joy. There is a well-known quote from the movie "When Harry Met Sally" that goes, "I'll have what she's having." Is your joy spilling out enough for others to want it too?

Thank you, Father, for infecting me with love for you. May I display that love so others will catch it from me.

July 11

Out of order

"I can do all things through Christ who strengthens me."

Philippians 4:13 (NKJV)

Some days when things aren't going well I feel like I have an "Out of Order" sign on me. A few years ago I was in the process of switching from an old computer to a new one and if that wasn't challenging enough I was hooking up a new wireless printer as well. New electronic equipment doesn't come with an instruction booklet so while I was following the instructions on the monitor, a message was displayed reading "make sure your device is plugged in." Well it was, but as I reflected on my day, I realized that I wasn't plugged in myself. No wonder I was "out of order".

When we get up in the morning, we need to connect with God before we begin our day. Otherwise, we're attempting to do everything on our own strength, which is like using a small battery that only runs for a short time. We are often in such a hurry to get things done that we forget to include God in our plans. He alone supplies us with the power we need to deal with our daily lives.

Father God, help me to remember you as I begin my day. Guide me through every decision and choice I make.

July 12

Splashing in the puddles

"Sing to the Lord with grateful praise; make music to our God on the harp. He covers the sky with clouds; he supplies the earth with rain and makes grass grow on the hills."

Psalm 147:7, 8 (NIV)

As I was scrolling through my Facebook page one morning, I saw pictures of children happily splashing in the puddles left by the rain. I was transported back to my childhood with happy memories of playing in the rain and stomping through puddles with my brother as we tried to outdo each other in creating the biggest splash. We're tempted to focus on what we see today and forget the blessings God offers us through each experience we have. Only a few days earlier, I had been bemoaning the rain and complaining about the inconvenience it was causing.

Oh to capture again the anticipation and excitement of children as they embrace each new experience and challenge. As we grow into adulthood, we become calloused to what each new, sometimes different or uncomfortable opportunity offers and as a result, we gloss over what we can gain from it.

Our days will bring sunshine and rain, heat and cold, gain and loss, but each one offers us an opportunity to find a blessing and develop our spiritual growth. God is the one who gives us each new experience and he watches to see how we use it. The rain in our life is what helps us to grow. Embrace it!

All-knowing God, you bring rain and sunshine into my life. Help me see your faithfulness through each of them.

July 13

Remember when?

"On my bed I remember you; I think of you through the watches of the night. Because you are my help, I sing in the shadow of your wings. I cling to you; your right hand upholds me."

Psalm 63:6-8 (NIV)

Each summer we enjoy a special time when my son, Steve, and his family come to Kokomo for their annual visit. Sometimes my other son Jeff will join us for a few hours. Whenever Steve and Jeff get together, their conversation inevitably migrates to "remember when?" They'll spend hours sharing the memories stored in their "memory bank." As they begin pulling them up, even more will come to the surface. I believe they could talk all night.

Occasionally during my devotions, I'll reflect on all that God has done in my life. I have a "Memory Bank" of his faithfulness through the trials I've faced. As I pull memories up and reflect on them, I'm comforted and encouraged, for I'm reminded that he has always been there to supply what I needed. The two years I spent writing my devotions, I tapped into those memories on a daily basis and started paying more attention to how God has worked in my life as well as the lives of my family.

Everyone has a "Memory Bank." Take time to withdraw some of those memories and look for God's hand in them. You'll be amazed when you see how he worked through every circumstance, using trials and victories to help you grow spiritually.

Merciful Father, thank you for memories of your faithfulness. Help me remember them each time I face a new challenge.

July 14

Billy Graham Library

"Put on God's complete armor so that you can successfully resist all the devil's methods of attack. For our fight is not against any physical enemy; it is against organizations and powers that are spiritual. "

Ephesians 6:11 (Phillips)

On our way home from Florida, we visited the Billy Graham Library. After the tour, we stopped by the prayer room in the facility and talked to a couple of volunteers. One of them asked if we had any prayer requests, so I shared about my writing and asked that it be lifted up. The volunteer pastor, prayed for an anointing on my devotions and I left there feeling good about having God's blessings on them. It didn't occur to me that we would come under attack. That evening we began to notice a strong, unpleasant odor in our RV. Jack tried to track it down but over the next two days, it grew so bad we had to leave the windows open and the exhaust fan on. During the night, God awakened me, and the smell was toxic. Jack went outside to investigate and discovered it was coming from the battery which was smoking by then. He removed it and we thought all would be fine. Then the next day we began to have problems with the truck, and ended up with an expensive repair bill. One week after arriving home Jack started feeling bad and ended up spending almost a week in the hospital.

Considering the timing of all that transpired after the anointing, I feel Satan was trying to discourage me. We have to be diligent about putting on the full armor of God for protection.

Defending Father, I don't always remember to clothe myself with faith and trust. Help me to make this part of my daily routine.

July 15

Blinders

"Lord, my heart is not haughty, nor my eyes lofty. Neither do I concern myself with great matters, nor things too profound for me. Surely I have calmed and quieted my soul, like a weaned child with his mother, like a weaned child is my soul within me."

Psalm 131:1,2 (NKJV)

"But Martha was distracted by all the preparations that had to be made. 'Martha, Martha,' the Lord answered, 'You are worried and upset about many things, but few things are needed—or indeed only one. Mary has chosen what is better'...."

Luke 10:40,41 (NIV)

When horses are racing, sometimes blinders will be put on them so they won't be spooked by what is happening around them. Wearing blinders helps them concentrate on the race.

As Christians we have access to blinders through the Holy Spirit, who keeps us from being influenced by what happens around us. However, we have to tap into this help by allowing him to direct us every day. As I grow in spirit and faith, I find myself less and less distracted by what the world thinks is important. I am learning to focus on the grace I have received, which helps eliminate most worry and the temptation to put other things ahead of my relationship with the Lord. I'll probably never be completely free from them but I am pressing on one step at a time with my eyes firmly fixed on the goal of completing this race in victory.

Holy Spirit, thank you for equipping me with your blinders so I can stand strong against the distractions of the world.

July 16

Get the word out

"For this reason I also suffer these things, nevertheless I am not ashamed for I know whom I have believed and am persuaded that He is able to keep what I have committed to Him until that Day."

II Timothy 1:12 (NKJV)

When we want to share news or plans we often use the phrase "Get the word out." I've spent a good deal of time lately thinking about how we can get the Word out. As believers we need to be in the Bible daily so that we'll be equipped to live a victorious Christian life. Social media such as Facebook can be an incredible tool for "getting the Word out." As I continue to post my thoughts on Facebook, it's encouraging to see others doing the same. Even when we are intimidated about witnessing in person, we can do it in our posts. I am challenging each of you to share your favorite scripture through social media and why it is important to you. Then start posting only thoughts that encourage others and bring glory to our Lord. Paul's letters include words that show me where I need correction, give me courage and strengthen my commitment.

Lord, infuse me with a desire to share your Good News in writing, posting or sharing personally. Help me share my joy and hope with the world.

July 17

My trust level

"Commit everything you do to the Lord. Trust him, and he will help you."

Psalm 37:5 (NLT)

When I first committed to writing and sharing my inspiration through social media back in 2013, I was challenged to be sure I was submitting my devotions to God. Each day as I thought and prayed about what to write, my trust level was put to the test. I couldn't have written the posts without the guidance of the Holy Spirit and sometimes relying on him was difficult. My earthly self tried to come up with ideas and write them ahead, but my spiritual self said to wait for inspiration from God. I had to learn to depend on his leading.

In our Christian journey, even when we say we walk in faith, we often charge ahead without waiting. Waiting is hard, especially in this day and age. We are accustomed to having everything done quickly and tend to grow impatient when our plans seem to be put on hold. Learn to wait for God's leading and while you are waiting, get into his Word, rest in his presence and he will direct your path.

Lord, when I don't know how to plan my day or what direction to go, walk before me and lead me to where you want me.

July 18

Gift of the Holy Spirit

"Therefore, there is now no condemnation for those who are in Christ Jesus, because through Christ Jesus the law of the Spirit who gives life has set you free from the law of sin and death."

Romans 8:1, 2 (NIV)

When we become Christians, God gives us the gift of the Holy Spirit. We're to live our lives guided by the Spirit but we are housed in a fleshly body, therefore we have an ongoing battle with our earthly body warring against our spiritual body. We do and say things that are carnal, and then wonder how we could have acted that way. We often neglect to do the things we know we should. The Spirit that lives within us is perfect but as long as we are housed in this body of flesh we will be tempted by Satan. Paul had this struggle and says in Romans *"with the mind I myself serve the law of God but with the flesh the law of sin."*

But, praise the Lord! Even if we don't always act the way we know we should, God doesn't count our sins against us because they are covered by the precious blood of our Savior Jesus Christ. Take time daily with prayer and study to prepare for this battle. Then quiet your mind and listen to the Spirit.

Forgiving Father, I know you've already won the war, but I still have battles to fight every day. Help me have victory and forgive me when I lose one.

July 19

Forgiving

"Since God chose you to be the holy people he loves, you must clothe yourselves with tenderhearted mercy, kindness, humility, gentleness, and patience. Make allowance for each other's faults, and forgive anyone who offends you. Remember, the Lord forgave you, so you must forgive others."

Colossians 3:12, 13 (NLT)

When we've been deeply hurt by someone, forgiving them is one of the hardest things God asks us to do. In my own life there was a lot to work through and get over so forgiveness didn't come easily. Sometimes it takes years to shed the heavy burden those feelings put on our heart. The anger that accompanies an unforgiving spirit is destructive and affects those around you, making it nearly impossible to heal from the hurt. When I finally was able to release that burden through forgiving, I had peace and God was able to use me to encourage others facing similar circumstances. What a blessing that has been. You see, forgiveness is not for those you forgive for they may never know about your hurt, or even care. It is for you. When you consider how much sin God has forgiven in you, how can you do any less?

Precious Lord, you forgave me, even though I didn't deserve it. Help me pass that gift of forgiveness on to those who have hurt me.

July 20

Swimming lessons

"Whoever heeds life-giving correction will be at home among the wise.

Proverbs 15:31 (NIV)

We enrolled our children in swimming lessons one summer when they were in grade school. After a couple weeks of lessons, the instructor took the class to the deep end of the pool and told them to jump in and swim to the edge. Both of my boys were fine with it but my daughter was afraid and wouldn't jump. After telling her a couple of times, the instructor tossed her into the pool. She floundered for a few seconds then made it to the edge. The instructor knew she had to see for herself that she could do it.

Sometimes we'll be under conviction to move in a new and perhaps scary direction. If we hesitate or balk when the Spirit is directing us, he may have to give us a shove. It could be away from something that's compromising our values or anything else that moves us away from our walk of faith. When it happens, you are upset and maybe angry as well, but later, in retrospect, you will see that it was the best thing that could have happened.

When Joseph was a teen his brothers threw him in a well and left him for dead. Later, even after circumstances turned around for him, he was sent to prison. All through this difficult time, God was working his will in Joseph's life. He has a plan for each of us, just as he had one for Joseph, and even though what we're enduring seems unfair or painful, trust in God for he will bring you to victory in due time.

Father, when the future looks uncertain and I cannot see the path ahead, take my hand and guide me.

July 21

A comfortable pillow

"In peace I will lie down and sleep, for you alone, Lord, make me dwell in safety."

Psalm 4:8 (NIV)

After a long, busy day filled with activities, nothing feels as relaxing as laying my head on a comfortable pillow. As the softness cradles my head, I begin to unwind and let sleep lull me away from all the ideas and problems that I encountered throughout my day. Sometimes, however, even when my weary body can rest, my mind can't. A couple of years ago I was asked to give a talk to a group of women at our church. I was prepared for the talk, but the night before, my mind wouldn't shut down and I was unable to fall asleep. Over and over, I rehearsed what I was going to say. Anxious thoughts poked at the peace I was seeking. Those times seem to come when we need a good night's sleep the most.

Recently I discovered a wonderful line in a hymn book published about 150 years ago. The words described Jesus as the pillow for a troubled soul. The phrase struck a chord with me. He gives us comfort and rest like no other as we lay our weary soul on him. As his peace settles over us, we find rest in our Savior's love.

Precious Jesus, you are the pillow that I can rest my weary, battle-scarred heart on. You offer unequaled contentment and relief for my troubled soul.

July 22

TV mysteries

"No, the wisdom we speak of is the mystery of God – his plan that was previously hidden, even though he made it for our ultimate glory before the world began. But the rulers of this world have not understood it; if they had, they would not have crucified our glorious Lord. But it was to us that God revealed these things by his Spirit. For his Spirit searches out everything and shows us God's deep secrets."

I Corinthians 2:7, 8, 10 (NLT)

I've always loved mysteries, reading many James Patterson and Patricia Cornwell novels through the years. I also enjoy watching "Without a Trace" and "Cold Case" so I was intrigued when Paul spoke of the mystery which is revealed in his epistles. How incredible that our God had plans for you and me before the beginning of time and kept it hidden until it was revealed to Paul. I didn't have to finish the novel or watch the end of the show to see the mystery explained. He knew us and our sinful nature even then, but loved us so much that he planned a way for us to be redeemed (even as Gentiles). This is awesome news for us and a revelation that I have only recently begun to understand. I encourage you to dig deeper in the Word for there are many mysteries revealed and they are exciting to discover.

O King of the universe, I am overwhelmed by the revelation that you made plans to redeem us before we were created. I cannot understand such love but I will be eternally grateful.

July 23

Planting an apple tree

"But what happens when we live God's way? He brings gifts into our lives, much the same way that fruit appears in an orchard – things like affection for others, exuberance about life, serenity. We develop a willingness to stick with things, a sense of compassion in the heart, and a conviction that a basic holiness permeates things and people. We find ourselves involved in loyal commitments, not needing to have our way in life, able to marshal and direct our energies wisely."

Galatians 5:22 (MSG)

If we planted an apple tree in our yard it wouldn't produce fruit the first year. It would have to grow and mature. It thrives because of sun and rain, eventually bearing a harvest of apples. It's the same way with the vegetables and flowers we grow in our gardens. We fertilize and water them to make sure they thrive and in time we will enjoy what they produce.

Our spiritual growth depends on our making the same effort. We have been planted with a strong root system through Jesus Christ but if we're going to produce the fruit he desires in us, we need to nourish our souls with God's Word and prayer. As Christians we are spiritual beings, but we possess a soul with a sinful nature that has to be tutored by the Spirit. Then as our soul matures in faith, our thoughts, speech and actions will produce the kind of fruit that sets us apart and brings glory to God.

God of the harvest, I want to bear the kind of fruit that displays your love and goodness to others. Help me to grow my roots deep through your Word and my faith.

July 24

Gold Rush

"Joyful is the person who finds wisdom, the one who gains understanding. For wisdom is more profitable than silver, and her wages are better than gold. Wisdom is more precious than rubies; nothing you desire can compare with her."

Proverbs 3:13-15 (NLT)

In the late 1850's my great-great-grandfather made his way from Indiana to California in a covered wagon during The Gold Rush. He left behind his wife and children, never to return to Indiana again. Unfortunately he never found the gold he was searching for. So many people search for an elusive treasure that always seems to be just out of their reach. Digging for gold, silver, diamonds or anything else we consider a treasure takes hard work and sometimes requires sacrificing everything else to find it, just as my ancestor did.

The treasure of really knowing our Lord is like digging for gold. It takes commitment and a lot of effort on our part, for the treasure we seek is buried in his Word. Like the gold, it will not be laying on the surface. There may be a nugget or two but most will be discovered piece by piece. Only then will we gain the true riches of God. The knowledge we gain enables us to understand, and our wisdom is gained by applying that knowledge in our life.

Father, plant in me a desire to search for the riches contained in your Word and teach me to use what I gain to change my life.

July 25

Feelings and emotions

He is my strength:
  "*The Lord is my light and my salvation – whom shall I fear?*"
  Psalm 27:1 (NIV)

God is on my side:
  "*The Lord is on my side; I will not fear. What can man do to me?*"
  Psalm 118:6 (NKJV)

God is with me:
  "*If God is for us, who can be against us?*"
  Romans 8:31 (NIV)

He will never leave me:
  "*I will never fail you, I will never abandon you.*"
  Hebrews 13:5 (NLT)

Sometimes I find myself trusting my feelings to gage how I should react. Feelings are based on emotions and they can be very deceptive. We hear bad news and we're swallowed up in fear. We accomplish something big and we succumb to pride. These are not feelings that are grounded in the Holy Spirit. We are told to "fear not" and cautioned against pride, or the feeling of "I can do it myself."

We are indwelt with the Holy Spirit which literally means that God himself is in us. He says he will never (ever, ever) leave us. It means he is there when we're walking in his will but it also means he is there when we slip out of his will and fall into sin. What a comfort to know that no matter what we are doing - good or bad - the presence of God guides us in our daily life but also nudges us when we're tempted. Don't depend on your feelings but rely on God's presence in you.

Father, thank you for dwelling within me even when I stray out of your will. I am grateful that you love me enough to prick my conscience when I need it.

July 26

Compulsive Christian Disorder

"I ask him to strengthen you by his Spirit - not a brute strength but a glorious inner strength - that Christ will live in you as you open the door and invite him in. And I ask him that with both feet planted firmly on love, you'll be able to take in with all Christians the extravagant dimensions of Christ's love. Reach out and experience the breadth! Test its length! Plumb the depths! Rise to the heights! Live full lives, full in the fullness of God."

Ephesians 3:16-19 (MSG)

I recently heard the term "Compulsive Christian Disorder" - a term used to describe Christians who are trying to gain something God has already given them. They become a Martha, so busy working to please God and score points that they miss out on the gift they've already received. Their lives become filled with the busyness of doing good things and they miss the best thing, an intimate relationship with Jesus.

God wants us, first and foremost, to rest in his presence and acknowledge him. To acknowledge means "add value to". His value in your life is immeasurable. There's no limit to it, and it will raise you to a whole new level of awareness. It isn't something you earn - it's a gift he presented to you. Learn to acknowledge his presence in everything you do.

Loving Father, help me take my eyes off what I can do for you and embrace the gift you've already given to me.

July 27

Being a family

"Set me as a seal upon your heart, as a seal upon your arm. For love is as strong as death. Many waters cannot quench love, nor can the floods drown it. If a man would give for love all the wealth of his house, it would be utterly despised."

Song of Solomon 8:6, 7 (NKJV)

I was filled with feelings of excitement and anticipation as Jack and I traveled to my daughter's home in Kentucky where our children, grandchildren, and great-grandchildren would be gathering. It would be the first time some of them had met and I could hardly wait. While they were greeting one another and sharing memories, I stood and watched, filled with joy and gratitude over this blessing that God had given me. What parent isn't filled with happiness when their children remain close after they become adults? While they were growing up, they had their differences and squabbles, but the glue that held them close was the love they shared with each other.

Our Heavenly Father rejoices when his children gather together in fellowship and unity. He loves it when we recognize him as our Father and share the closeness that only comes as a family. He smiles proudly when we treat each other with love and respect and forgive hurts and offences. He is filled with pleasure when we talk to him and include him in our memories and plans.

As believers, we are a family. God calls us his children. We're secure in his love forever. There is no greater blessing.

Loving Father, thank you for the gift of families, both the earthly ones and the spiritual ones, for both remind me of your love.

July 28

Eastern Kentucky

"When I consider your heavens, the work of your fingers, the moon and stars, which you have set in place, what is mankind that you are mindful of them, human beings that you care for them? You have made them a little lower than the angels, and crowned them with glory and honor."

Psalm 8:3-5 (NLT)

As we were driving through the gently rolling hills of Eastern Kentucky, I was in awe of the beauty of God's creation. He provides the rain that enables the trees and grass to be lush and green and the sun to help them grow. That reminds us of his incredible love and care for us. He wants us to recognize that it's his handiwork and we're to enjoy it.

When you are camping, as we were that week, you are nestled in the midst of it. In the evening you hear the crickets and other creatures filling the air with their songs and peeking through the trees is a garden of stars. In the morning you arise to a new day with the sun bringing warmth and light into the quiet, peaceful park. It's an opportunity to pause and reflect on God's majesty and power. Everywhere you look you see God's workmanship.

Thank you God for creating what we too often take for granted and abuse. In the busyness of our daily lives, we need to pause and appreciate the beauty around us that only you could provide.

July 29

Suffering

"Whenever we're sick and in bed, God becomes our nurse, nurses us back to health."

Psalm 41:3 (MSG)

"Tell the world what He's done - sing it out."

Psalm 107:21 (MSG)

The longer I live, the more I see some of our close friends suffering from illnesses, chronic pain and serious health issues. There've been times in my own life when I've dealt with pain that seemed to go on forever.

During these times, even when others comfort and encourage you, it's tempting to feel alone and isolated. We may even feel like God doesn't care - or at least he's not paying attention. He assures us that he does feel our pain and is in us, helping us to grow in dependence on His mercy. When we recognize his presence in our affliction, we're able to grow spiritually and even though we may not be healed physically we emerge victorious. In our victory, we can pass on to others how wondrous and merciful our loving Father is. Some of the most inspiring testimonies I have read are from people who have endured unbelievable illnesses or injuries and yet they never gave up. Their stories give us hope and encouragement.

Father of healing, strengthen me, even when I don't have physical healing, for I know you will fill me with the medicine of peace and acceptance.

July 30

Surprises

"You saw me before I was born. Every day of my life was recorded in your book. Every moment was laid out before a single day had passed."

Psalm 139:16 (NLT)

Life is full of surprises, and all of us have had plenty of them. Some are wonderful and bring happiness and others aren't so pleasant. We're often taken by surprise by what goes on around us.

My birthday was coming up so Jack took me on a trip to Southern Indiana to visit friends. I didn't know it, but he had planned a surprise birthday party for me. He told me we were to stop by my former church to meet our friends. When we got there, he went in to find them. A few minutes later he returned saying they wanted to show me something, so I followed him in, grumbling about the delay. I entered the room and was delighted to see some of my closest friends. In a few minutes my family walked through the door. Later that evening we were joined by other friends whom I hadn't seen for a few years. I was overwhelmed with joy and totally surprised.

God is never surprised. He knows every move we'll ever make. He knows our thoughts and all the secret things we do. We sometimes act and talk like we think he's not watching but he already knows about it. Nothing we could ever do will catch God off-guard but he loves us in spite of our failings, so much so that he had a plan to rescue us from our sins before we were formed. I'll never be able to fully understand a love that deep.

Father of surprises, thank you for the blessings you surprise me with each and every day.

July 31

Waiting again

"I wait quietly before God, for my victory comes from him. He alone is my rock and my salvation, my fortress where I will never be shaken."

Psalms 62:1-2 (NLT)

One activity I find extremely tedious is sitting in a waiting room. It seems as though I spend a lot of time every year waiting to be seen by the doctor, the dentist, and on a few occasions in the ER. The magazines are usually outdated and if there's no one to talk to, time seems to drag by. Usually I'm not excited about being there anyway.

Waiting on God isn't easy either. A lot of the time he has us waiting for what we think we need right now. So we sit in his waiting room trying not to worry or get discouraged. He's there with us, reminding us how much he loves us, encouraging us to trust him, and assuring us that the answer is coming in his time. Although the wait can sometimes test our faith, it develops our patience and trust. Most of my spiritual growth developed while I was in his waiting room.

Lord help me learn that I don't need answers to my prayers immediately and trust that your timing is perfect.

August

*Your rod and your staff,
they comfort me.*

*Father, I feel secure knowing
that you are leading me, not
pushing me from behind. You
know the way and I am
following in obedience.*

August 1

This week

"Those who wait on the Lord shall renew their strength; they shall mount up with wings like eagles, they shall run and not be weary, they shall walk and not faint."

Isaiah 40:31 (NKJV)

It had been a week of wide-ranging emotions and lots of activities for me. Even though the days had been wonderful, I needed to pause and allow the Spirit to refill me.

Sometimes, when there is so much going on, we neglect to fill our spiritual fuel tank and all of a sudden we're running on empty. There are warning signs when we reach that point. We begin to think more about our activities and concerns and less about our Lord. Our patience may wear thin. God understands and waits for us to come back and rest in him. He restores our peace and refills us.

Lord, help me to slow down today and spend time with you. Enable me to put aside all other thoughts, memories and concerns so I will be open to your Spirit's leading. Quiet my soul and mind so that I can find rest.

August 2

Talk about peace

"Peace I leave with you; my peace I give you. I do not give you as the world gives. Do not let your hearts be troubled and do not be afraid."

John 14:27 (NIV)

"For Christ is our living peace..."

Ephesians 2:14 (NLT)

There's a lot of talk about efforts to establish peace through agreements and treaties between our country and others. With the conflicts in the Middle East, Ukraine and other parts of the world, finding that elusive peace becomes increasingly more difficult. Even if they manage to obtain a ceasefire between two warring countries, it is an uneasy truce, not real peace.

Conflict has been a part of our existence on this earth since the fall of man in the garden. Even though Americans today have not lived through all-out war on our own soil akin to our Civil War, we're still unable to have the tranquility we so desire. We walk out our doors often wondering where in our country the next radicalized extremist will strike. Some face violence every day in homes and neighborhoods plagued with crime and unrest. We have loved ones serving in war-torn countries all around the world.

God doesn't promise peace to those who live their lives in opposition to him. But we, as believers, can have real peace in our hearts, even in the midst of all the uncertainty and conflict around us. That peace transcends anything the world can throw at us. It will lift us above all the trouble and hurt, ushering us into the very presence of our Lord and Savior Jesus Christ.

Giving Father, thank you for bathing me in peace when I rest in your presence.

August 3

Tyler's accident

"My brothers, I do not consider myself to have fully grasped it even now. But I do concentrate on this: I leave the past behind and with hands outstretched to whatever lies ahead I go straight for the goal – my reward the honor of being called by God in Christ."

Philippians 3:13,14 (Phillips)

I had just received news that my grandson had been in an accident. I tried not to worry but it's difficult when you're not sure what is going on. Fortunately the only things really hurt were his car and his pride. The car can be replaced and his pride will recover. Being involved in an accident is upsetting and the memory lingers for a long time.

I've had to learn some hard lessons through the experiences in my life. One very important thing to remember: *we cannot change what has already happened.* We will have disappointments, make mistakes we regret, make bad choices and have many bumps in the road. The hurts and mistakes I experienced in my own life still linger in my memory, but I moved beyond anger, regret and bitterness. Those experiences became a catalyst leading to the person I am today. .

Paul had much in his past that could have caused him guilt and regret but he chose not to dwell on it. When he did refer to his actions in the past, he used them to point to a merciful God who changes lives. Paul tells us to concentrate on living with God in the "now" and keep our eyes on the hope we have in eternity.

Father of mercy, thank you for wiping my slate clean of offenses. Help me to erase them too so I can concentrate on living a life that is pleasing to you.

August 4

Mental check list

"A good person produces good things from the treasury of a good heart... what you say flows from what is in your heart."

Luke 6:45 (NLT)

I have a mental check list of what I need to have with me when I leave the house: the keys, my purse, my cane or any other items that I think I might need. On a few occasions I've been in a rush and forgotten something. Jack left his billfold at home a couple of times but that's not a problem if I have my purse with me. However, there's one essential thing that we sometimes forget to take as we head out the door, and that's our Christian witness. Consequently, if another driver cuts us off, Jack might honk his horn impatiently and grumble. In response, I'll snap at him for his reaction. Maybe one of us picked up the basket of complaints sitting by the back door waiting to be disposed of, and we began to go through them while we were out. These should have been put in the trash where they belong. What happened to our witness?

We can go out the door with everything in our pockets and purses, but if we don't pick up the love of our Savior, we've left the most important thing behind. Only by allowing his influence to permeate our actions will we be able to shine a reflection of his glory on a lost and broken world. You never know what opportunity will be presented and if you're not dressed with his character, you will miss it. Fasten his love firmly in your heart so it will always be with you, wherever you are.

Gracious Father, help me to clothe myself with your character so that when I'm around others my actions will reflect your love.

August 5

Scattering words

"If you claim to be religious but don't control your tongue, you are fooling yourself, and your religion is worthless."

James 1:26 (NKJV)

I once heard a sermon on the tongue and it caused me to think about words I had spoken in haste, carelessly or in anger and then later regretted. Even though it is small, a tongue can cause enormous damage or it can lift someone up. Have you ever considered the number of words you speak in a 24-hour period? Most of it is idle chatter but now and then we'll say things that are hurtful and they'll be the words others remember. Words carelessly spoken can never be recalled and cause relationships to be damaged. By the same token, encouraging words lift you up and can later be brought to mind when you need positive thoughts.

When I was a teenager my dad, whom I only saw once a year, told me he thought I had a lot of common sense. At a time in my life when I was struggling with self-confidence his words meant more than he realized. He said many other things to me but I don't remember them. The words we remember are the ones that touch us emotionally whether positively or negatively. As Christians we have a responsibility to speak in a manner that brings honor to God. That may be the only witness we'll have with some people.

Lord, guard my tongue today so I will say things that bring honor to you. Everyone is precious to you and I don't want my language to hurt others or disappoint you. Help me to muzzle my tongue and allow your Spirit to permeate my words.

August 6

My limp

"Three times I begged the Lord for it to leave me, but his reply has been, 'My grace is enough for you; for where there is weakness, my power is shown the more completely.' Therefore, I have cheerfully made up my mind to be proud of my weaknesses, because they mean a deeper experience of the power of Christ.....For my very weakness makes me strong in him."

II Corinthians 12:8-10 (Phillips)

As a teenager, dancing was one of my favorite things to do. When I married Jack, we danced quite often on the weekends but after two knee surgeries, we found other things to spend our time on. Over the course of the last few years, though, I developed a limp. When doctors told me that my limp couldn't be corrected through medical means, I was shocked. All along I had hoped surgery or therapy would be an option that would allow me to walk normally again. It took me several weeks to get over the disappointment. Since that time I've learned to accept it as just a part of who I am and I know when I get to heaven I'll be able to sing and dance with the other saints as we worship our Lord and Savior.

Sometimes we are given thorns in our life and it's not easy to understand why. They can pull us down so that we become self-involved and resentful or they can be used to show that God works through every circumstance. Paul prayed three times for his thorn to be removed but that wasn't God's plan. What thorn do you have in your life that God can use? Through the pain and stress over something that will never change, you will grow into a greater dependence on his grace. Life becomes even more precious as we learn to rest in Him.

Lord, help me accept what I cannot change. Use my thorn to show others that true life is not about the physical but comes through trust in you.

August 7

His everlasting arms

"You will keep in perfect peace, all who trust in you, all whose thoughts are fixed on you!"

Isaiah 26:3 (NLT)

"He will feed his flock like a shepherd, he will carry the lambs in his arms, holding them close to his heart. He will gently lead the mother sheep with their young."

Isaiah 40:11 (NLT)

"For he himself is our peace..."

Ephesians 2:14 (NIV)

One morning as I was sitting quietly contemplating God's mercy and love, the song "Leaning on the Everlasting Arms" was running through my mind. Usually when I get a song in my head I'll wish I could turn it off, but this one brought good memories and a feeling of security. *"What have I to dread, what have I to fear, leaning on the everlasting arms? I have blessed peace, with my Lord so near, leaning on the everlasting arms."*

In our weakness we have a tendency to try and solve problems on our own, only going to God as a last resort when we run out of options. He tells us to come to him first. He will then either work his miracle, direct us in what to do or give us peace till the storm passes. What a comfort to know that it's not all up to us. Daily I'm learning to lean more on his everlasting arms.

Lord of my day, help me to lean on you whatever today holds for me. Give me patience and compassion so I will walk confidently, trusting in your faithfulness.

August 8

The rest of the story

"What we believe is this: If we get included in Christ's sin-conquering death, we also get included in his life-saving resurrection. We know that when Jesus was raised from the dead it was a signal of the end of death-as-the-end."

Romans 6:5, 6 (MSG)

I always enjoyed listening to Paul Harvey's "The Rest of the Story." During a time when the media didn't saturate us with so much information, it was fun to hear him tell how a certain story ended. Now most of the news is speculation and opinions about what might happen in events that aren't always that important.

We have a story to share and we already know the ending. However, most of the world doesn't know or care about what will someday play out as "the rest of that story." We're always eager to relate the news we've heard but we have difficulty sharing the good news that could transform lives and change someone's future. Life is brief and we only have a short time to share the greatest news that has ever been known.

Lord, help me have the courage to respond to the spiritual needs of those I come in contact with. Enable me to share the life-giving words that can change lives and alter futures. I am thankful that someone shared "the rest of the story" with me.

August 9

Rosie

"'What are you so frightened about, you of little faith?' he replied. Then he got to his feet and rebuked the wind and the waters and there was a great calm. The men were filled with astonishment, and kept saying, 'Whatever sort of man is this---why, even the wind and the waves do what he tells them!'"

Matthew 8:26, 27 (Phillips)

As far back as I can remember I've gone to church on Sundays. I have fond memories of a special lady named Rosie who took care of the toddlers on Sunday mornings at my grandma's church. I was so enamored with her that I named my first doll "Rosie". Going to church each week was something we did - no excuses. At the time I didn't understand the significance of attending but I knew that it was important to my grandma and my mother. Developing that habit as a child carried me through difficult times as an adult, keeping me connected to God even though I didn't comprehend the enormity of who he was and what he did for me. At one of my lowest times, I reached out to God and he became real to me. Only then did he become my personal Savior.

Sometimes it takes a major crisis in our life to show us how much we need him. He alone can calm the storm and give us peace. Our need to express our love wells up when we sense his presence through heartaches and trials.

Lord, help me to understand more fully how much you have done for me. I am so thankful you've always been here, leading and sometimes carrying me. I thank you for being patient when I cruised along my road in life, taking you for granted.

August 10

Grandma's stories

"Forget about self-confidence; it's useless. Cultivate God-confidence. No test or temptation that comes your way is beyond the course of what others have had to face. All you need to remember is that God will never let you down; he'll never let you be pushed past your limit, he'll always be there to help you come through it."

I Corinthians 10:12-13 (MSG)

When I was a child, my Grandma Smith told me stories of her parents and grandparents. I was intrigued by my family's history which gave birth to a lifelong desire to research my genealogy. Discovering my ancestors and seeing the way their lives were shaped by trials strengthened my courage. Most of their challenges lay in surviving in remote, sometimes unforgiving areas. They worked hard all day without modern conveniences. They took no vacations and had no grocery stores. With all they faced every day, they learned to rely on God to provide for and protect them.

We have different kinds of challenges to face in our lives and we can become overwhelmed. We run to God with health concerns, job losses and family issues, but ignore him when we spend our money, choose our friends and decide how to occupy our time. We're inclined to think we can handle temptations on our own. We can't isolate ourselves from the world, but to lead a victorious life we have to arm ourselves daily, feeding on his Word, praying and fellowshipping with other Christians so we'll be equipped for a safe journey.

Father, thank you for the courage and persistence of my ancestors. Help me learn from them and trust you in my trials.

August 11

New environments

"Have I not commanded you? Be strong and courageous. Do not be afraid; do not be discouraged, for the Lord your God will be with you wherever you go."

Joshua 1:9 (NIV)

August is the month that parents are sending their children back to school. When children begin their journey in a new environment, they may be nervous about how they'll adapt. Whether they're starting kindergarten, middle school, high school or college, their life is going to change with new experiences. They'll be filled with excitement and anticipation yet will have some fear as well. As parents, we try to reassure them and tell them everything will be fine and they will like it.

When I first left home at eighteen to study at a business college in Fort Wayne, Indiana, I was thrilled about the new adventure and yet intimidated by the prospect of attending a school where I didn't know anyone. None of my friends would be there so new friendships would have to be forged. Fortunately, I had an aunt and cousins in the area to encourage me and invite me over occasionally.

Now and then God calls us into a new area of serving him that's different from what we're familiar with. It may take us completely out of our comfort zone, but God won't call us to serve without equipping us for the task. He promises to be with us wherever he leads us, guiding us as we learn to trust. Each new adventure with God creates growth in our faith and displays his love and care to those around us.

Lord, it's the unknowns that fill me with fear and dread. Infuse me with faith for I know you are with me.

August 12

Learning to walk

"So speak encouraging words to one another, Build up hope so you'll all be together in this, no one left out, no one left behind."

I Thessalonians 5:11 (MSG)

When our babies were first learning to walk, they'd take a cautious step or two, then fall. We would stand them back up and they would walk another step or two. Even though they didn't understand it, they had a goal to walk like their parents or siblings. At first they needed a helping hand, but as they practiced they became more confident and eventually walked on their own.

When we first become a believer our walk is much like a baby's first steps. We may stumble and fall a lot. The spiritually mature Christians walk alongside us to pick us up and get us going again. The Spirit in us urges us on, saying, "You can do this. Let me hold your hand for a while." After falling a few times, we become more confident and ready to walk in faith. The growth of our faith takes time and effort but we have to be willing to take the steps. Like the first steps of a toddler, we, as new Christians, took cautious steps as we learned to pray, study the Word, fellowship with other believers and develop our relationship with the Lord. Then, much like our parents who helped us learn to walk, we're equipped to walk alongside those who are just beginning their faith journey.

Lord, thank you for the people you placed in my life who encouraged and walked with me as I began my faith walk. Help me be sensitive to those who are still learning and need someone to walk with them.

August 13

Camping

"Take delight in the Lord, and he will give you your heart's desires. Commit everything you do to the Lord. Trust him, and he will help you."

Psalm 37:4, 5 (NLT)

Several years ago a few of our friends at church who shared a love of camping, began a ministry called "Chapel Hill Campers." As the planning began for our first outing, we had some uncertainties and fears about how it would be received and if it was God's will. One of the major concerns was the weather.

Reservations had to be made well in advance so we had no assurance that weather would be favorable. The day before we were to leave on our first trip it was raining. We stopped at the grocery to pick up something and while I waited in the car, I prayed for good weather and God's blessings on the campers. When I finished and looked up there was a beautiful rainbow. I had a sense of peace and knew he was with us in this ministry.

The Camper's Club always kept God at the center of their activities. The highlights of each weekend were the shared meal, the worship service and communion which were a strong witness to other campers. We camped for seven years and never had a weekend spoiled by bad weather.

I have learned through the years that any activity or ministry must have God at the center in order to succeed. We, as a team, did the planning and made the arrangements but trusted in God to make it a success. We could then go with confidence in His blessings.

Faithful Father who always guides our steps, thank you for blessing the efforts we place in your hands.

August 14

Shipshewana

"Here is a last piece of advice. If you believe in goodness and if you value the approval of God, fix your minds on the things which are holy and right and pure and beautiful and good. Model your conduct on what you have learned from me, on what I have told you and shown you, and you will find that the God of peace will be with you."

Philippians 4:8 (Phillips)

One warm summer day Jack and I drove to Shipshewana to meet friends for dinner at a local restaurant. As we strolled up the walk to the restaurant, we were enjoying the beautiful flowers that were planted around the building and noted that someone was taking good care of them, making sure no weeds would spoil their beauty or crowd them out.

Our mind is like a flower bed. If we are not diligent, worldly and negative thoughts will be planted and take root. Each of us are responsible for weeding out those thoughts that don't center on God and maintaining the garden of joy, peace and contentment that he's planted. We cannot draw others to Christ if our hearts and lives aren't reflecting His glory. Our thinking should be so filled with beauty that there is no room for anything else. Proverbs 23:7 says *"For as a man thinks in his heart, so is he."*

Lord, help me to fill my mind with positive, uplifting thoughts. May I always keep your Word in my heart and mind so that I'm not tempted to think as the worldly do.

August 15

Lunch with a friend

"Hear my cry O God; hear my prayer! From the ends of the earth I cry to you when my heart is overwhelmed. Lead me to the towering rock of safety, for you are my safe refuge, a fortress where my enemies cannot reach me."

Psalm 61:1-3 (NLT)

Some of my most treasured times are sharing lunch with one or two good friends. We know each other well enough to share openly and honestly without feeling judgment or disapproval. Only friends that have proved themselves can share moments like these.

That's the kind of relationship Jesus desires to have with us. He doesn't want stiff, formal prayers that don't come from our hearts. He wants a relationship that fosters real communication. He welcomes our joys, our tears, our concerns and even our anger when we're struggling. Talk to him like you would with your closest friend - for he is that and so much more, and he will not judge or condemn you. When you've been derailed because of something that's happening in your life tell him you don't understand. When you're honest and open with your Lord, you'll be given the peace and comfort you need.

Lord of my time, you already know my fears and struggles, but you want me to bring them to you anyway. Help me make time to pray, for in you I find strength and victory.

August 16

Debbie's new glasses

"Jesus stood quite still and called out to them, 'What do you want me to do for you?' 'Lord, let us see again!' And Jesus, deeply moved with pity, touched their eyes. At once their sight was restored, and they followed him."

Matthew 20:32-34 (Phillips)

When our daughter was seven years old she began having some difficulty seeing the blackboard at school, so we took her to get her eyes checked. After she was fitted for her new glasses and we walked out to the car, she exclaimed in surprise "I can see the leaves on the trees now!" Her new glasses gave her a new perspective on the world around her.

Before we become believers we see the world blindly. There's a film over our spiritual eyes called unbelief. All we see is the hopelessness and despair around us and it leaves us feeling empty and unfulfilled. What a difference having God's grace makes. When you believe and have a Savior, the film is removed and your eyes are opened. You have a new hope and joy in your life. I love the song "Amazing Grace." The words tell us:

"Amazing grace, how sweet the sound,

That saved a wretch like me.

I once was lost but now I'm found,

Was blind but now I see."

Loving Jesus, I will be forever thankful for the grace you have extended to me.

August 17

Written in stone

"For no one can ever be made right with God by doing what the law commands. The law simply shows us how sinful we are. So we are made right with God through faith and not by obeying the law."

Romans 3:20, 28 (NLT)

Sometimes I'll hear the term "It's written in stone" meaning it will not change. It could be rules about something or a situation that has come up, but I know that nothing I can say or do will alter it. I imagine the term derived from the Ten Commandments carved in stone on Mount Sinai. The Israelites were given an impossible set of laws to live by and if they broke even one point in the law they were guilty - no exceptions. The laws became like millstones around their necks weighing them down, for the laws were given to make them aware of their sinfulness.

How blessed we are that those impossible laws were put aside! Jesus died to remove that weight and give us freedom. The commandment he left for us, to love God and to love our neighbor as we love ourselves, is written on our hearts. Praise God for his indescribable gift of grace!

Loving Father, thank you for offering us the gift of forgiveness even while we were still sinners.

AUGUST

August 18

Baby's firsts

"The Lord is like a father to his children, tender and compassionate to those who fear him. For he knows how weak we are; he remembers we are only dust."

Psalm 103:13 (NLT)

"Like newborn babies, you must crave pure spiritual milk so that you will grow into a full experience of salvation. Cry out for this nourishment now that you have had a touch of the Lord's kindness."

I Peter 2:2-3 (NLT)

One of our granddaughters and her husband were expecting their third child and each of us in the family was excited about the prospect of a new addition. Each new baby is different, presenting new joys and sometimes challenges. The first time they recognize you, that first smile, their first steps and hearing the first "Da Da" and "Ma Ma" brings so much pride. When I was a young mother, I watched in fascination at each of God's creations, reluctant to take my eyes off them for fear I'd miss an important "first" moment.

God feels the same pride in our growth as we did for our children. When we were "born again" into his family, he watched us as we grew spiritually. He put his Spirit in us to nourish and help us. When we stumbled or fell while we were learning to walk in our new faith, he reached out to help us back up. He placed people in our life to encourage and sometimes correct us. He wrote a book for us and planned our future. When we grow in faith and pattern our life after our Savior's example, he is a proud Father.

Father, thank you for accepting me into your family and watching over me as I learn each new measure of faith and trust.

August 19

List-maker

"Open your mouth and taste, open your eyes and see—how good God is. Blessed are you who run to him. Worship God if you want the best; worship opens doors to all his goodness."

Psalm 34:8-9 (MSG)

I'm a list-maker by nature. I enjoy being organized and love marking things off my list as I complete them. The list may consist of chores I want to take care of today or at least by the end of the week, all things that need to be done. Having a list keeps me focused.

In my morning quiet time I try to list all the blessings God has already sent into my life: the many answered prayers; times he's held me up during trials; the people he's put in my life; my children, grandchildren and great-grandchildren, and the wonderful husband he sent me. I don't think I have enough paper to write them all down. Every good thing that comes into my life is by God's design and when I do face trials and struggles he promises to see me through them. When I think about what God has already done in my life, I can face the future without fear for I am confident that his goodness and mercy will continue to amaze me as I live each day.

Lord, thank you for always being here for me, even when I fail to recognize your watch care. Help me to walk in complete trust for your promises and love never fail.

August 20

Posting problems

"Be strong. Take courage. Don't be intimidated. Don't give them a second thought because God, your God, is striding ahead of you. He's right there with you. He won't let you down; he won't leave you."

Deuteronomy 31:6 (MSG)

Computers are wonderful tools for communicating, organizing and storing information and I'm constantly learning how to master all the processes. However sometimes I'll run into a roadblock which nearly causes me to crash and burn. One weekend I was trying to save my daily social media posts into a Word document. After wasting several hours with no success, I had sunk into a bad mood and was totally frustrated. Ever get like that? What I was trying to master had become my master! I had become so involved in what I was doing that I had failed to include God in my struggle. I finally called out to him in desperation and he sent someone to show me how to save the posts.

How often we try to resolve problems on our own without taking them to God first. We waste our time and energy which affects our mood. We're good about taking big issues to God but we think we can handle the small stuff. He wants to walk with us through EVERYTHING!

Lord of my time and tasks, be with me in everything I do today. Help me to trust you even in my mundane tasks, resting in the promise that you never leave me.

August 21
People who influence us

"So here's what I want you to do, God helping you: Take your everyday, ordinary life - your sleeping, eating, going-to-work, and walking-around life - and place it before God as an offering. Embracing what God does for you is the best thing you can do for him."

Romans 12:1, 2 (MSG)

As I sat during my quiet time one morning, I thought about the people who had the most influence on my Christian walk, the ones who set examples that I want to emulate in my own life. They include: my mother who would never say anything unkind about anyone; Esther, Mother's friend, who was so patient and uncomplaining through many years of pain; my daughter who sacrifices so much of her life taking care of her grandchildren; my husband who spends much of his time meeting the needs of others; Jeff Newton, leader of Kokomo Urban Outreach, who has given his life over completely to helping the underprivileged; Carolyn, a dear friend from Clarksville, who displayed courage and perseverance in spite of spending most of her life in a wheelchair.

These people displayed, and some still do, the unselfish love and commitment to living as Christ did without realizing the impact they have on others. They don't look for recognition or honor but simply live their lives in obedience.

Reflect on your own life and see the people you can use as your role models.

Lord, help me to live a life that exemplifies your love. I want your righteousness to be evident in everything I do and say.

August 22

Please, please

"Then he said, 'Imagine what would happen if you went to a friend in the middle of the night and said, "Friend, lend me three loaves of bread. An old friend traveling through just showed up, and I don't have a thing on hand." "The friend answers from his bed, "Don't bother me. The door's locked; my children are all down for the night; I can't get up to give you anything."

But let me tell you, even if he won't get up because he's a friend, if you stand your ground, knocking and waking all the neighbors, he'll finally get up and get you whatever you need. Here's what I'm saying: Ask and you'll get; seek and you'll find; knock and the door will open.'"

Luke 11:5-9 (MSG)

When our children were young and wanted something, they often pestered us saying, "Please, please, please!" Even if we didn't give in right away, usually one of us would cave in to the request just to get them to stop begging.

There've been times that I've prayed about a concern and am tempted to give up because God hasn't answered as quickly as I want. As adults, we tend to lose the intensity displayed by children, forgetting that persistence in our prayer life guarantees an answer. God tells us to ask and ask and ask. He has all the resources. Perhaps he's waiting to see the depth of our dependence on him; therefore we need to continue asking. He does hear and honor our prayers!

Father, sometimes I feel like I'm pestering you when I repeat the same prayer every day. I am torn between being persistent or giving it to you once and leaving it there. I do trust that you will answer but I will continue to lift them up so I am reminded that some things are out of my control.

August 23

Double jeopardy

"...that if you confess with your mouth the Lord Jesus and believe in your heart that God has raised Him from the dead, you will be saved."

Romans 10:9 (NKJV)

Several years ago there was a much-publicized trial of a man in Louisville who had been charged with murdering his fiancé. Although there appeared to be no question of his guilt, the prosecuting attorney had no concrete evidence to prove it. Consequently, the jury found him not guilty and he was acquitted. Several months later, evidence was discovered that proved his guilt. However, because he had been tried and found "not guilty," he couldn't be tried again. That would have been double jeopardy.

We become a Christian by believing that Jesus paid our sin debt on the cross, died and rose again. We are then declared "not guilty." We will not be tried again because our sins: past, present and future are off God's record and we'll never be judged for them. Our names are written in the Lamb's Book of Life and we are God's righteous children. That is reason to celebrate!!!

Father, I'm so blessed to be called your child. I live in peace and joy knowing that I am forever secure in your hand. I thank you that I have been declared innocent through your amazing grace.

August 24

Attached at the hip

"You have searched me, Lord, and you know me. You know when I sit and when I rise; you perceive my thoughts from afar. You discern my going out and my lying down; you are familiar with all my ways. Before a word is on my tongue you, Lord, know it completely."

Psalm 139:1-4 (NIV)

We may know two people who are especially close and we'll say "they're attached at the hip." After our first grandson, Tyler, was born, our daughter and her one-month-old baby came to live with us. She went to work and it became my responsibility to take care of Tyler. He was my constant companion no matter where I went, so we became very close - "attached at the hip." I tried to plan things that would please and engage him. When you spend that much time with someone you develop a sense of what they need before they even let you know.

The moment we become a Christian God moves in with us - I mean really moves in! He takes up permanent residence inside us and is more than "attached at the hip." He knows everything about us: our words, our actions, even what we're thinking. As we become more aware of His presence we start changing the way we act, the way we talk and our thoughts. Others begin to see Christ through the way we speak and act.

Lord, I want to be so close to you that others will get a glimpse of who you are through the way I live my life. Help me to stay aware of your presence in me.

August 25

Defining blessings

"Blessed are the poor in spirit, for theirs is the kingdom of heaven, blessed are those who mourn, for they will be comforted. Blessed are the meek, for they will inherit the earth. Blessed are those who hunger and thirst for righteousness, for they will be filled. Blessed are the merciful, for they will be shown mercy. Blessed are the pure in heart, for they will see God. Blessed are the peacemakers, for they will be called children of God. Blessed are those who are persecuted because of righteousness, for theirs is the kingdom of heaven."

Matthew 5:3-10 (NIV)

How do we define our blessings? We're quick to claim that God has favored our life because we have a great job, beautiful children, good health, and many others things that we enjoy, defining those as the way He bestows blessings. What about the committed believers who struggle just to make ends meet and sometimes can't pay their bills? How do we explain a believer who daily battles declining health? Does that mean God hasn't blessed them? Absolutely not!

Jesus catalogued our blessings, but they're not the kind we want to showcase. Look carefully at his list, for these are the blessings that display God working in your life and are the ones that give us an abundant life in Christ. The Bible tells us that the sun shines on the righteous and the unrighteous but the blessings given to us by God cannot be claimed by those who don't know him as their Savior.

God of blessings, help me to recognize and embrace the true blessings of my walk with you.

August 26

Dehydrated

"The high and lofty one who lives in eternity, the Holy One, says this: 'I live in the high and holy place with those whose spirits are contrite and humble. I restore the crushed spirit of the humble and revive the courage of those with repentant hearts.'"

Isaiah 57:15 (NLT)

One very hot August day a number of years ago, we attended an air show with some friends. The only space left to sit was in the sun so we settled in to watch the planes, drinking a lot of water and trying to stay cool. We'd been there about three hours when suddenly I passed out, overcome by the heat. The medics transported me to the first-aid center where they were treating a number of other people for heat-related problems. I had become dehydrated and didn't realize what was happening to me until it was too late.

If we fail to drink the living water that Jesus offers us, we can become spiritually dehydrated and not see what is happening to our hearts. We begin to feel like he's not close anymore and all of a sudden life becomes harder. The sad part is, the lack of spiritual refreshment weakens us without our even realizing it. The Holy Spirit is like a medic for our soul, reviving it with the living water that only our Savior can offer. I'm so thankful he is always with me to prod me to read God's Word and pray so I will stay refreshed.

Father God, fill me today with your living water for I am thirsty and need you to refresh my soul.

August 27

Donating blood

"Yet God, with undeserved kindness, declares that we are righteous. He did this through Christ Jesus when he freed us from the penalty for our sins. For God presented Jesus as the sacrifice for sin. People are made right with God when they believe that Jesus sacrificed his life, shedding his blood. His sacrifice shows that God was being fair when he held back and did not punish those who sinned in times past. For he was looking ahead and including them in what he did in the present time. God did this to demonstrate his righteousness, for he himself is fair and just, and he declares sinners to be right in his sight when they believe in Jesus."

Romans 3:24-26 (NLT)

My husband, Jack, has been donating blood regularly for over 35 years. He's been told that each pint he donates will help save the lives of three people. If a person gives six times a year for over 30 years, that comes to around 550 people. Multiply 550 times the hundreds of others who donate and you have an impressive number. But that need for blood is never really satisfied. It has to be replenished constantly.

Thankfully, Jesus only had to shed his blood once and his sacrifice was for everyone. Our donations of blood help three people. The blood of Jesus covered the entire human race. He doesn't have to shed it again and again. On the cross he said "It is finished." It didn't just help save lives like the blood donations we make, but it guarantees salvation for all eternity. All he asks from us is that we believe that he died on the cross for our sins, was buried and rose again.

Precious Savior, thank you for loving me so much that you were willing to die for me.

August 28

Walking in my shoes

"Yea, though I walk through the valley of the shadow of death, I will fear no evil, for You are with me; Your rod and Your staff, they comfort me."

Psalm 23:5 (NKJV)

I've heard people say "If you had to walk in my shoes, you'd understand how I feel." Literally speaking, you cannot walk comfortably in someone else's shoes, for after they've worn them for a while the shoes form to the shape of their feet and won't fit anyone else the same way. Our life experiences affect the way we handle our circumstances the same way our shoes form to our feet. No one else can completely understand how you react to what is going on in your life. They may say "I understand" but they really cannot.

Jesus is the only one who has walked in everyone's shoes. Think about it! He wore the shoes of a child, the shoes of a carpenter, waded into the water barefoot with Peter, and donned the shoes of a hated tax collector, the sandals of an outcast leper, the barefoot, disgraced prostitute and even a thief on the cross. He gave up His royal shoes in heaven to come to earth and walk in our shoes. That's how much he loves us. He, alone, knows how we feel. Think about him today when you put on your shoes, for he's walking in them with you.

Jesus, thank you for walking in my shoes so you would understand my deepest feelings.

August 29

Believing

"Your love for one another will prove to the world that you are my disciples."

John 13:35 (NIV)

"Three things will last forever---faith, hope, and love---and the greatest of these is love."

I Corinthians 13:13 (NLT)

Our Christian journey begins with believing what Jesus did for us. He's the rock we build our faith on. That faith leads us to the hope we have: an eternity in heaven. Both faith and hope are internal, and lead us to a relationship with our Lord. But then Jesus gave a new commandment - *"A new commandment I give to you, that you love one another: as I have loved you, that you also love one another."* (John 13:34). This time the word becomes a verb and it requires action on our part. It's a whole new level for us and a lot more difficult. Jesus said, "love as I have loved". This is not just affection for one another but a new, forgiving, sacrificial, "putting others' needs ahead of ours" kind of love. This new commandment now becomes our marching orders! We're to move beyond our internal love for God to loving others the way Jesus did.

Before Paul's conversion on the Damascus road, he persecuted and murdered believers without any feelings of guilt or remorse. However, once he met Jesus, he made a 180-degree turn and became totally committed to showing love toward those he once considered enemies.

Lord, help me to love others the way you have loved me. Strengthen me when I struggle with showing love to people who are difficult and challenging.

August 30

Jesus comes for a visit

"You will show me the way of life, granting me the joy of your presence and the pleasures of living with you forever."

Psalm 16:11 (NLT)

What would you do if Jesus showed up at your front door this morning? You weren't expecting him so you've done nothing to prepare for such a guest. You invite him in while wondering if there's anything sitting out that you should hide. Well, he already knows about it. Should you tell him how often you're going to church and how much work you've done there? He's not concerned about that. Do you confess that sin you've been hiding? He's already forgotten about it. He sees you sitting there nervously and then says with a smile, "I just came to visit with you for a while. We haven't talked lately and I thought today would be a good time to catch up." A warm feeling of love and awe washes over you. Then it dawns on you that this is the God of the universe and he wants to sit with you and talk!

Sound too farfetched to happen? Well, guess what? He's already there - in your home and heart 24/7. He sees your tears, your frustrations, your sins, your struggles, and loves you anyway, with a love so deep that we cannot comprehend it. He just wants you to know him more intimately and that will only happen if you spend time together.

Lord, I'm sorry I spend so much time on things that aren't really important and neglect the One who desires to be at the center of my life. Help me learn to sit quietly in your presence for there I will find real joy

August 31

Is God even listening?

"I cry out to you, O God, but you don't answer. I stand before you, but you don't even look."

Job 30:20 (NLT)

"Just as you cannot understand the path of the wind or the mystery of a tiny baby growing in its mother's womb, so you cannot understand the activity of God, who does all things..."

Ecclesiastes 11:5 (NLT)

Do you ever feel like God isn't listening to you? Sometimes I'll have long conversations with God, venting my feelings and asking why some people have to endure so much heartache and challenge. I know in my heart that he's not going to give me an answer, but he does hear my anguished groanings. When I see friends face one challenge after another, with no relief in sight, it breaks my heart. So I cry out, "Why?" Some answers will never be revealed, so we need faith that God has a plan beyond our understanding, and that he will bring it to fruition in his own time.

So what can we do when we hurt for those we care about? We can continue to pray for them. We can encourage them and help them when they need it. My prayers now consist mostly of asking God to pour out his peace upon those who are suffering. This blessed peace equips them to stand strong in the midst of their pain and trouble. God didn't promise us that our lives would be easy or without valleys to go through, but he did promise he would always be with us and give us his peace.

Loving Father, you hear all my pleas for mercy. Grant me patience as I lay my petitions on your altar for I know you listen when I call to you.

September

*You prepare a table
before me
in the presence of
my enemies.*

*Lord, I am overwhelmed that
you invite me to your table in
the midst of enemies,
even when I don't deserve it.*

September 1

Stand your ground

"Be prepared. You're up against far more than you can handle on your own. Take all the help you can get, every weapon God has issued, so that when it's all over but the shouting you'll still be on your feet. Truth, righteousness, peace, faith and salvation are more than words. Learn how to apply them. You'll need them throughout your life."

Ephesians 6:13-16 (MSG)

A few years ago a controversial law was passed which has been used as a defense in seemingly unjustified killings. It is the "Stand Your Ground" law and it has been used in a couple of high profile trials, one of which resulted in an acquittal. As with any law, it can be used in a good way or in some cases abused.

In His Word, God has told us to "stand our ground," not with weapons that will kill or injure, but with the protection of righteousness, truth, the gospel of peace and, more importantly, faith. Without these elements of defense we cannot stand against the attacks of the evil one.

All of us are, and will continue to be, under attack because the world we live in is full of evil. We can only have victory if we're diligent to equip ourselves with his armor each morning. We have the ultimate defense for "Greater is He that is in me than he that is in the world." (I John 4:4, NKJV)

Father, you are the defender and protector of the helpless. May your Spirit enable me to stand my ground when I face the enemy.

September 2

Shaving off his beard

"You've been with me all this time, Philip, and you still don't understand? To see me is to see the Father. So how can you ask, 'Where is the Father?' Don't you believe that I am in the Father and the Father is in me? The words that I speak to you aren't mere words. I don't just make them up on my own. The Father who resides in me crafts each word into a divine act."

John 14:9, 10 (MSG)

Recently a friend shaved off the beard he had been sporting for a few months. He told me his beard was gone for two days before his wife even noticed. Then when he went to church, no one there noticed either. Sometimes when we look at our family and our friends, we don't really see them. Either our mind is somewhere else, or we're so accustomed to seeing them in a certain way, that we don't actually pay attention.

When we think about our Savior, we visualize the pictures we've seen of Jesus. That's not really him, just an artist's idea of what he looks like. We're so used to the way we worship, read the Bible and pray that we fail to focus our heart on the One we're worshipping. We don't see the author and creator of the universe, the One who planned for us before we were even conceived, the One who picked up our load of sin and carried it to the cross, the One who is getting our home ready in heaven, the One who is waiting to take us home. I really cannot imagine what Jesus will look like but I believe I will recognize him.

Beautiful Savior, I can't see your face yet, but I know your character, your personality, your love, your patience and your forgiveness and that will be enough for me to recognize you.

September 3

Exploring grandma's attic

"Don't you know that you yourselves are God's temple and that God's Spirit dwells in your midst?"

I Corinthians 3:16 (NIV)

While I was growing up, one of my favorite pastimes was exploring my grandma's attic. The things she stored up there were from our family's past and to me they seemed like treasures. There were trunks tucked away in a storage area, old clothes in a little closet, books piled up in boxes, furniture, toys and all sorts of fascinating things to investigate. Being allowed to go up there was a child's dream come true. Realistically, most of it had no monetary value anymore, but she couldn't let go of it.

Our hearts and minds are sometimes like my grandma's attic. We hang on to old ideas, guilt, bad memories, failures, grudges we should have gotten over, doubts and all the other negative stuff we store in our heart and have so much difficulty getting rid of. These things are a hindrance and keep us from having the close, personal relationship with Jesus that we so long for. We're his temple and he wants our hearts and minds to be filled with him. It's time to clean out our attics and put a lock on the door. An attic, after all, is only a place to store what we don't need anymore.

Lord, help me to throw out all the things I harbor in my heart and mind that keep me from focusing on you. Fill me with so much of your presence that nothing will uproot the joy and peace I have in you.

SEPTEMBER

September 4

Unlocking the door

"See, I stand knocking at the door. If anyone listens to my voice and opens the door, I will go into his house and dine with him, and he with me."

Revelation 3:20 (Phillips)

A familiar picture of Jesus shows him knocking on a door with no doorknob. When our son, Steve, was a little over two, he managed to lock himself in the bathroom. We didn't have a key to open the door and we tried explaining how to unlock it from the inside but he couldn't understand. Finally his daddy had to climb through a small bathroom window to rescue him.

Why is there no knob on the door in the picture of Jesus? Before we accepted Him as our Savior, he was knocking at the door of our heart. For some of us, he'd been there a long time, waiting for us to open the door and invite him in. But, like the bathroom door that kept us from Steve, it has to be opened from the inside - by us. He stands at everyone's door but most people don't want to open it. Some have even put a deadbolt on their heart's door. They're content to stay in the darkness of unbelief, not realizing that light would shine in their lives if they would only open the door and invite him in.

Father of patience, thank you for waiting so long for me to open the door of my heart. I am so grateful that you never gave up on me.

September 5

Each child is different

"This means we will not compare ourselves with each other as if one of us were better and another worse. We have far more important things to do with our lives. Each of us is an original."

Galatians 5:26 (MSG)

When I think about my three children, I'm amazed at how each one of them is so different. Even though they came from the same parents and were raised in the same home, their personalities and passions are unique to each one and they allowed those passions to lead them as adults. They are all driven but one is in constant motion in caring for the needs of family; one is open to being a leader and is creative, and one is totally focused.

God made each one of his children uniquely different, with his or her own capabilities and gifts. When we allow him to direct our path, he puts us in a place designed just for us. Even though I didn't realize it when I was hired, being a church secretary was a great fit for me because I love detail work, having things organized and doing some writing.

God knows your strengths, even if you don't, and can put you in a place where they can be used by him. If you have a passion for something, pray about it, for using your gift gives your life purpose and brings glory to God.

Creator God, thank you for giving each of us gifts that we can use to further your kingdom.

SEPTEMBER

September 6

Life is a book in progress

"You will keep in perfect peace all who trust in you, all whose thoughts are fixed on you."

Isaiah 26:3 (NLT)

The moment we're born our life stretches out before us like a book yet to be written. Sadly, some books are short; but most go on for many chapters, each one representing a specific time in our life. Early chapters are filled with growing and learning and later ones with the joys of achieving our goals. Some will chronicle our struggles and sorrows, but each chapter will end as a new one begins. The experiences we face and the trials we endure develop our character and form us into the person we become. If we have put our trust in Jesus, the author and finisher of our book, we can face the final chapter with hope in eternity where our name is already written in The Lamb's Book of Life. Then, when our book is finished, those we leave behind can cherish the chapter we completed and embrace their book that is yet to be finished.

Father, you are the author of life and you have already written the end of my book. Help me fill my life pages with things that bring honor to you.

September 7

Unfaithfulness

"The Lord is close to the brokenhearted; he rescues them whose spirits are crushed."

Psalm 34:18 (NLT)

"Remember your promise to me; it is my only hope. Your promise revives me; it comforts me in all my troubles."

Psalm 119:49, 50 (NLT)

My first husband and I had been married thirteen years when I learned he was being unfaithful. I was in shock and felt a deep sense of betrayal. We were involved in a church, but I had no real relationship with the Lord. One night, in deep despair, I picked up my Bible and sat down on the couch. I knew it contained words of comfort but I didn't even know where to begin looking. I didn't realize it at the time but my Lord was just waiting for me to submit to him. After a few months of struggling I found God's amazing grace and, through the powerful prayers of friends and the Lord's compassion and love, I was saved. My husband found salvation soon after, and through that dramatic transformation our life as a family was turned around and restored.

Sometimes it's necessary to go through painful trials before we realize how much we need a Savior. He's the Great Physician, healing broken hearts, restoring tattered dreams and filling empty lives. We'll have times when we cannot fix things on our own. He has a plan for each of us, but we have to come to the end of ourselves and submit to him before our circumstances will change. He is the glue that binds our shattered lives back together.

You are the Father of families and I will be eternally grateful that you healed mine when it was dying.

September 8

Old cars

"He will take our weak mortal bodies and change them into glorious bodies like his own using the same power with which he will bring everything under his control."

Philippians 3:21 (NLT)

One evening after spending some time with us, our grandson Petar started up his old car to head home to Indianapolis. Jack mentioned that it sounded pretty rough. He asked Petar how many miles it had on it - over 250,000 - so guess it had a right to sound a little rough. It had a few dings and scratches, but it ran and got him where he needed to go.

Jack and I are beginning to feel like that old car. We've put a lot of miles on our earthly bodies and sometimes they don't run as efficiently as we'd like. We've accumulated some bumps and bruises along the way and the finish is showing wear and tear. We're still chugging along though, and they're getting us where we need to be - at least most of the time.

When he can afford it someday, Petar will trade his old car in for a new one but that will come at a cost. Someday our worn-out bodies will be traded in for new ones, and everything on them will work efficiently and never need repairs. The best part - it's already paid for and will be delivered when we're ready for it - God alone knows that time.

Father, I look forward to the day when I'll have a new body and can celebrate with the One who gives it to me.

September 9

I have a dream

"You will show me the path of life; in Your presence is fullness of joy; at Your right hand are pleasures forevermore."

Psalm 16:11 (NKJV)

A famous quote from Dr. Martin Luther King is "I have a dream..." His dream wasn't fulfilled in his lifetime, but it set in motion a movement that has changed our nation.

We all dream of doing big things, going on exciting adventures and achieving significant goals in our lives, but most of us are too fearful to give it a try.

There are many people who dared to pursue something extraordinary in their senior years: Grandma Moses, Phyllis Diller, Ronald Reagan, Mother Teresa and KFC's Harlan Sanders to name a few. Others go on mission trips, start businesses, run a marathon, write a book, take up painting or go back to school. We are never too old to learn and try new things. A couple close friends of ours planned and successfully completed skydives a couple of years ago. Other friends took an extended RV trip to Alaska. All these people dared to dream big.

If God is the guide in your life, don't be afraid to step out in faith. He rewards the faithful with blessings and joy in the fulfillment of those dreams.

Father, thank you for the blessings that accompany fulfilled dreams.

September 10

I'm Reminded

"The Lord is my shepherd; I have all I need."

Psalm 23:1 (NLT)

"Long before he laid down the earth's foundations, he had us in mind, had settled on us as the focus of his love, to be made whole and holy by his love. Long, long ago he decided to adopt us into his family through Jesus Christ."

Ephesians 1:4-5 (MSG)

Daily, I'm reminded of God's love for me and how he cares about all the details of my life. I don't have to go outside to see his handiwork.

I'm reminded every time Jack holds me in his arms, for God is the one who brought him into my life.

I'm reminded when I see the food in the cabinet and refrigerator, for God promises to provide for our needs.

I'm reminded when I look at the sun filtering through our curtains, because he is the One who brought light into my life.

I'm reminded when I take a shower, for Jesus washed my sins away with his cleansing blood.

I'm reminded as I think of our debt-free home, for he paid my sin debt completely with his forgiving grace.

I'm reminded when I look at our earthly home, for he has an even better one waiting for me in heaven.

Lord, everywhere I look, I see your indescribable grace. It surrounds me every day. Help me to look at where I am, what I have and who I am, with new eyes.

September 11

9/11

"But there's far more to life for us. We're citizens of high heaven! We're waiting for the arrival of the Savior, the Master, Jesus Christ, who will transform our earthly bodies into glorious bodies like his own. He'll make us beautiful and whole with the same powerful skill by which he is putting everything as it should be, under and around him."

Philippians 3:20, 21 (MSG)

Today marks the anniversary of the devastating attack on the Twin Towers and our nation's capital in 2001. It's hard to believe how long it's been, for time slips by so quickly. Much has happened since that day and memories become blurred by other things that are going on. We've pushed to the back of our mind any thoughts of the three thousand people killed and the thousands more who were left picking up the pieces of their lives after losing their loved ones.

When we face a tragedy such as 9/11, it's tempting to wonder why God allows this kind of atrocity. He didn't ordain suffering, pain, grief - all of the other trials that make life so difficult. We live in a fallen world and as long as we are housed in our earthly tents these things will happen. But this is not really our home. We're pilgrims here on a journey, and one day we will be ushered into our real home in heaven where we will live in the peace and joy of God's presence forever.

Father, shelter us in the cradle of your arms when we're fearful and overwhelmed by the evil that surrounds us.

September 12

Namedroppers

"That is why God has now lifted him so high, and has given him the name beyond all names, so that at the name of Jesus 'every knee shall bow,' whether in Heaven or earth or under the earth."

Philippians 2:9, 10 (Phillips)

The term "namedropper" refers to those who try to impress others with a list of important people they've met or are acquainted with. I've known a few "namedroppers" and no doubt have been guilty of doing it myself.

What we usually don't tell others is that we have a close, intimate relationship with the creator of the universe. We don't mention that we are talking to him every day, that books have been written about him and he inspired his own book. We don't relate all the things he has done for us, including paying our sin debt and building us a home in His neighborhood. It's as though we're embarrassed to mention we even know him. He wants us to tell others about our relationship, so they will want to meet him as well. That's the best kind of "namedropper" to be, and a name we all need to "drop" more often.

Lord, help me to be bold in telling others about our friendship. I want others to have this kind of relationship with you.

September 13

Climbing over the fences

"God has given each of you a gift from his great variety of spiritual gifts. Use them well to serve one another."

I Peter 4:10 (NLT)

One evening, when our children were young, we were given a puppy which we named Herbie. We got him from a young man who had come to our door looking for someone who would adopt the adorable little pup that was tucked in his jacket pocket. Of course the kids had to have him. As Herbie got older, we went to a great deal of expense putting up a chain link fence to keep him in the yard. The first day we let him play outside he figured out how to climb the fence. On one occasion he almost hung himself when his collar got caught on the fence. In desperation we started leaving the gate open. He was free-spirited and would not be bound in by barriers.

As Christian, we're not fenced in by rules and laws. I have freedom in my Christian walk, but it hasn't always been like that. For years I felt like God was judging every move I made and measuring my works. What a joy it was when I realized that I was accepted because I believe in what Christ did for me, not because of my effort. Learning to trust in my Lord has given me the courage to explore "outside the fence."

You're one-of-a-kind and no one else can duplicate what you bring into your service. The joy comes when you are able to serve your Lord in your own special way because you love Him.

Father, what joy I found when I climbed over the fences others put around me and explored your world.

SEPTEMBER

September 14

A jigsaw puzzle

"I will praise the Lord, who counsels me; even at night my heart instructs me. I keep my eyes always on the Lord. With him at my right hand, I will not be shaken."

Psalm 16:7, 8 (NIV)

I used to enjoy putting jigsaw puzzles together. As I would spread the pieces out on the table, it seemed almost overwhelming. Puzzles don't come with instructions and all I had as a guide was the picture on the box. One piece at a time, the picture would come together and when it was finished it was beautiful (at least to me).

Sometimes life may feel like the pieces of a puzzle, scattered and incomplete, and we don't know how to put it together. Jesus is the picture we have to go by and if we follow the pattern he has set before us, it will come together one piece at a time. The puzzle doesn't come with instructions but we do have a guideline for putting our life together in God's Word as well as help from the Holy Spirit and we end up mirroring his beauty in our completed transformation.

Father, thank you for giving me a pattern to follow for my life. Help me continue putting the pieces together faithfully until my picture is complete.

September 15

Staying connected

"I love the Lord because he hears my voice and my prayer for mercy. Because he bends down to listen, I will pray as long as I have breath!"

Psalm 116:1, 2 (NLT)

Today's Christians have multiple options to help them stay connected with each other. Often those devices get in the way and keep them from spending time with their Lord. It takes discipline to pick up your Bible instead of the newspaper or a book. It's tempting to text or phone a friend instead of praying and communicating with God. We find excuses for missing Sunday School or small group. A lot of people are satisfied with giving God one hour a week and then wonder why he doesn't feel close or personal to them.

When you have a close, personal friend you make an effort to spend time together, discussing what's going on in your lives, problems, plans and other things that you share an interest in. God wants that kind of fellowship with you as well. Deep friendships don't happen overnight. They develop over time. If you really want that closeness with God then give it a chance to grow by spending some time together every day. He already considers you His BFF (best friend forever) so make Him yours as well.

Lord, it is so tempting to pick up my iPad or iPhone instead of pausing to spend time with you. Help me overcome my addiction to this form of communication.

September 16

Diversity

"Then God looked over all he had made, and he saw that it was very good."

Genesis 1:31 (NLT)

"Everything God created is good, and to be received with thanks. Nothing is to be sneered at and thrown out. God's Word and our prayers make every item in creation holy."

I Timothy 4:4, 5 (MSG)

We fuss and complain because things aren't the way we're used to and we want our surroundings to be structured around what we're comfortable with. We feel uncomfortable around people that aren't like us.

How boring our world would be if all the flowers looked and smelled the same or all the trees were exactly alike. How amazing that God created each of them to show their own uniqueness. We enjoy them because they display their beauty without competing with one another. The rose doesn't say to the daisy, "Why can't you look like me?"

What we enjoy individually doesn't mean all other ideas and styles are wrong. We won't all look alike or think alike. We're created the way God planned and we have his blueprint imbedded in our DNA. Celebrate the way God created you by loving and embracing the diversity of personalities and gifts that others display.

Lord, you created each of us with in a special way with special abilities. Help me learn to appreciate what they have to offer without comparing them with myself and what I like.

September 17

Knocked to our knees

"The Lord says, 'I will rescue those who love me. I will protect those who trust in my name. When they call on me, I will answer; I will be with them in trouble. I will rescue and honor them. I will reward them with a long life, and give them my salvation.'"

Psalm 91:14-16 (NLT)

Sometimes events happen in our life that will knock us to our knees. We might struggle with "why", but we manage to pick ourselves up and get going again. Then something else occurs and we're down again. How do you cope when it seems as though you've just recovered from the first trial?

That happened to Seaside Heights in New Jersey. The popular park and boardwalk was destroyed in Hurricane Sandy, and yet the people managed to come together and rebuild in time for the tourist season. And then they suffered another devastating blow in a fire that wiped out all their efforts. Yet most of them were determined not to be defeated.

When we're faced with several trials in a row, we may not have answers, but we have a God who understands and is there to lift us up, even carry us at times. We need to go to God first for he has a big lap and wants to hold you when you're hurt and feel like you've lost your way.

Lord, sometimes I have a hard time accepting what happens in my life and the lives of my loved ones. Your Word says that you will never leave me, but when I'm hurting I'm not always able to feel your presence. Help me to trust in your promises even when I'm weak.

SEPTEMBER

September 18

He's one step ahead of us

"Have mercy on me, my God, have mercy on me, for in you I take refuge. I will take refuge in the shadow of your wings until the disaster has passed. I cry out to God Most High, to God, who vindicates me."

Psalm 57:1, 2 (NIV)

Our faith grows as we experience the way God works in our life. He knows each step we will take even before we begin our journey. If we're going to need help or assistance, he's already planned for it. This has happened to me a number of times. Once, when I was on my way to my mother's in Marion, I was driving alone on the interstate in the dark, about 9:30 in the evening, with less than twenty miles left to my destination. The car began to cut out on me and I managed to get it to the side of the road before the engine died. I put my head down and prayed for God to send someone to help.

As soon as I looked up, a semi pulled up in front of me and stopped. The driver got out and walked back to see if he could help. I had put it in God's hands so, in faith, I rolled down the window and told him where I was going. As it turned out he was going to Marion too. I decided that God had sent him, so I got in his truck and he took me to a service station in Marion, gave me the name of a towing service to call and waited to make sure arrangements were made. I trusted my God and knew he was watching over me. God knew I would need help before I left home that evening.

Each time he intervenes when we face an unexpected trial, it strengthens our faith and we're able to stand stronger when we face the next one.

All knowing Father, thank you for walking ahead of me on my journey.

September 19

Rationing

"A devout life does bring wealth, but it's the rich simplicity of being yourself before God. Since we entered the world penniless and will leave it penniless, if we have bread on the table and shoes on our feet, that's enough."

I Timothy 6:6-8 (MSG)

During the 1940's, when we were growing up, rationing was a part of the way we lived. Because of the war, many of the things we take for granted were in short supply. After the war the economy recovered and took off and the more it grew, the more purchasing power people had. Now it seems as though acquiring more stuff has become the norm. We no more than get the latest phone, computer, TV, clothes, car or anything else we think we can't function without, and we decide it's out of date, out of style or doesn't include the latest technology. TV ads convince us that we can't have a good quality of life without the latest new "stuff". Consumerism has overtaken our culture and as a result many families struggle with debt and stress.

God doesn't want our hearts to be focused on acquiring more stuff all the time, for those things may become the idols that draw us away from our Lord. The way they hook us is subtle and we don't realize how much we're tied to them.

God designed each of us with an empty place that can only be filled by him and we have to make that the top priority so that His fellowship means more than anything else.

Lord, help me ration the things that have no lasting value and focus on the spiritual blessings that offer eternal value.

September 20

Sunday attitudes

"My child, don't lose sight of common sense and discernment. Hang on to them, for they will refresh your soul. They are like jewels on a necklace. They keep you safe on your way, and your feet will not stumble."

Proverbs 3:21, 23 (NLT)

When our children were growing up, getting all of them up, fed, dressed and out the door on Sunday mornings was often a challenge. Sometimes everyone would be in a bad mood by the time we arrived, but when we walked in the door each of us put on a happy face. Ever happen to you? All of us needed an attitude adjustment. As parents, we had neglected to think about the reason we were going to church. We didn't pause to reflect on who we were there to worship. In retrospect, I think the "going" had become more of a duty instead of a privilege. We didn't want others to see our bad mood, but God knew and I'm sure he was disappointed. We can't really worship if our minds are divided.

When we get up each morning, we can decide what our mood is going to be that day. If we focus on being upbeat and cheerful it changes the way we'll handle situations we encounter.

Lord, help me to react in a loving, compassionate way when I face times that are stressful, for I know with the help of Your Spirit, I can be patient and speak and act with wisdom.

September 21

Cleaning out my closet

"Therefore, since we are surrounded by such a huge crowd of witnesses to the life of faith, let us strip off every weight that slows us down, especially the sin that so easily trips us up. And let us run with endurance the race God has set before us."

Hebrews 12:1 (NLT)

Spring and fall are typically seasons when I'll decide to clean out closets and drawers. Each time, as I fill up bags to take to Goodwill, I ask myself "Where does all this stuff come from?" It seemed important when I bought it. Styles, needs and desires all change from year to year. What a wonderful feeling to know that the unneeded and unused items are gone for good! My mother had a rule about her closet. If she bought something new, something old had to go. I've never been successful in following her example.

I've noticed now and then that my mind and heart become cluttered and crowded with outdated, useless and often harmful ideas and feelings, so I need to start ridding myself of those things that tend to pull me down or rob me of peace. There's resentment over something that happened long ago, but it's still buried in the recesses of my heart. I've hung onto feelings of hurt over a betrayal. There are remnants of greed, discontent, pride and worry that are tucked away in the corners of my mind. They need to go in the trash, which is what they are. Now there's room for all of the good things the Lord wants me to fill my heart with.

Father, help me shed any negative, critical thoughts so I can fill my mind with love and compassion.

SEPTEMBER

September 22

Defining moments

"And we know that all things work together for good to those who love God, to those who are called according to His purpose."

Romans 8:28 (NKJV)

I learned early in life that hurt and disappointment inevitably show their ugly faces and when they do, I have a choice to make. I can allow them to derail me and bring me down, or I can rise above them. It becomes a defining moment and the decision could affect the rest of my life. When my parents divorced (I was thirteen), I decided to make the best of it and I grew to love my stepmom. When my first husband was unfaithful, I chose to stay with him and as a result he eventually accepted the Lord.

Then, when he passed in 1983, I started a new chapter which eventually led me to Jack, the love of my life. None of these transitions came overnight and they all involved many tears and adjustments. Through each of them I drew closer to God. I learned to trust in his promise that he would never leave or forsake me and discovered through my trials that God is the only one that is able to offer that kind of assurance.

All of us will face seemingly insurmountable obstacles in our faith walk. Some of them we won't be able change, but we do have control over how we react. These are the trials than can bring the greatest growth in our Christian walk.

Abba Father, you are the rock I stand on. Thank you for walking with me through my journey.

September 23

Adding a family room

"So we have not stopped praying for you since we first heard about you. We ask God to give you complete knowledge of his will and to give you spiritual wisdom and understanding. Then the way you live will always honor and please the Lord, and your lives will produce every kind of good fruit. All the while, you will grow as you learn to know God better and better."

Colossians 1:9-12 (NLT)

When Jack and I were newly married we had some remodeling done, adding a family room to our home. We found the process to be disruptive and not conducive to a peaceful existence. Both of us grew weary of the mess, but looked forward to the time we could enjoy the new room. When it was finally ready to occupy around Thanksgiving that year, we were thrilled to be able to share it with family members at our traditional gathering. It was then we knew it had been worth all the grief we had endured.

When we first accept our Savior's grace, he begins the work of remodeling us. The process is painful at times as he works at rearranging everything in our hearts and minds, using trials to mold us into the person we were designed to be. Sometimes that can be almost overwhelming, but he stays with us and we grow steadily. Someday his work will be complete and we'll be called home to be with the Lord forever. Then all the discomfort of the growing process will have been worth it

Father, help me be patient as you work daily on changing my heart and mind.

September 24

Waiting Rooms

"We wait in hope for the Lord; he is our help and our shield. In him our hearts rejoice, for we trust in his holy name."

Psalm 33:20-21 (NIV)

The year was 1978. Mike and I sat in the waiting room of a hospital in Louisville, Kentucky, anticipating the arrival of our first grandchild. For several hours I stayed in the labor room with my daughter, comforting her and rubbing her back. Even though I didn't like seeing her in pain, I knew what she was enduring would be worth it once the baby was delivered. When Tyler finally made his appearance, the hours of waiting and pain were forgotten. We were filled with joy the moment we saw this tiny blessing filling the room with his lusty cry.

God has a waiting room too. Many times we have to sit in this room, suffering and anxious, waiting for God to answer our prayers. Waiting is hard and we long desperately for relief from our troubles. As we sit there trying to be patient, we anticipate the joy we'll feel when his answer finally comes. Like the wait for the birth of Tyler, the time we spend in God's waiting room will soon pass and the answer he brings will infuse us with renewed faith and hope. Then we'll rejoice in his unfailing love and care for us.

Father of hope, bathe me with perseverance when my life seems to be on hold.

September 25

Being in a race

"You've all been to the stadium and seen the athletes race. Everyone runs; one wins. Run to win. All good athletes train hard. They do it for a gold medal that tarnishes and fades. You're after one that's gold eternally. I don't know about you, but I'm running hard for the finish line. I'm giving it everything I've got. No sloppy living for me! I'm staying alert and in top condition. I'm not going to get caught napping, telling everyone else all about it and then missing out myself."

I Corinthians 9:24-27 (MSG)

We have friends and family members who compete in races. One nephew has done a number of bike races and others in our family have competed in marathons. There are things they do to be prepared physically. No matter what kind of race they're in, they wear light-weight clothes and shoes and load up on carbs so they'll have the extra energy their body needs.

Paul tells us we are in a race, and if we are to finish in victory there are two very important steps we need to take. First, we have to shed those things which distract us and cause us to lose our focus on the crown that awaits us when we complete our race. Some of these distractions aren't necessarily bad but if they consume us, we're tempted to put aside our run and work toward a different goal. The second essential element of victory is loading up on God's Word to give us added strength when the run gets tough, which it will! At some point in our race we'll "hit a wall" and won't be able to continue without the strength found only in God.

Lord, equip me through your Word and strengthen me with your Spirit so I can complete my race in victory.

SEPTEMBER

September 26

Our precious Lord

"So be strong and courageous! Do not be afraid and do not panic before them. For the Lord your God will personally go ahead of you. He will neither fail you nor abandon you."

Deuteronomy 31:6 (NLT)

As we're walking in our faith journey, life will become challenging at times. No one's journey is guaranteed to be problem-free. When we were young parents we dealt with so much activity that we sometimes felt as if personal time for us was an elusive dream. Then as we grew older, the frenzy was replaced with the realization that the family didn't need us like they used to. Life slowed down, but so did we. I'm so thankful that God gave us children when we were young because I'm realizing how challenging it would be as I grow older. However through all of the ups and downs of life, we had the assurance that God was always with us, holding our hand and giving us the strength we needed.

I have family and friends who are caring for grandchildren, great-grandchildren and sometimes other members of their family. I'm sure there are times they feel overwhelmed but God enables them to endure and he continues to walk with them. Even though the challenges are still there, he promises to hold them close and walk with them until they have completed the task set before them. They'll emerge stronger and have the satisfaction of serving as God's hands and feet each time they offer their help to others.

Precious Jesus, thank you for being a light in my life when I can't see the path ahead of me.

September 27

Saying you're sorry

"I know I distressed you greatly with my letter. Although I felt awful at the time, I don't feel at all bad now that I see how it turned out. The letter upset you, but only for a little while. Now I'm glad - not that you were upset, but that you were jarred into turning things around. You let the distress bring you to God, not drive you from Him. The result was all gain, no loss."

II Corinthians 7:8-11 (MSG)

Having three children pretty close in age often led to disagreements among them. Once in a while, when the arguments became too heated or physical, I would intervene and make them tell each other they were sorry. Usually they would glare at each other with clenched teeth and "apologize".

Saying you're sorry isn't easy, even as an adult. It's hard to admit you were wrong or that you behaved badly. Sometimes we have to reflect on what happened for a while. The Spirit convicts us, then we feel regret and long to set things right. I missed a lot of teaching opportunities with my children, because I could have explained what being sorry really involves and how it can restore peace to a relationship. God has already forgiven us when our behavior disappoints him, but if we allow the Spirit to guide us, we want to act in a manner that reflects his love.

Paul chastised the Corinthians about the disputes and fighting in their church and the Holy Spirit led them to repentance.

Forgiving Father, sometimes it's really hard for me to say "I'm sorry" Forgive me when I fail to reach out to restore a relationship.

SEPTEMBER

September 28

Learning discipline

"You realize, don't you that you are the temple of God, and God himself is present in you?"

I Corinthians 3:16 (MSG)

"Keep vigilant watch over your heart; that's where life starts."

Proverbs 4:23 (MSG)

We have to do certain things to maintain our physical and spiritual health. It's hard for me to get excited about the physical part. Jack is very disciplined, committed to reading the Bible every morning, walking twice a day and going to the gym regularly. Sometimes I need a prod to get me to the gym. My favorite part of the gym (ordeal) is when we're finished and are walking to the car. However, I can spend hours meditating and writing.

Learning to be disciplined isn't easy. We're responsible for keeping ourselves healthy spiritually as well as physically, for we're God's temple while here on earth. It's important to develop and grow our faith with the same dedication we have in keeping ourselves physically strong. If we train ourselves to spend time with our Lord daily, we'll sense his presence in whatever we do. That motivates us to have conversations with him throughout the day, sharing joys, lifting concerns, expressing thanks and simply enjoying his company.

Father, help me learn to be more disciplined in every aspect of my life.

September 29

Losing my song

"The Lord is my strength and my song, and He has become my salvation. He is my God, and I will praise Him; my father's God, and I will exalt Him!"

Exodus 15:2 (NKJV)

For a while after my husband died in 1983, I felt as though I'd lost the song in my heart. I no longer looked forward to facing a new day. My life seemed bleak and flat, like a barren desert. Gradually the emptiness and loneliness I was experiencing began to diminish and as spring approached, each day became a little brighter. That spring was filled with a lot of activity as I sold our home, bought a house in town and helped my daughter prepare for her upcoming wedding. When all the activity finally settled down that summer, I felt a new song being composed in my heart. Another chapter had begun and life was good again.

There will be days when troubles eclipse the song in our heart and we feel abandoned and alone. If we do hear a tune, it's a haunting, sad one that brings no joy to us. But that will pass, for God has a new song to replace it and soon it will fill our soul with joy again. The song we lost is replaced by the Creator of all music, our Lord and Savior Jesus Christ.

God of music, help me recognize your voice in the melody of a dirge as well as songs of joy. Draw me closer to you through each note.

SEPTEMBER

September 30

A brand new day

"The faithful love of the Lord never ends! Great is his faithfulness; his mercies begin afresh each morning."

Lamentations 3:22, 23 (NKJV)

Each morning we wake up to a brand new day spread out before us like a blank sheet of paper. We have the opportunity to write whatever we want on it. If we choose to fill it with positive, uplifting thoughts, the day will be blessed even in the tough times. However, if we get up feeling negative and defeated, that's the way our day will be. We make the choice.

For myself, I try to look forward to each morning. When I take the time to commune with God, he starts me off with a feeling of peace. This might be the day God has a surprise in store for me: it could be going out to lunch with Jack, an unusually beautiful day, being able to balance the check book; anything pleasant that I hadn't expected. His blessings come in all shapes and sizes.

For you, it could be a chance to take a break from a hectic schedule, an encouraging call from a friend, getting all green lights on your way home, a prayer answered or any of the other little ways God uses to smooth out your path. Rejoice in every new day, for who knows what surprises lay in wait.

Father, thank you for a brand new day. Give me an opportunity to pass on some of your blessings to others.

A Thankful Heart

Today I sat reflecting
on the beauty all around,
as leave of gold and crimson
drifted lazily to the ground.

I thought how I take for granted
the blessings God sends my way,
and I fail to thank him each morning
for giving me a brand new day.

A day I should use for his glory,
in prayer and in his word.
Perhaps a chance to share his message
with someone who's never heard.

What can I do to let God know
how deep my love has grown,
how his spirit lifts and comforts me
so I never feel alone.

I will learn to trust God every day
and release what I grip with my hand.
He always supplies just what I need
so on his promises I'll forever stand.

October

*You anoint my head
with oil;
my cup runs over.*

*Father, thank you for declaring
me righteous and filling my cup
to overflowing. I cannot contain
my love and gratitude.*

October 1

In a war

"Soldiers don't get tied up in the affairs of civilian life, for then they cannot please the officer who enlisted them."

II Timothy 2:4 (NLT)

"And everyone here will know that the Lord rescues his people, but not with sword and spear. This is the Lord's battle......"

I Samuel 17:47 (NLT)

Jack and I grew up during World War II when most battles were fought by soldiers who were dug into trenches for days, sometimes even weeks at a time. Their job was to hold the front and advance whenever possible. They suffered through the cold, ate meager rations and faced the threat of enemy fire constantly. Often they would gain some ground only to be forced to retreat. However, they were determined to defeat the enemy so they endured, always following the orders of their sergeant. Because of the bravery of all our military the enemy was finally defeated and they returned home to their families.

As Christians, we're in a battle with Satan. His weapons are more subtle than the ones used by the soldiers in a war. He attacks with feelings of guilt, greed, doubt, unclean thoughts and other devious ways, but unlike the soldiers who followed their generals' orders in World War II, God is our commander and protector. He will defeat the enemy and win this war for us. Our job is to dig into the trenches and stay committed to letting him lead us safely through. Someday Satan will be defeated, the war will be over and God will take us to a new home in heaven.

Protector Father, I seem to be in a battle every day but I know you've already won the war. Help me to trust you and rest in the hope that someday I'll finally go home.

October 2

Licking the beaters

"Taste and see that the Lord is good; blessed is the one who takes refuge in him."

Psalm 34:8 (NIV)

"Who wants to lick the beaters?" I would call out and my three children would come running. They loved cleaning out the bowl and licking the beaters when I baked a cake. They tasted the batter, but the cake that would come out of the oven would be so much better.

God has prepared many good things for us out of his vast storehouse of treasures. When we enjoy our blessings, we are only getting a taste of what he wants to give us. All he asks is that we put him first in our life. If we are holding on to our things too tightly, we may be asked to let go and let him use them. Then blessings will pour in like a spring of fresh water producing a stronger faith, a deeper appreciation for who God is and an ability to trust him more. What's in your life that has become so important that it takes all your time and attention? That may be the very thing he wants to use. How many opportunities and blessings we miss when we are afraid to step out in faith.

God has an abundance of everything we will ever need - he owns it all. He doesn't really need what we have to offer but wants us to trust him with it. The only way we can do that is to let loose of what we are holding on to so tightly. Taste his goodness for it is only a sample of what He has prepared for you.

Father, you have already given me a taste of your goodness. Help me to want more than just a sample of what you have stored up for me.

October 3

What is love?

"I have become absolutely convinced that neither death nor life, neither messenger of Heaven nor monarch of earth, neither what happens today nor what may happen tomorrow, neither a power from on high nor a power from below, nor anything else in God's whole world has any power to separate us from the love of God in Jesus Christ our Lord!"

Romans 8:38, 39 (Phillips)

Love is a word we toss around like a ball. We say we love our home, our new computer or the book we just read. These loves fade and new ones come on the scene. On a deeper level, we love our family, our friends and our church. These loves endure longer, but circumstances sometimes cause that love to diminish. But who can understand the love of God? It goes beyond what we can comprehend. The Spirit works within us bringing us to maturity so we can love each other in a greater way, but we will still never be able to love the way God does.

I cannot envision the vastness of space and God says his love is greater than that. I will never completely absorb how he loves even the vilest of all men and yet he does. I cannot grasp the enormity of the sacrifice our Savior made when he left his throne in heaven to come to earth and offer his life on the cross for my sin debt, but he did. We don't deserve that kind of love, but he offers it to us freely. That's worth shouting about!

Loving Father, thank you for a love so complete that nothing I can do will cause you to withdraw it.

October 4

Staying positive

"Encourage the limp hands, strengthen the rubbery knees, tell fearful souls, "Courage! Take heart! God is here, right here, on his way to put things right, and redress all wrongs. He's on his way! He'll save you!"

Isaiah 35:4 (MSG)

"Have mercy on me, my God, have mercy on me, for in you I take refuge. I will take refuge in the shadow of your wings until the disaster has passed."

Psalm 57:1 (NIV)

Every day when we watch the news on TV or read the newspapers, we're bombarded with reports of violence, threats of war, dissension in governments and scandals. Most of the world has drifted away from any moral values and shut God out and the result is what we are seeing all around us.

We need to be on guard against becoming fearful and pessimistic for thinking in a negative way can become a slippery slope and erode our faith. It tends to feed on itself and permeates our mind so that we neglect to rely on the source of our strength. The only way to combat these attacks on our mind is to focus on the hope we have in Christ. He restores peace to our soul when we take our eyes off the world and seek refuge in the shelter of His wings.

Lord of all hope, because of you I can face each morning in peace.

October 5

Forgetting God in my plans

"Trust God from the bottom of your heart; don't try to figure out everything on your own. Listen for God's voice in everything you do, everywhere you go; he's the one who will keep you on track."

Proverbs 3:5-7 (MSG)

I made a lot of plans in my life without talking to God about them first. Some worked out and some didn't but I was relying on myself too often. We're tempted to put "I" and "me" in the middle of everything we do. Parents of toddlers deal with the "I can do it myself" kind of attitude. With them it is a normal response to learning independence. If we're not careful as adults, we carry that same tendency to take control and consequently we make our plans and choices without praying about them first. Then, if it doesn't work out the way we hoped, we run to God for help. We act like God only wants to be included on the major decisions we make, but he's even interested in the little choices we make every day. We miss opportunities for blessings when we leave him out. The Bible says God knows the number of hairs on our head and if he cares about something as insignificant as how much hair we have then he cares about choices that seem mundane to us.

As parents we strive to teach our children how to become responsible, independent, and make wise choices, and we then neglect to explain the importance of including God in their decision-making. We should be saying "Let's pray about it" instead of "I can do it myself."

Lord, thank you for being so patient when I don't include you in my plans.

October 6

Sitting on the end of the bed

"I love the Lord because he hears my voice and my prayer for mercy. Because he bends down to listen, I will pray as long as I have breath!"

Psalm 116:1, 2 (NLT)

Each evening as I tucked my children in, I tried to spend a few minutes sitting on the end of their beds before they drifted off to sleep. We would spend some time talking about what had happened that day, their plans and any struggles they were having. It was a precious time for me, and gave me the opportunity to encourage and guide them. Spending these special moments with each of them developed the ability to have an open communication which has carried into their adult lives. It is such a blessing when we can be comfortable expressing our deepest feelings and struggles with each other.

Now in my life, I'm the one going to bed at night and it's my Father who is "sitting on the end of my bed" having a conversation with me. We discuss how my day has gone, my plans and struggles, and he offers me comfort and guidance. He values our time together just as I did with my children.

Father, thank you for listening to me each night. Because of your love, I am able to end my day in peace and comfort.

October 7

A makeover

"Nothing between us and God, our faces shining with the brightness of his face. And so we are transfigured much like the Messiah, our lives gradually becoming brighter and more beautiful as God enters our lives and we become like him."

II Corinthians 3:18 (MSG)

On a couple of occasions while I was a Mary Kay consultant, our Senior Director held a gathering of consultants, their guests and a photographer. When the guests arrived, they removed all their makeup and were photographed. After that picture was taken, they returned to their consultant and applied new makeup. Then their picture was taken a second time to showcase the difference. Seeing what a change the makeup made was startling. It was a "before and after" hard copy.

As Christians, we have a "before and after" heart. Before our salvation, our hearts were stained and ugly with our sin. We were outside of our Lord's presence. The moment we accepted the saving grace that Jesus offered, the stains were removed and we became beautiful in God's sight. The best part is, unlike the makeup that needs to be reapplied every day, we are remade permanently. Even though the world may splash us with the dirt of sin, God washes it off so we remain pure and righteous in His sight. That renewed life reflects the "before and after" of God's grace, a "hard copy" for the world to see.

Precious Jesus, thank you for transforming me into a new person. I'm so thankful you don't keep a picture of my life before I was washed with your grace.

October 8

Who's holding your hand?

"I am the Lord your God who holds your right hand, and I tell you, "Don't be afraid, I will help you."

Isaiah 41:13 (NKJV)

When I was four years old, my parents took me to Cincinnati to see a concert. Later that evening as we walked back to the car, I let go of Daddy's hand and ran ahead. In a little while I reached up and grabbed his hand and began walking with him again. But I wasn't paying attention and had the hand of a stranger. When I realized what I had done, I ran back to Daddy immediately. Of course my mom and dad were watching me the whole time.

Isn't that like our Christian walk? Sometimes we let go of our Father's hand and run ahead of him, putting our trust in someone or something else and don't realize it until we don't feel his presence anymore. If we're not vigilant, we take our eyes off God and without thinking, place our trust somewhere else: a person, our bank account, or perhaps our job; and if we trust them, we aren't trusting him. We are lulled into thinking they can meet a need or give security. God never lets us out of his hand but we stop depending on him. He is watching us just like my parents were watching me, waiting for us to come back and take his hand again.

Father, thank you for taking my hand again even when I have dropped it for a while.

October 9

Only twelve years

"The steps of a good man are ordered by the Lord, and He delights in his way..."

Psalm 37:23 (NKJV)

"When the Lord takes pleasure in anyone's way, he causes their enemies to make peace with them."

Proverbs 16:7 (NIV)

One of the most exciting truths I've discovered through the years is how God orchestrates what happens in our life. After my first husband Mike met Christ in late 1969, he attacked his faith with gusto, knowing God had literally saved his life and his family. He attended Bible college, taught, and served at church and youth camp. Our life together was also flourishing. Mike had only twelve years to get to know his Savior before he was taken home to meet him face to face on this day in 1983.

Mike died suddenly, early on a Sunday morning. During the week prior to his passing, he had contact with over thirty friends, some of whom he hadn't seen for a long time. He shared meals, led a Bible study, played golf, had a committee meeting, stopped by to see his mom and even had the communion meditation that week. To top that off, he shared his last evening in fellowship with all his children, a grandchild and me. In hindsight, I saw how that evening brought a measure of closure to all of us. God can bring people together to heal hurts, mend fences or rekindle friendships. We may not realize we are getting together for the last time. Reach out and seize these moments when they come and be thankful for a loving God that directs the course of your life.

Lord, I am so grateful that you know the path I will take before I even start on it. Thank you for all the times you arrange the circumstances I face. When I consider how much you love and care for me, I can rest in faith because you are always one step in front of me as my guide and protector.

OCTOBER

October 10

Patterns

"This is my instruction, then, which I give you from God. Do not live any longer as the Gentiles live. For they live blindfolded in a world of illusion, and are cut off from the life of God through ignorance and insensitiveness. No, what you learned was to fling off the dirty clothes of the old way of living, which were rotten through and through with lust's illusions, and, with yourselves mentally and spiritually remade, to put on the clean fresh clothes of the new life which was made by God's design for righteousness and the holiness which is no illusion."

Ephesians 4:17, 21-24 (Phillips)

When I was a senior in high school I took a sewing class. Our final assignment was to make a suit. Each girl in the class picked out a pattern hoping her finished product would look as good as the picture on the pattern envelope. After carefully cutting the pieces out of the fabric we had chosen, the sewing began. If we followed the instructions carefully, our suit turned out well and we received a good grade and something special to wear.

God has given us a pattern for our life as believers. The instructions are laid out in his Word and if we follow them carefully, we'll be transformed into the finished work he began in us. In my sewing project, I had to read all the instructions and then, after I cut out all the pieces I needed, I discarded the scraps. We need to cut away the useless things in our life that don't bring glory to our Lord, and work on making our Christian journey a reflection of him.

Father, you gave me a pattern to follow so I could reflect my Savior. Each day I want to work on myself so others will see Jesus in my life.

October 11

His love is forever

"Give thanks to the Lord, for he is good. His love endures forever. Give thanks to the God of gods, His love endures forever, Give thanks to the Lord of lords, His love endures forever, Give thanks to the God of heavens, His love endures forever."

Psalm 136:1-3, 26. (NIV)

"For even if the mountains walk away and the hills fall to pieces, my love won't walk away from you, My covenant of peace won't fall apart." The God who has compassion on you says so."

Isaiah 54:10 (MSG)

Sometimes love is like the wind. It can brush over you like a gentle breeze bringing comfort and a feeling of contentment like the love a husband and wife share after years of a successful marriage. When you first fall in love it may come like a sudden burst, almost knocking you over, or it may be a gust of wind that dies down quickly as the relationship that falters and fades.

But who can describe the love God has for us? It is like a breeze, caressing us, sometimes bringing us to our knees as a gust passes through, and then it will settle into a refreshing flow, energizing us and gently moving us along our path. You can't see it or touch it but you feel it as it washes over you, leaving you with a feeling of peace. He is the air I breathe. His Spirit fills me and inspires me to love in response.

Loving Father, thank for the unconditional and unending love you have given me. Help me display that kind of love toward others.

October 12

Healing

"The righteous cry out and the Lord hears them, he delivers them from all their troubles. The Lord is close to the broken-hearted and saves those who are crushed in spirit."

Psalm 34:17, 18 (NIV)

I ran everywhere when I was little so I tripped and fell a lot, often scraping my knees. My mother usually treated it with iodine, which burned like fire and left an ugly brown stain. After a few days a scab would form over the wound and eventually my skin would look as good as new. That is, if I left the scab alone and didn't pick at it. The scab was there to protect the scrape while it was healing. When I wouldn't leave it alone, the healing process took longer.

When we've been hurt by someone or something that's happened to us, the healing process can be painful. God comforts us like a gentle antiseptic lotion (not like the burning iodine). Then His Spirit soothes our wounded hearts and we recover without any scars. But if we revisit those hurts over and over (like picking at a scab), the healing process takes much longer. God's peace acts like a scab, shielding us while we heal.

Lord, thank you for your soothing touch when I am healing from my painful wounds.

October 13

And then there were three

"For I know the plans I have for you," says The Lord. "They are plans for good and not for disaster, to give you a future and a hope."

Jeremiah 29:11 (NLT)

When our granddaughter and her husband were expecting their third child, she announced her pregnancy on Facebook by showing the ultra sound and stating "and then there were three." The next few months were filled with doctor appointments and planning decorations for the room that would be shared by a new baby boy and his three year old sister.

Before my babies were born I remember wondering who they would look like, whether it would be a girl or boy and what their temperament would be. We dreamed about what their future held and the direction they'd take in life. Sometimes the plans we have for our children don't turn out the way we hoped. Although the way we parent them affects the how our children develop, they will have choices to make as they mature, and so we pray fervently that they make the right ones.

God formed each of us before we were born. He had plans for our life before we took our first breath. He made plans for me and already knew if I would be someone who would follow his will in my life. He molded me and shaped me into a vessel that he could use for his glory. God makes a "life blueprint" for each of us; but we have choices to make and it's up to us whether his plans come to fruition.

Father, thank you for charting my course in life. Forgive me for the times I strayed off that course.

October 14

Dead to the world

"He died, because of sin, once: he lives for God forever. In the same way look upon yourselves as dead to the appeal and power of sin but alive and sensitive to the call of God through Jesus Christ our Lord."

Romans 6:11 (Phillips)

There is an old Hoosier saying, "dead to the world," meaning you are sleeping so soundly that nothing fazes you. One time when my children were playing with their cousins in the bedroom, my four-year-old son, Jeff, who was sitting on the bed, flopped back on the pillow, sound asleep. In the midst of all the noise and activity, he tuned everything else out and did what his body told him to do. He was "dead to the world."

With all that's going on around us: the greed and corruption, the bickering and dissension in politics, the immorality and the unrest in the Middle East, we need to learn from my son's example and shut out the sounds of sin that surround us. That doesn't mean we don't reach out to those we can help or influence, but we're not to feel helpless or without hope. With the help of his Spirit, we can rise above the turmoil and have peace, secure in God's love and protection.

The Bible reminds us that we are not of this world; we are strangers and aliens; our citizenship is in heaven. We are "dead to the world" (sin) and alive in Christ.

Lord, help me shut out the world and focus on you today.

October 15

Divided hearts

"You will keep in perfect peace all who trust in you, all whose thoughts are fixed on you."

Isaiah 26:3 (NLT)

Our world is filled with so many distractions, it has become challenging to focus completely on one thing at a time. We've become so accustomed to these distractions it's hard to be "present" where we are. We'll be in one place physically and yet be miles away in our thoughts or attention. I see people with cell phones up to their ears, completely oblivious to their surroundings. Breaking news can pull us away from other activities. As convenient as these newest tools are, we managed to survive without them while we were growing up. A divided heart and mind will not succeed for it is neither here nor there.

As a child I wasted a lot of time daydreaming which sometimes kept me from paying attention in school. Time wasted cannot be reclaimed.

The time we spend with our Lord, whether morning, evening or tucked somewhere in between, should be undivided. If we're thinking about our day or what's next on our "to do list" then we're not really connected to him. We need to be in his presence in our heart, mind and body. God wants more than the crumbs of our attention.

Lord, it's hard to put down the tools I've embraced and focus on you alone. Help me break habits that often enslave me.

October 16

God looks at the heart

"But God told Samuel, 'Looks aren't everything. Don't be impressed with his looks and stature. I've already eliminated him.' God judges persons differently than humans do. Men and women look at the face; God looks into the heart."

I Samuel 16:7 (MSG)

Before my first knee replacement, I went to a water therapy class. Most participants were seniors, but there was one young man in the group who was covered in tattoos. He was trying to regain the strength he had lost in a bad motorcycle accident. I decided he was a redneck and made no attempt to get acquainted. About a year later I saw him again in a local Bible book store, dressed in plaid flannel pants and a tee shirt. This time I struck up a conversation and, to my surprise, found out he was a strong Christian who ministered to street people.

Believers come in all sizes, all colors, dress differently, are all ages, have tattoos and piercings, and all kinds of backgrounds. But we are all brothers and sisters in Christ. We're a family and we have the same Father. Since that encounter in the book store, I have worked hard on accepting believers just the way they are. I no longer look at their attire, their hair, their taste in music or any of the other stuff that tends to separate us, and it has been freeing to me. I cannot judge their faith walk by how they appear on the outside. God looks beyond the exterior and sees what is in the heart.

Father, thank you for not judging us by how we look or dress. Help me to look beyond the outward appearances the way you do.

October 17

Brain Freeze

"For our light and momentary troubles are achieving for us an eternal glory that far outweighs them all. So we fix our eyes not on what is seen, but on what is unseen, since what is seen is temporary, but what is unseen is eternal."

II Corinthians 4:17-18 (NIV)

One of my favorite cold beverages is a McDonald's Mocha Frappe. Nothing tastes quite as good so when I get one I usually take two or three big swallows very quickly. That leads to "brain freeze" resulting in a sharp, temporary headache. As much as I dislike the pain, the drink is worth the discomfort.

Many of the things we take on as we serve our Father can cause us pain and discomfort as well. Even when we have a deep desire to serve, getting out of our comfort zone in new areas such as teaching, leadership and especially witnessing may bring on feelings of anxiety and fear. God has promised that he will equip us with what we lack. The end result will bring glory to our father and fill us with joy.

Father, teach me to trust in you more when I share your love and mercy with others in whatever role I play. Help me be authentic and to walk in confidence and faith.

OCTOBER

October 18

Backseat driver

"The path of the right-living people is level. The Leveler evens the road for the right-living. We're in no hurry, God. We're content to linger in the path sign-posted with your decisions. Who you are and what you've done are all we'll ever want."

Isaiah 26:7, 8 (MSG)

When Jack and I are going somewhere in the car and he is driving, he wants to be in control and sometimes I can be a backseat driver. Most of the time he just ignores me, but once in a while he reacts. I'm really trying to leave him alone and not say anything unless he misses a turn. I guess I'm like my mother who sometimes told me where I should turn even when I was driving around the town I grew up in - as if I didn't know where we were.

In our faith journey, we are tempted to tell God how we want things to work out, how we want our prayers answered, telling him to change someone, or to alter our circumstances. He has the road map and already knows the road we're traveling in this life. He's aware of the roadblocks and detours and is the best navigator we could ever hope for. Our journey will go so much smoother when we quit being backseat drivers and let him be in the driver's seat. Then we'll be free to enjoy the trip.

Lord, you already know the path ahead of me. Help me trust your Spirit as he moves me along.

October 19

Footprints to follow

"Young people are prone to foolishness and fads; the cure comes through tough-minded discipline."

Proverbs 22:15 (MSG)

As a young parent raising three active children, my life was so full of activity that I rarely stopped to consider the footprints I was leaving for them to follow. Most days I didn't think beyond tomorrow. I was consumed with all the distractions that were demanding my time and attention. I usually cleaned all day Friday, and would be upset if they came in and messed anything up. I didn't want all my work to be for nothing.

When we're raising a family, it's easy to become so involved in the physical aspect of it that we neglect to guide them spiritually. I was often short-tempered and impatient, yelling and spanking - two things the world tells us will damage their self-esteem. However, in spite of mistakes I made, they became responsible, mature Christians.

It is important to leave footprints for them to follow. Demonstrate in your own life how to be patient, set priorities and establish reasonable boundaries. Give them strong guidelines while allowing them opportunities to explore. They may make a few mistakes and bad choices, but that's how they learn and grow. Help them to set goals and teach them that they can't always be the winner. Most important though, let them see that your faith is real and demonstrate how to walk in it.

Father, I made so many mistakes as I was raising my children. Thank you for working in their lives even when I was out of your will.

October 20

Dying a little every day

"That is why we never give up. Though our bodies are dying, our spirits are being renewed every day. For our present troubles are small and won't last very long. Yet they produce for us a glory that vastly outweighs them and will last forever! So we don't look at the troubles we can see now; rather, we fix our gaze on things that cannot be seen. For the things we see now will soon be gone, but the things we cannot see will last forever."

II Corinthians 4:16-18 (NLT)

Some years seem to be more challenging than others. Within a 10-month period we were sick twice with what was going around. The first time mine developed into bronchitis, and the second round I contracted Enterovirus 68, which also affected my lungs. That spring, Jack developed a bleeding ulcer that sidelined him for a while, and shortly before Christmas he had a knee replacement. "The Big 8-0" seemed to be a turning point for our physical bodies!

Someday you'll discover that our bodies deteriorate a little every day. None of us can escape it. We can exercise, eat the right foods, get face lifts, joint replacements and tummy tucks, but nothing stops the aging. We expect our stuff to wear out but have a problem recognizing that our bodies won't last forever.

The blessing that accompanies slowing down is that we now have more time to spend communing with our Lord and growing spiritually. Take time to reflect on how he has worked in your life, bringing you to where you are today. He has always been there and will see each of us through to the end. Each day he will become more real to you.

Loving Father, thank you for walking through the difficult times with me.

October 21

Still under construction

"I pray that out of his glorious riches he may strengthen you with power through his Spirit in your inner being, so that Christ may dwell in your hearts through faith. And I pray that you, being rooted and established in love, may have power, together with all the Lord's people, to grasp how wide and long and high and deep is the love of Christ, and to know the love that surpasses knowledge - that you may be filled to the measure of all the fullness of God."

Ephesians 3:16-19 (NIV)

As you can tell from my posts, I'm "still under construction" and have a long way to go before I become the kind of person God wants me to be. Some days are good - some not so much but I move forward, one step at a time, toward the day when I will no longer have to deal with temptation and failure.

We're created in God's image, made to love him and grow in the example Jesus set before us. However, sometimes we act as though we were created to satisfy our own wants: to achieve fame, or at least recognition; to excel at sports; to get to the top of the ladder. When we do, our pride runs interference with God and we don't mature spiritually.

All God asks is that we keep our eyes on him and become so filled with his presence that our trust will grow steadily as we move forward. We hardly notice our progress, but he does. Nothing pleases God more than our Christian growth and he loves it when we stop to thank him for just being there with us. He is saying "good job" when we share our faith with others.

You are God the Builder of my life. Help me keep my eyes on you as I walk my journey of faith.

October 22

Dr. Spock

"Every part of Scripture is God-breathed and useful one way or another - showing us truth, exposing our rebellion, correcting our mistakes, training us to live God's way. Through the Word we are put together and shaped up for the tasks God has for us."

II Timothy 3:16, 17 (MSG)

Dr. Spock's book on how to care for babies had just become popular when my daughter was born. I had little to no experience with babies so I bought it right away. I wanted to be the best mother I could be for the precious little bundle we brought home from the hospital. That book was an invaluable tool, giving me instructions on all the little details I needed to learn very quickly. I personally think all first babies should come with an instruction manual.

When we become Christians we do have an instruction manual, the Bible, detailing all we need to know in order to grow strong in our faith walk. If you try to navigate your Christian walk without God's Word, it is like putting an engine together without reading the instructions first. You're probably not going to be successful and even if you manage to put all the pieces someplace, it won't run like it's supposed to.

The world will tell you that you don't need the Bible - it's not relevant, or they found a better way, but when you look at the state of humanity, you know they are being deceived. We do need God's Word to successfully navigate our journey here and reach our destination.

Father of all that's good, thank you for your Word. Help me be more disciplined in the time I spend reading about your love for your children.

October 23

Chloe's "Gotcha Day"

"But to all who believed him and accepted him, he gave the right to become children of God. They are reborn—not with a physical birth resulting from human passion or plan, but a birth that comes from God."

John 1:12-13 (NLT)

"But when the right time came, God sent his Son, born of a woman, subject to the law. God sent him to buy freedom for us who were slaves to the law, so that he could adopt us as his very own children."

Galatians 4:4, 5 (NLT)

Several years ago on this date I received a phone call from China at about 3:00 A.M. My son and his wife had just picked up their baby and he was over the top excited and happy as he said, "Mom, she's beautiful." The whole family rejoiced at the news. It was their baby's "Gotcha Day" which they celebrate as much as an actual birthday. Since that first trip to China in 1998, they have gone back for two more girls as well. Each event was reason for rejoicing as a new child was brought into their lives.

As exciting as these adoptions have been, they pale in comparison to the joy felt in heaven when a new believer comes into the fold. They are now adopted into God's family and their new Father is King of the Universe. Being his child comes with unlimited access to him and the security of knowing a love beyond description. It doesn't get any better than that!

Father, thank you for loving me enough to adopt me as your child.

October 24

In God's image

"There are different kinds of spiritual gifts, but the same Spirit is the source of them all. There are different kinds of service, but we serve the same Lord. God works in different ways, but it is the same God who does the work in all of us. A spiritual gift is given to each of us so we can help each other. It is the one and only Spirit who distributes all these gifts. He decides which gift each person should have."

I Corinthians 12:4-7, 11 (NLT)

We're created in God's image but each of us is unique. How unbelievable that God has made billions of people and none are exactly alike. We may resemble each other but there will be something different in each of us, especially our fingerprints. He has given each of us a special gift as well.

A lot of us spend much of our life trying to emulate someone else's gift and we never recognize or utilize the one God gave us. What is it that you have a passion for? What do you like to do that seems to come easily and naturally? There used to be a song called "Doin' What Comes Naturally"; that title describes what using your gift feels like. Whatever your gift is, God wants you to use it.

Lord, teach me to utilize the gift you've given me. I want to use it to bless others and bring glory to you. Thank you for making me in a special way and help me embrace my uniqueness.

October 25

Campfires

"Then they said to each other, 'Weren't our hearts glowing while he was with us on the road, and when he made the scriptures so plain to us?'"

Luke 24:32 (Phillips)

"And the special gift of ministry you received when I laid hands on you and prayed – keep that ablaze! God doesn't want us to be shy with his gifts, but bold and loving and sensible."

II Timothy 1:6, 7 (MSG)

One of our favorite activities in the Campers Club was gathering around a campfire in the evening. Watching the flames dance and listening to the crackle of the wood as it burned mesmerized and calmed me. It was a time of fellowship and bonding with other campers as we relaxed at the end of a busy day. The fire became almost hypnotizing, but if it wasn't tended, it would die down and have to be poked and more logs added. When neglected, the fire would eventually go out.

New Christians are often described as being "on fire for the Lord" in their newfound faith. If they are diligent to feed their faith by praying, reading the Bible, and becoming involved in a church, the fire will continue to burn within them. Many who have been in their Christian journey longer have trouble keeping the excitement going. The new, amazing change that came over them at first begins to slip into glowing embers instead of a vibrant fire. If not tended, it will slowly die down like our campfire. We have all the fuel we need to keep that fire burning within us but we have to be willing to use it. As the old song says, "It only takes a spark to get a fire going."

Gracious Father, thank you for the spark that ignited my love for you. Help me keep that fire burning brightly.

October 26

The center ring

"God resists the proud, but gives grace to the humble."

Proverbs 3:34 (NKJV)

"But among you it will be different. Whoever wants to be a leader among you must be your servant, and whoever wants to be first among you must be the slave of everyone else."

Mark 10:43, 44 (NLT)

There is an old movie, "The Greatest Show on Earth," which is a story about two trapeze artists competing for the center ring in a circus. For those of you who never experienced the thrill of attending a circus, the center ring is reserved for the performer who draws the biggest crowd. In this movie, one of the performers was taking risks and endangering her life in order to win over the crowd. Even though I knew it was only a movie, watching it was stressful.

In my own life, I have to be careful in my writing. It's tempting to be focused on who reads it and not on the reason why I write. I want to use my writing to bring glory and honor to my Lord. I have a daily battle over who occupies the center ring in my heart. My desire is to use my words to point to what God offers us: forgiveness, mercy, love, strength, peace, but pride is always there on the sideline trying to worm its way into the center. God alone deserves the center ring in my heart and it's only through his grace that I'm able to write.

Father, you know how I struggle with pride. Help me keep you on the throne in my heart.

October 27

Getting a new truck

"But it was to us that God revealed these things by his Spirit. For his Spirit searches out everything and shows us God's deep secrets. No one can know a person's thoughts except that person's own spirit, and no one can know God's thoughts except God's own Spirit. And we have received God's Spirit (not the world's spirit), so we can know the wonderful things God has freely given us..."

I Corinthians 2:10-13 (MSG)

A few years ago we bought a new truck which came equipped with satellite radio. That was an added bonus we weren't expecting and we were excited about the choices it offered. We enjoy having the radio on when we're in the truck and it's great to be able to pick up a good signal wherever we are; we don't have to search for a station and can always hear clearly, without static. I don't understand the technology, but the signal is always available when you turn it on.

When we become a Christian, we're equipped with the Holy Spirit. When we tap into all he has to offer, he's able to change us or help us to grow spiritually. The Spirit enables us to mature in the Lord. With his guidance, we learn to understand the scriptures and draw closer to our Father. We can't accomplish this on our own.

We have the option of using our satellite radio or letting it be silent. It won't turn itself on, and the Spirit doesn't force his will on us either. But he is there whenever and wherever we go.

Lord, thank you for the incredible gift of your Spirit who guides and strengthens me every day.

October 28

In unison

"His gifts were made that Christians might be properly equipped for their service, that the whole body might be built up until the time when, in the unity of common faith and common knowledge of the son of God, we arrive at real maturity- that measure of development which is meant by "the fullness of Christ."

Ephesians 4:13 (Phillips)

"Above all, clothe yourselves with love, which binds us all together in perfect harmony."

Colossians 3:14 (NLT)

One of the things I enjoy the most about a football game is when the halftime show features a marching band. I love watching synchronized band members crisscrossing the field, never missing a step and coming together again in unison. They weave in and out, sometimes marching in different directions yet always in sync with the beat. This doesn't happen without weeks of practice and a skilled band director leading them as they learn to march to his directions.

As Christians, marching together in God's church, we should be working in unity. Even though we won't all be moving in the same direction as we serve with varying gifts and skills, we're all marching to the beat of The Lord of our life. We come together again in shared love when we gather to worship the One who directs our life. Band members have to focus their attention on the director or they'll soon be out of step. We need to keep our eyes and heart on our Lord as he directs us so we'll be a unified body of believers, perfectly in harmony with his will.

Lord, you direct my life every day. Help me keep my eyes focused on you so I won't be out of step with your will.

October 29

A project for tomorrow

"Command those who are rich in this present world not to be arrogant nor to put their hope in wealth, which is so uncertain, but to put their hope in God, who richly provides us with everything for our enjoyment."

I Timothy 6:17 (NIV)

My mother often told me she daily gave herself a "project for tomorrow" so that she would look forward to getting up in the morning. That gave her hope that her day would be a good one, and kept her active until she died at the age of 94.

Every day most of us wake up hoping for something. Perhaps it's good weather, a phone call from someone special, that new job we want; anything which gives us a lift in spirit. Hope offers us something to look forward to. However these hopes are temporary, and when things don't happen the way we want we're disappointed and begin looking for something new, our own "project for tomorrow". None of these things will completely satisfy us, which is why sometimes we fall into a dangerous hole of hopelessness, a hole that can only be filled by Jesus. Knowing him gives us "strength for today and bright hope for tomorrow", as the song "Great is Thy Faithfulness" says.

When we focus on the hope Jesus offers, we're able to face each day equipped to handle whatever happens. Maybe the weather won't be good, we might not get that call we were counting on, the job we applied for goes to someone else, but nothing can take away the hope that becomes our anchor and gives us a solid rock to stand on.

Lord, thank you for the hope that you shine before me even in the storms.

OCTOBER

October 30

I see you!

"But the Lord is in his holy Temple; The Lord still rules from heaven. He watches everything clearly, examining every person on earth."

Psalm 11:4 (NLT)

"His own iniquities entrap the wicked man, and he is caught in the cords of his sin."

Proverbs 5:22 (NKJV)

"I see you!" Jack said, grinning as he observed the activity going on outside the bedroom window of our fifth wheel. A couple of our friends had crept back in the dark to TP our lawn chairs. They thought we had gone to bed, but as Jack raised the blind, he saw our friend Kathy. Needless to say, they were startled at being caught "red-handed."

Isn't that how we often view our actions? We think if we don't make a lot of noise about our little sins, God won't notice. We'll say something off-color, engage in a little gossip or retaliate in anger when someone upsets us. We make excuses thinking God won't notice or care that much, but, like Jack when he saw Kathy, God is there with us and already knows what we're going to say or do. We cannot hide from him. But even when we mess up, he forgives us. All we have to do is ask. His love for us is beyond anything we could ever imagine.

Father, I know I disappoint you sometimes when I think you aren't watching. Please forgive me for I am sorry.

October 31

Hiding behind a mask

"We refuse to wear masks and play games. We don't maneuver and manipulate behind the scenes. And we don't twist God's Word to suit ourselves. Rather, we keep everything we do and say out in the open, the whole truth on display, so that those who want to can see and judge for themselves in the presence of God."

II Corinthians 4:2 (MSG)

My children always looked forward to Halloween when they could don a mask and costume and go trick-or-treating and to parties. When my son Steve was 11, our church youth group held a Halloween party. The children got to dress up so he decided to dress like a girl; he borrowed clothes from his sister and put on a blond wig and mask. Even though he was with the youth sponsors every week, he deceived them until the end of the evening when the children revealed who they were.

All of us hide behind a mask once in a while. We say we're OK when inside we are falling apart. We want to blend in with others so we pretend to be someone we're not. Being honest and open isn't easy because we don't want to be seen as vulnerable or weak. But we can have victory over these weaknesses and trials through the loving care of our Lord. We need to show those watching us that they can have hope by taking off our masks and being honest about our troubles. We need to show those watching us there is hope through our Savior who forgives and brings peace. If we're wearing a mask, acting self-righteous, and doing it all on our own, they'll never really know us, or our Lord.

All-knowing Father, help me be genuine with those I have contact with so they'll believe I serve a risen Savior that accepts us as we are, broken and sinful.

November

Surely goodness and mercy shall follow me all the days of my life,

Father, you have declared me forgiven and have made me your child forever. Help me to remember that promise when I am weary and struggling.

November 1

The Great Depression

"Be ready with a meal or a bed when it's needed. Why, some have extended hospitality to angels without ever knowing it!"

Hebrews 13:2 (MSG)

Our country was recovering from the Great Depression when I was in elementary school. My grandma had an alley that ran along the back of her property. Times were still difficult for a lot of people so now and then a hobo would come down the alley and stop at Grandma's house. She always took time to fix them something to eat. They would wash up a little with the hose and then sit on the back stoop to eat their food. Sometimes they offered to do a little work in the yard for her. The hobos must have had some way of marking which homes would be receptive, for they came to her house and didn't usually stop at the neighbors.

Grandma's home was always open to relatives and a few others who lived there at some point over the years. Among them were my Great-Aunt Lizzie, my Great-Grandma Barnard, my cousin Margaret, a couple of teachers, and finally my mother, brother and I moved in when Grandma was in her middle 70's. I'm sure our moving in was a big adjustment but she handled it very graciously, displaying the kind of hospitality the Bible talks about. She took pride in what she had but knew it wasn't for her only, but was for sharing.

The more we pass on what we have, the more God gives us to share. The joy we experience when we use it to reach out makes it all worthwhile.

Loving Father, thank you for filling my life with abundance, so that I can share with others.

NOVEMBER

November 2

Letting go

"You know when I sit down or stand up. You know my thoughts even when I'm far away. You see me when I travel and when I rest at home. You know everything I do."

Psalm 139:1, 2 (NLT)

As parents, our job is to teach our children to nurture their natural abilities and learn how to handle independence responsibly so they can make the right kind of decisions. Every parent's hope is that their children will become happy and productive adults.

I moved North after Jack and I were married so I'm farther away from my children and consequently don't see them as often as I would like, but I've made the decision that I'll "take what I can get." I know they love me and I understand they all have busy lives. Their responsibility is to guide their own children into the future. I'm grateful they're passing on what I showed them by my own faith walk. My job is finished and I still love and enjoy all of them, even if it's from a distance.

God understands that our lives are busy, and as our Father, he is pleased when we take time to talk to him even if it's not as often as he would like. He knows our hearts and our love for him and that we're often distracted by all the activity and busyness that surrounds us. Someday we'll have unlimited time with him. In the meantime, he loves hearing from us and is content to "take what he can get." Before you know it, the responsibility of raising a family will come to an end and you can develop an even greater relationship with your Lord.

Father, thank you for being patient with me when I seemed to be too busy for you. Thank you for giving me a family to nurture and guide.

November 3

Climbing the sand dunes

"Patient endurance is what you need now, so that you will continue to do God's will. Then you will receive all that he has promised."

Hebrews 10:36 (NLT)

Have you ever tried climbing up a sand dune? When my kids were young we went to the Indiana Dunes. Ascending them was very challenging for we'd climb up two steps and slide back one - sometimes climbing one and sliding back two. There were a few scrubby trees to grab ahold of which helped stabilize us. It took a lot of effort and determination to make it to the top, but when we finally did we felt a rush of pride and sense of accomplishment! We had overcome the challenges.

There've been times of trial in my life when I felt like I was sliding back one step for every two I took forward. The friends that encouraged me and steadied me along the way were like the little trees at the dunes. They gave me the boost I needed at the time. All the while, the Spirit was telling me "You can do it, just concentrate on one step at a time." What a feeling of release and joy when you finally have victory. If we learn anything at all through our hard times, it's that we will overcome with God's help.

Lord, thank you for the friends who encouraged and walked with me when I was climbing mountains of hurt and disappointment.

NOVEMBER

November 4

Stretching

"For if a man is in Christ he becomes a new person altogether – the past is finished and gone, everything has become fresh and new."

II Corinthians 5:17 (Phillips)

"Put on your new nature, and be renewed as your learn to know your creator and become like him."

Colossians 3:10 (NLT)

It seems as I get older, I've become so comfortable doing things the way I've always done them, that I'm sometimes intimidated by change. I like my comfort zone and I'm cautious about venturing out of it.

The times I have embraced a new or challenging ministry, I've been blessed by the experience. I've also learned that God won't call me to do a job until he equips me to do it. That often doesn't happen until I have taken a step of faith and begun.

We serve a God who is the author of "new". Each creature born, each flower that blooms, every baby conceived is new when making its entrance. We have new seasons every year, new experiences every day, and a new heaven to look forward to. Best of all he made us new when we believed him and has promised us a new body when we give up this earthly one.

My hope is that, no matter our age, we'll continue to expand our horizons, trying new ways of serving him and trusting in the Spirit's leading. When we're in God's will, he promises new blessings every morning.

Loving Father, thank you for a brand new day. Help me use it wisely and live it joyously.

November 5

My source

"Trust God from the bottom of your heart; don't try to figure out everything on your own. Listen for God's voice in everything you do, everywhere you go; he's the one who will keep you on track."

Proverbs 3:5, 6 (MSG)

There were times when I couldn't come up with an idea as I was writing my devotions. I learned that I had to come to the end of myself and rely completely on the leading of my Lord. He is the source of my strength and ability. If I try to do it without him I come up blank and get discouraged. What a comfort to know he's always there for me. I can only go down the path of my life one step at a time and he lights my way when I place my trust in him.

Don't try to see too far ahead on your journey. We are to walk at the pace he set for each of us. We don't know what each new day will bring but we can trust God's promises. He has said he will never leave nor forsake us and that is enough for us to move forward with confidence and hope.

Father, shine your guiding light on my path today.

November 6

We won't always win

"Pay close attention, friend, to what your father tells you; never forget what you learned at your mother's knee. Wear their counsel like flowers in your hair, like rings on your fingers."

Proverbs 1:8, 9 (MSG)

One important lesson we learn as children is that we are not always going to be first in everything. Learning to accept defeat graciously is as important as coming out on top. Some parents put so much emphasis on winning that the children never learn some valuable lessons. The fact that they put forth their best effort is something to be praised. Learning to congratulate the winner even amidst their own disappointment develops character.

There are many Biblical lessons we can teach our children but they often get lost in the moment because our culture places so much emphasis on being the top dog. One thing we tried to teach our children was that when you started something, you saw it through until it was finished, and if the finish was out of your control then adjust to it and move on. That lesson has carried each of them through some tough times.

God is pleased with our endurance and the commitment to stick with a struggling marriage, a difficult job, schooling that seems to consume you or anything we take on even if we don't seem to have success. He is more concerned about our motive and what's in our heart than how we finish. You don't need a trophy to show you have victory.

Father, help me accept my setbacks and failures with grace and patience.

November 7

Close friends

"Friends come and friends go, but a true friend sticks by you like family."

Proverbs 18:24 (MSG)

"I call you friends, now, because I have told you everything that I heard from the Father."

John 15:15 (Phillips)

We are blessed when we have close friends who patiently listen when we vent, encourage us when we are struggling, and have wisdom to share when we need it. They are like a tether that keeps us connected and close.

I have several very close friends who are like that, but my best friend is my Savior Jesus Christ. I have days when I just want to sit in silence and let his presence fill me and bring me peace. Sometimes situations or people cause turmoil in our life and all we can do is run to our Lord and let him comfort us.

When I draw close to him, his peace surrounds me. He reminds me that I am valuable and that he loves me. He understands my hurts and disappointments because he faced them too. What joy it is to have a friend like my Lord.

Precious Jesus, you are my best friend, but thank you for putting earthly friends in my life as well, for they encourage and bless me with their love.

November 8

Can you hear me now?

"Listen to my words, Lord, consider my lament. Hear my cry for help, my King and my God, for to you I pray. In the morning, Lord, you hear my voice; in the morning I lay my requests before you and wait expectantly."

Psalm 5:1-3 (NIV)

"Can you hear me now?" became a well-known line from a commercial a few years ago. Communicating with another person can be challenging. You can go through a dead spot with cell phones. In a noisy room, other sounds may drown out voices you're trying to hear. Sometimes one of you is simply not paying attention. Whatever the reason, you might have to try two or three times to get your message across. Even then it may not be understood.

It's not that way with God. He hears the smallest whisper. He knows when you are thinking about him. He senses the stirring of your heart and he is instantly alert and listening, for he understands that you are reaching out to him. God is never more than a thought away. When you're hurting, he's there immediately to comfort you. When you're celebrating, he's right alongside rejoicing with you. He listens when you cuddle your child or comfort an aging parent. Rest in the assurance that God will always hear you!

Father, thank you that I always have a direct line to you.

November 9

Helping the homeless

"For you have been called to live in freedom, my brothers and sisters. But don't use your freedom to satisfy your sinful nature. Instead, use your freedom to serve one another in love. For the whole law can be summed up in this one command: "Love your neighbor as yourself."

Galatians 5:13, 14 (NLT)

My son Jeff was home from Bible College, his summer "break" winding down with only a couple of weeks left before he headed back to school. After working all summer he planned to relax for the remaining time, gearing up for another demanding school year. Those plans were about to change. As I left choir practice one evening in late July, I noticed a family walking down the street by the church and recognized the young man as one of our choir members. His wife and their three young children had come in by bus from Illinois that day and he was unprepared to care for them. They had no place to stay, so I loaded them into the car and took them home with me.

It was a big change for Jeff and me. I worked every day, so Jeff ended up babysitting while the couple worked and looked for an apartment. This was something Jeff hadn't planned on, and it was hard for him. The family stayed with us a little over two weeks before finding a place of their own. Later my son told me how upset he had been at the time, but after reflecting on the experience he realized it was one of the best things that could have happened to him. We both learned a valuable lesson from the experience.

When God puts opportunities in our path, we have a choice to make. Do we stay comfortable where we are, or do we take a chance and react in love? I am so glad I reached out that time.

Father, give me the courage to step of my comfort zone and extend a helping hand when I see a need.

NOVEMBER

November 10

"Take care of Wanda"

"Even to your old age and gray hairs I am he, I am he who will sustain you. I have made you and I will carry you; I will sustain you and I will rescue you."

Isaiah 45:4 (NIV)

"There's more to come. We continue to shout our praise even when we're hemmed in with troubles, because we know troubles can develop passionate patience in us, and how that patience in turn forges the tempered steel of virtue, keeping us alert for whatever God will do next. In alert expectancy such as this, we're never left feeling short-changed. Quite the contrary- we can't round up enough containers to hold everything God generously pours into our lives through the Holy Spirit."

Romans 5:3-5 (MSG)

After our children have grown up and are on their own we, as parents, still hurt for them when they go through trials. We long to protect them from troubles and worries but they need to experience pain and difficulty just as we did. We may not have answers for what they're enduring or ways we can help, but we can encourage them and pray. I'll carry that desire to protect my children until I am in the grave. I was 68 when my own mother passed away. One of the last things my mother said to Jack before she died was "Take care of Wanda" and she was 94 years old.

The most important lesson our children can learn from us is how God works in our lives and takes care of us. We can remind them of the times God met their needs as well. God, our Heavenly Father, hurts for us when we suffer. He encourages us and walks with us, but he lets us experience trials, for they're our "growing pains" as we mature in our faith and trust.

Loving Father, even though my children are on their own, I continue to bathe them in prayer. Hear my prayers and work in their lives so that they might grow in their faith and trust.

November 11

Honoring the veterans

"I saw Holy Jerusalem, new - created descending resplendent out of Heaven, as ready for God as a bride for her husband. I heard a voice thunder from the throne. 'Look! Look! God has moved into the neighborhood, making his home with men and women! They're his people, he's their God. He'll wipe every tear from their eyes. Death is gone for good - tears gone, crying gone, pain gone - all the first order of things gone.' The enthroned continued, 'Look! I'm making everything new. Write it all down - each word dependable and accurate.'"

Revelation 21:2-5 (MSG)

Today is set aside to honor the veterans who have served our country so faithfully, sacrificing their time with families, their jobs, sometimes limbs and often their lives. Because of their sacrifices, we can celebrate the freedom we enjoy today.

Since sin entered the garden, conflict has been something all of us have had to contend with. Millions have lost their lives defending homes, villages and countries from the enemy. Even if secured, peace and liberty weren't guaranteed to last. As long as we're in this world, war will be part of life. What a comfort to know that God has promised us peace in the midst of the fighting and suffering in this world. His peace enables us to stand amidst the battles around us. Someday we'll join faithful believers in a paradise that is beyond anything we could imagine. There'll be no more need for military protection for sin will be nonexistent and God's love will be in all of us.

Father, thank you for the men and women who sacrificed so much to defend our freedom. May you send a special blessing on each one who served so unselfishly.

November 12

Tear down that wall!

"When you were stuck in your old sin-dead life, you were incapable of responding to God. God brought you alive - right along with Christ! Think of it! All sins forgiven, the slate wiped clean, that old arrest warrant canceled and nailed to Christ's cross. He stripped all the spiritual tyrants in the universe of their sham authority at the Cross and marched them naked through the streets."

Colossians 2:13-15 (MSG)

"Mr. Gorbachev, tear down that wall!" demanded President Reagan when the two of them met in Berlin as the Cold War was winding down. The wall had divided Berlin for many years, separating the East and West sides of the city. On the East side the people lived under communist rule and had no freedom. It was a drab, dreary place without hope or joy. The West side of Berlin was just the opposite with people living normal lives in freedom. That wall was the divider, often keeping friends and sometimes families apart.

Until you accept Jesus as your Savior, you have a wall separating you from God. You might think you have freedom, but that wall is the sin in your life and it keeps you from God's presence. The moment you become a believer, that wall is removed, your sins are forgiven and you live in the freedom bought for you by the blood of Christ. As meaningful as tearing down the Berlin wall was, it was nothing compared to the wall brought down at Calvary. Praise God for His mercy and grace!

Forgiving God, thank you for Jesus who tore the curtain through his death and resurrection giving us access to your presence.

November 13

A wayward child

"...The prayer of a person living right with God is something powerful to be reckoned with."

James 5:16 (MSG)

Have you ever felt so low that you couldn't pray and, even if you did, you felt like your prayers weren't going anywhere?

When my daughter was twenty, she left our home one morning and didn't return. We had no idea where she was. Her father and our minister searched for her throughout the night as I waited, worried and prayed from home. She had been unsettled and restless, as many young people are at that age, but we weren't prepared for the decisions she made that morning. Fortunately, in a couple of days we were notified of her whereabouts and knew she was safe, but our hearts were broken. I had faced many trials in my life before but nothing had equipped me for the emptiness and depression that washed over me. As days turned into weeks, then months, I prayed - but nothing seemed to help. I was unable to find peace and felt totally helpless.

I finally shared with my mother about how I was doing. She told me she had been praying for our daughter but instead was going to pray for me. By the next morning, I felt as though a weight had been lifted off my shoulders and I had peace for the first time in months. It would be another long year before our daughter would return home, but during that time we re-established communication and grew close again.

Sometimes, when others ask us to pray, we'll say yes and then forget, or we pray half-heartedly. I know without a doubt that earnest, heartfelt prayers of others can make a huge difference. It might not remove the problem but it will change the attitude about it.

Father, thank you for those who have taken the time to pray for me.

November 14

Shrinking Scars

"Thank God, the Father of our Lord Jesus Christ, that he is our Father and the source of all mercy and comfort. For he gives us comfort in our trials so that we in turn may be able to give the same sort of strong sympathy to others in theirs. Indeed, experience shows that the more we share Christ's sufferings, the more we are able to give of his encouragement."

II Corinthians 1:3-5 (Phillips)

When you are going through trials in your life, you don't see how God is preparing you to minister to others down the road. You are being trained in God's "Survival School."

I've dealt with a number of heartaches in my life: growing up without a dad in our home, an unfaithful husband, a runaway child, and becoming a widow. Each time I emerged stronger in my faith and better equipped to encourage and lift up others facing similar trials, but I still bore the scars of those heartaches.

When I shared my story with others, they saw that it was possible for them to emerge in their own victory. At times I felt as though God purposely put people in my path so I could minister to them. I learned that the more I shared with and encouraged hurting people, the smaller my own scars became. Now, the only purpose for those scars is to show someone else how to have victory. I like to say that "I am who I am today because of where I was yesterday."

Father, continue to use me to encourage others who are hurting.

November 15

Mixed blessings

"He will feed his flock like a shepherd. He will carry the lambs in his arms, holding them close to his heart. He will gently lead the mother sheep with their young."

Isaiah 40:11 (NLT)

One of the reasons we love our property is having a creek bordering the back yard, but that can be a mixed blessing. Sometimes when the weather is dry for a long spell, the water level in the creek bed gets so low that it barely moves, but it never completely dries up. On the other hand there have been a few times, during heavy storms, it came out of the banks. It would be wonderful if it had a reasonable water level all the time – never too low or too high.

Our spiritual lives are like the creek. Now and then we'll have a dry spell and lack the living water he promises us. God doesn't cut off our supply, but we've put up a dam of complacency or worries so his living water is not reaching us. We feel out of touch and wonder why we're not excited about our faith walk anymore. Yet there are occasions when we're flooded with an overwhelming sense of his presence and it spills out and touches those around us.

It's hard to remain up and on fire all the time. We'll all have ups and downs in our walk but God is always the same. He is the one constant we can put our faith and trust in. He promises to be there to lead us through the dry spells and he rejoices with us when we're flooded with love and excitement in our walk.

Loving Father, thank you for the floods I have in my spiritual journey. When my living water level is low, send a shower of your precious presence to replenish it.

November 16

Window shopping

"I've learned by now to be quite content whatever my circumstances. I'm just as happy with little as with much, with much as with little. I've found the recipe for being happy whether full or hungry, hands full or hands empty. Whatever I have, wherever I am, I can make it through anything in the One who makes me who I am."

Philippians 4:11-13 (MSG)

A favorite activity in high school was going downtown to window shop with my mother on Sunday afternoons. Shops were closed on Sundays but the drugstores remained open. The downtown square was lined with a variety of stores and many windows were displaying the latest fashion and shoe styles. We never had much money but it was sure fun to look and dream. After walking around the square, we would top off our excursion with a root beer at a local drug store.

For those of you too young to know about window shopping - it involved admiring displays in store windows and wondering if you could ever afford it. During a time when you either paid cash or put your items in layaway, we were realistic and usually content with what we had. How different it is today. We're tempted to buy whatever is the latest and greatest. We have to fight the urge to replace what we already have with something we don't really need. We can only resist these temptations by allowing the Spirit to guide us daily. Paul tells us that he has learned to be content whether he has much or little. Our focus needs to be on walking close to our Savior not on what we can acquire

Lord, I sometimes struggle with the desire to buy what I don't need. Help me learn to be content with what I already have.

November 17

Tornado Warning

"Let us then approach God's throne of grace with confidence, so that we may receive mercy and find grace to help us in our time of need."

Hebrews 4:16 (NIV)

On this day in 2013, our Sunday had begun as a normal day. We had planned to relax in the afternoon and later wash supper dishes at Kokomo Urban Outreach. After getting home from church, we got a call informing us the meal had been cancelled because of a severe weather forecast. About 3:40 a tornado warning came on TV and on our cell phone telling residents a tornado had been spotted and to take shelter immediately. We grabbed our shoes, coats and cell phones and headed for the basement. Within a few minutes we lost our power. Over the years I've watched TV coverage of many disasters and wondered how people survived physically, not to mention emotionally.

You cannot prepare for an event such as a tornado, for it comes with very little warning. Even a "safe place" to wait out the storm may not be safe at all.

God never promised us a life free of trials, but his promise is that he will walk through them with us. We can make reasonable preparations and use good judgement but ultimately he is in control of what happens and will supply what we need. I am so thankful that I have a loving God who never leaves me stranded or without hope. I can face each new day with confidence knowing, whatever comes my way, I do not walk this path alone.

Father, thank you for walking by my side through the storms I face.

November 18

Life is a see-saw

"But you asked God for help and he gave you the victory. God is always on the alert, constantly on the lookout for people who are totally committed to him...."

II Chronicles 16:9 (MSG)

When I was a child we used to like to visit Matter Park in Marion, Indiana. I liked getting on the see-saw. Once in a while someone bigger than me would be on the other end and I would spend much of my time up in the air. If someone smaller would be on the other side, I had a hard time getting my end off the ground. It was rarely balanced.

During the week of the tornado, our life seemed like a see-saw. Even though our power was out (down), we were comfortable and rejoicing that nothing had been damaged in our neighborhood. We had everything we needed to get by (up). Then, like a see-saw, Jack began "coming down" with something. In spite of that, he reached out to help another family move their belongings. He was feeling pretty sick when I came down with the same bug. So, our end of the see-saw was up on Monday and came crashing down later in the week. There was a blessing in Jack getting sick because then he had to stay home and take care of himself.

Life is like that, rarely on an even keel. I've learned though, whether you are up or down, God will bring the balance back. We just have to trust him.

Lord, even when life seems upside down, you are there to stand me up again.

November 19

The best and worst in people

"Share each other's burdens, and in this way obey the law of Christ."

Galatians 6:2 (NKJV)

Any disaster seems to bring out the best and worst in people. There were looters after the tornado that took advantage of the situation, not only in stores that were damaged, but in homes as well. Thankfully there weren't many of them. However there were hundreds, maybe thousands who stepped up to help with clean up, moving possessions, bringing in meals and some offering places to stay. Power companies from all over the Midwest sent workers and supplies to get electricity restored. The unselfish generosity that was displayed reached across the state and even beyond.

There's something about seeing others face overwhelming destruction that brings out the best in us. Each community facing trials think they are unique in this, but each of us has the gift of "helps" in us, the ability and willingness to provide support, to lend a hand, to "help". We just need to tap into it.

We'll have many opportunities to help carry someone else's burden. It might not be the destruction such as we had, but anytime you can reach out and share the load someone else is carrying, you are honoring God.

Father, thank you for those who step up to help when I face unexpected trials.

November 20

Seeing a big shadow

"Do not be afraid or discouraged, for the Lord will personally go ahead of you. He will be with you; he will neither fail you, nor abandon you."

Deuteronomy 31:8 (NLT)

"Cast all your anxiety on Him because He cares for you."

I Peter 5:7 (NKJV)

A few times my fears have loomed large and made me want to run and hide. Later, when the seemingly insurmountable crisis had passed, I would reflect on it with a more realistic view. What had seemed like a monster was only a mouse. Now, granted, I'm not particularly fond of mice either but they don't frighten me. There is a Swedish Proverb which says: "Worry often gives a small thing a big shadow." It seems as though most of what we expend our energy worrying about never happens, and even if it does, it isn't nearly as bad as we imagined.

Unbridled fear is the result of failing to put our complete trust in God. If someone asks Jack to do a job for them, they don't come back later and say they don't trust him and they'll do it themselves. They know he will do it. Why is it, we seem to put more trust in people than we do in our Heavenly Father? We say we have left our concerns with God, but then we often pick them back up and struggle with carrying them ourselves.

Lord, help me learn to leave my fears and concerns at your feet and trust you more. Your promises never fail and your love carries me faithfully every moment of every day. Thank you for always being there for me.

November 21

Nicknames

"...And I will give to each one a white stone, and on the stone will be engraved a new name that no one understands except the one who receives it."

Revelation 2:17 (NLT)

Names are so important! I never really cared much for my name and always wished I could have a nickname but there isn't much you can do with "Wanda". That was the name my mother selected and she liked it. I did have an Uncle Dick who called me "Pumpkin" and I loved that.

Names reflect who we are in other people's eyes. I try to remember the names of new people I meet but I'm not always successful. It gives us a good feeling when others address us by our name because that means they cared enough to remember us.

Jack and I each have a son named Steve and a good friend of ours is named Steve as well. When I say to Jack, "I talked to Steve today" he'll ask, "Your Steve, my Steve or our Steve?"

God's Word tells us we will be given a new name when we get to heaven. That new name will be known only to us and God. No one else will share that name and that tells me I am special to my Lord.

Father, thank you for loving me enough to give me a special name in heaven.

NOVEMBER

November 22

God provides

"Do not worry, saying "What shall we eat?" Or "What shall we drink?" Or "What shall we wear?" For the pagans run after these things, and your Heavenly Father knows that you need them. But seek first His kingdom and His righteousness, and all these things will be given to you as well."

Matthew 6:31-33 (NKJV)

Through my years as a widow, I learned what trusting God meant. After selling our house in the country, I wanted to move into town. Even though I had no job or credit history, I was able to purchase a house in Clarksville. Later God provided me with a job that I loved, but the most amazing thing he did was to send people to me who needed a place to live. At first I hesitated a little then decided to give it a try. The extra income would be helpful. I never advertised or indicated that I wanted to rent out my upstairs, but during the next twelve years I had thirteen more people come to me to rent the room.

I had a single mom and her baby for eighteen months, a high school senior, several who had just graduated from college, an engineer on a work-study program and a young father whose wife had just left him. Each time I learned more about sharing and was able to encourage the ones God placed in my home. It didn't feel like it was my house anymore, but in a sense it wasn't, for I believe he allowed me to buy it so it could be used to help others.

God had a two-fold plan for me. He supplied a financial need by providing extra income and because there was always someone else sharing the bath, kitchen, laundry and sometimes the living room, I never viewed it as "my space only" so when I married Jack I was able to adjust quickly.

Father, you are awesome, for you arranged help for me before I even had a need. Thank you for orchestrating my life.

November 23

Peace through trials

"The Lord is the everlasting God, the creator of the ends of the earth. He will not grow tired or weary, and His understanding no one can fathom...Even youths grow tired and weary, and young men stumble and fall; but those who hope in the Lord will renew their strength. They will soar on wings like eagles; they will run and not grow weary, they will walk and not faint."

Isaiah 40:28, 30-31 (NKJV)

During the days following the 2013 tornado, many who had lost everything and the volunteers who worked tirelessly to help victims, reached the end of their physical and emotional strength. They had run out of reserves.

In the summer of 2003 when we had the flood, Jack and I had around three hours to save what we could from our finished basement. We were exhausted and drained emotionally. Our neighbors, who had suffered loss as well, suggested we all go get some breakfast together; there wasn't anything else we could do until the water subsided. As we waited for our food, we thought about the enormous task ahead of us. Having a time to commiserate and share with each other was a welcome relief. Later friends began showing up to see what they could do to help and a peace settled over us. We'd have a lot to do in the coming months, but in the light of day it didn't seem so overwhelming.

The peace God gives during times of trial makes the stress almost worth it. I have to fight the temptation to worry when we have a prolonged and heavy rain storm, but I know God is always with us and we will get through whatever happens.

Father, help me release my fears and trust you in the storms.

November 24

Escalators

> "And now, compelled by the Spirit, I am going to Jerusalem, not knowing what will happen to me there."
>
> Acts 20:22 (NIV)

> "For the love of Christ compels us..."
>
> II Corinthians 5:14 (NIV)

When I was approaching my teens, Mother took my little brother Billy and me on a trip to Indianapolis so we could visit the L. S. Ayres and Block's department stores, back before there were malls, when going shopping downtown in a big city was an event. For me, it was as if we we're be transported into a world of fantasy, full of exciting new sights and sounds. My brother and I were especially fascinated by the escalators. To be carried along with no effort on our part seemed magical. Billy was so intrigued by them that he slipped away and was on his way up again before Mother could stop him. By the time we hurried to the top to catch him, he had started down again.

The Holy Spirit works like that in our life. We have to step out in faith and trust, just as we had to step onto the escalator, but very soon he is moving us to a new level. I've experienced this on a few occasions when I felt led to start a ministry that was completely new to me. When I let the Spirit lead me, the ministry would be successful and bring glory to God. If I start something without his guidance, I will probably be on a down swing.

When we align our will with the Holy Spirit's, he enables us to rise to new heights.

Father, thank you for your Spirit who moves me to new heights and opens up my understanding. Help me keep my heart open to his leading.

November 25

Under warranty

"This truth gives them confidence that they have eternal life, which God—who does not lie—promised them before the world began."

Titus 1:2 (NLT)

"If you are faithless, He remains faithful. He cannot deny Himself."

II Timothy 2:13 (NKJV)

"Do not let your heart envy sinners, but always be zealous for the fear of The Lord. There is surely a future hope for you, and your hope will not be cut off."

Proverbs 23:17-18 (NIV)

When you purchase a new vehicle, a large or small appliance, computer or TV, it comes with a guarantee, commonly known as a warranty. Sometimes the warranty will be good for a few months and in the case of vehicles, parts of the engine may be guaranteed for several years, but eventually it will run out. I've noticed a number of times that whatever you purchased won't have a problem until the warranty expires. Much of what we purchase today is not built to last, for the need to replace these things is the engine that drives the economy.

God offers us a guarantee that never expires. When we accept Jesus as our Savior, believing he died for the forgiveness of our sins and rose again, we are his forever. In our faith walk, we may become bruised and battered; disappoint God at times and even struggle with questions, but God's promise can be counted on, for God cannot lie.

Thank you Father that you are faithful, even when I am not. I rejoice that I can rest in your promises.

November 26

My shoes

"For shoes, put on the peace that comes from the Good News so that you will be fully prepared."

Ephesians 6:15 (NLT)

There is a common joke around our house about my love of shoes. Jack tells people that someday our trailer won't be able to pull out of the drive because of the weight of all my shoes. I've loved shoes since I was a little girl. One of the things that I remember most about starting school in the fall was the wonderful smell of my new leather shoes. Jack is content with just a few pair, two or three for dress, a couple for casual, and then there are the ones he works in. They have to be falling apart before he will get rid of them.

The shoes you wear need to be appropriate for the activity you will be engaged in. A ballerina will wear small slippers built for dancing, but a nurse will wear comfortable shoes that enable her to be on her feet for long periods of time.

Paul tells us in Ephesians that we are to dress for a spiritual battle. Specifically, we are told to fit our feet with the gospel of peace which should be strong enough to equip us for dealing with conflict so we'll be able to stand firm and fully prepared for whatever we face. This is the peace of God which transcends all understanding. (Philippians 4:7)

Lord, help me be as concerned about my spiritual shoes as I am with my earthly ones.

November 27

Funnels

"God saved you by his grace when you believed. And you can't take credit for this; it is a gift from God. Salvation is not a reward for the good things we have done, so none of us can boast about it. For we are God's masterpiece. He has created us anew in Christ Jesus, so we can do the good things he planned for us long ago."

Ephesians 2:8-10 (NLT)

When we need to put a large amount of liquid into a small opening we use a funnel. That way none of it is spilled or wasted.

In our community we have a servant leader, Jeff Newton, who is acting as a funnel for food, meals and help to hundreds of people in our community who otherwise would have little hope. Most are families with children and little access to transportation. Donations pour into his ministry, Kokomo Urban Outreach, where he is the director, and are distributed to those who need it. Through his contact with the people, he is demonstrating God's love. Jeff is a godly example how God can direct and use each of us to do his good work. He began the KUO several years ago when he felt God's leading to start this ministry. From its inception in a small local church, it has grown to nearly a city-wide service with around ten sites where they serve meals on Sunday evenings and distribute food.

God planned good works for each of his children. These works probably won't be on the scale of KUO and may not attract attention here on Earth, but they will be fulfilling God's purpose in our lives.

Lord, help me to become a funnel through which you can pour out your help and blessings to those around me.

November 28

Son of God

"God created human beings; he created them godlike, reflecting God's nature."

Genesis 1:27 (MSG)

"The angel answered, "The Holy Spirit will come on you and the power of the Most High will overshadow you. So the holy one to be born will be called the Son of God."

Luke 1:35 (NIV)

A few years ago I spent several months researching my genealogy. As I followed the footsteps of the generations, the father's name was the one I found the easiest to trace. The father's last name is the one parents hope will continue through their sons. I was able to trace my father's ancestors back to the late 1700's. I had hoped to discover someone famous in my search but they were all ordinary, hardworking people. We all share a common genealogy, though. The Bible tells us we are children of God - all part of his family. God adopts us into his family when we accept Jesus as our Savior.

Luke 3:23-38 lists the complete genealogy of Jesus all the way back to Adam (76 generations), going backwards from Jesus, son of Joseph to Seth, son of Adam, son of God! Adam was the son of God and Jesus was the son of God. When God created Adam he breathed his own life into him, and through Mary God had a son named Jesus. All of the translations list Adam as the son of God. Each one of us has a King in our genealogy. How cool is that!

Eternal Father, thank you for the heritage I gained when I became your child.

November 29

Show and tell

"Direct your children onto the right path, and when they are older, they will not leave it."

Proverbs 22:6 (NLT)

When my children were in the first or second grade they occasionally had "show and tell" days. They could bring in a treasured item and tell the class something about it. My middle son once took in a little model car and explained how he would run it down our driveway. The teacher later told me how proud he was of that little car.

When you think about it, you have "show and tell" time with your children every day. By your actions you can show them how to treat others. With your words you are able to teach them to speak kindly and gently, without anger. When you make commitments and keep them, you are letting them see how to be responsible and trustworthy. Making your faith walk a central part of your daily life lets them see how important it is to you.

Showing our children how to grow into godly adults is often challenging. They're faced with opportunities and often pressures to participate in other activities instead of worship and/or church. When we allow this to become a pattern, we're telling them that putting God in second place is OK. We only have a short time to steer them in the right direction, so every day counts.

Father, even when our children are grown, we have opportunities to demonstrate our faith and perseverance to them. Help me stay positive and joyful in my walk with you so they will see that aging isn't a threat.

November 30

Our mirror image

"Your fame soon spread throughout the world because of your beauty. I dressed you in my splendor and perfected your beauty, says the Sovereign Lord."

Ezekiel 16:14 (NLT)

How do you like standing in front of one of those mirrors that distort your image? As a child, I was fascinated when I saw myself very tall with little short legs. Another mirror would show me short and very wide. At that time in my life, I could see that image and not be too concerned about how I looked. However as we grow up, we tend to be more focused on how we look in the mirror and begin to wonder what other people think about our bodies and whether we look old or out of style. When I check myself in the mirror every day, I see the wrinkles, the thinning hair, the limp and all the other imperfections and I spend a lot of time trying to improve the image I see.

God doesn't see us that way. Everything he creates, he declares good. When he says it's good that means there is nothing he would do to improve it. We are made in his image and he calls us beautiful. He doesn't see all the imperfections we tend to focus on.

Someday, when we're finally with him, we'll look in his mirror and see the beauty that he created and we won't be prideful, just eternally grateful.

Father, help me view myself with value because of what you have done for me and not because I consider myself worthy.

Is it December already?

Like sand, time has slipped through my fingers,
While I lived my life helter skelter.
The years flew by like geese in the fall
On their way to a warmer shelter.

There were people I wanted to see
And places I had wanted to go.
Somehow I never found the time
With all my running to and fro.

I wonder if I gained any wisdom
In this life I've been given to live.
Did I share enough with those I met
Or have I been too insensitive?

As I head into life's December
And my journey's end draws near,
I'm reflecting on God's plan for me,
And my responsibility is becoming clear.

There are hurting souls around me
Dying of thirst for some living water.
They don't know their thirst could be quenched
If they'd trust in the Master Potter.

He molded me into a vessel
To be used to carry the message
That God's love and grace are offered
So they can face the future with courage.

I cannot waste the time that's left
Worrying whether or not to share.
God offers salvation to each of them.
I want people to know that I care.

December

And I will dwell in the house of the Lord forever.

Psalm 23

Father, you have prepared a place for me to abide in your presence forever.

No words can adequately express my gratitude and love.

December 1

Old clothes

"Even though on the outside it often looks like things are falling apart on us, on the inside, where God is making a new life, not a day goes by without his unfolding grace."

II Corinthians 4:16 (MSG)

Jack loves hanging around the house and working on a project, usually wearing old, worn work pants or jeans and shirts full of stains, holes or frayed collars. Sometimes I have to bite my tongue to keep quiet about it. If we're going out to the grocery or gym, he sometimes waits until the last minute to change. Occasionally he refuses to change saying, "Nobody is going to see me." However, on Sunday and occasions when we're going to be around other people, he takes a lot of pride in his appearance.

I am learning to be comfortable in my body, even though it is getting worn like Jack's old clothes. It's the body God gave me and since it wasn't designed to last forever, I have adjusted to the wear and tear that life has brought upon it.

The Jack that wears the old, worn clothes and the Jack that dresses in a coat and tie is the same man in his heart and soul. I am the same in my aging body as I was in my younger one. I'm so thankful the Lord looks at my heart and not my outward appearance. That's what being in Christ does for us.

Lord, sometimes my body doesn't function the way I wish it would and my mind has trouble recalling all the stuff it once held but I want to be content with where I am in the winter of my life. I feel your presence more keenly than I used to and that closeness far outweighs the loss of youth.

DECEMBER

December 2

Tartar sauce

"For the Lord grants wisdom! From his mouth comes knowledge and understanding. He grants a treasure of common sense to the honest. He is a shield to those who walk with integrity. He guards the paths of the just and protects those who are faithful to him."

Proverbs 2:6-8 (NLT)

When my youngest son was in his mid-twenties, some of our family went to a local buffet. As he was checking out the choices on the food bar, he saw what he thought was tapioca (which he loved) and put a generous helping on his plate. Almost as soon as he sat down, he picked up his spoon and took a big bite of it. Much to his surprise and dismay, it wasn't tapioca; it was tartar sauce. He hates tartar sauce and he had a big bite of it in his mouth with no choice but to make the best of it and swallow.

Every day we are faced with multiple choices, some good and some that will negatively affect our faith walk. We often reach out to sample something that looks appealing and it ends up not being what we thought it was. Like the food on the buffet, it is designed to tempt you. The enemy knows where your weakness is and he is adept at disguising his bait so you don't realize what you're getting until you've already sampled it.

We can only be prepared to make wise choices by gaining wisdom - discovering God's truths and applying them to our lives.

Father, help me to make wise choices today. Give me wisdom so I will recognize truth.

December 3

Stains

"Come now, and let's reason together," says the Lord; though your sins are like scarlet, they shall be as white as snow; though they are red like crimson, they shall be as wool."

Isaiah 1:18 (NKJV)

Once in a while Jack or I will get a stain on our clothes. If I treat it right away it might come out. Sometimes it will be difficult and occasionally impossible to remove. I've tried advertised products and a few home solutions. Some were effective, some weren't, but there aren't any guarantees that they'll do the job. However, even if the garment is ruined, you have others or it can be replaced so it's not a huge loss.

Before we accept Christ as our Savior, we are stained with our sins and no matter what we do to try and remove the stain by our own efforts, we will fail. There are all kinds of self-help books telling you how to clean up your life, but the stain will remain. Unless it's removed, it will keep you from God's presence for all eternity.

Jesus is the only permanent stain remover. When you accept his saving grace, he removes all your stains - past, present and future - and you can walk in confidence knowing that you have been washed clean and are righteous in God's sight.

Forgiving Father, thank you for removing the sin stains from my life and making me white as snow.

December 4

Laws are to protect us

"Do you think all God wants are sacrifices - empty rituals just for show? He wants you to listen to him! Plain listening is the thing, not staging a lavish religious production."

I Samuel 15:22 (MSG)

When our children were growing up, no one had seatbelts or safe, secure car seats. Consequently many children were injured in sudden stops, or even killed in car crashes. The one car seat we had was cloth and attached to a metal frame that hooked over the back of the front seat.

Two of the best laws ever passed were the ones on seatbelts and car seats. We follow these laws because they're for our protection and safety. However, there are still some who refuse to obey and will not buckle up, resisting any kind of restrictions on their freedom to choose.

God set up guidelines for our protection and to help us stay focused on him; obeying those "laws" doesn't earn salvation or points with God. Like seatbelt and car seat laws, they were set up for our benefit and to keep us connected to our Lord. There have always been people who don't want to follow God's guidelines, thinking they're too restrictive or take away one's freedom to choose what they want. However, because God loves us so much and knows us so well, he knew from the beginning we would need strong guidelines to live a victorious life.

Father, thank you for the guidelines you established for us to live by. I know they are for our spiritual health and protection.

December 5

Put criticism in the basket

"Finally, brothers and sisters, whatever is true, whatever is noble, whatever is right, whatever is pure, whatever is lovely, whatever is admirable—if anything is excellent or praise-worthy—think about such things."

Philippians 4:8 (NIV)

Before I married Jack and moved north, I was a Mary Kay consultant for thirteen years. The senior director in the area had monthly meetings so all of the consultants could meet together. She was a positive, upbeat person and had a rule that all negative, complaining, or critical attitudes were to be placed in a basket by the door. They weren't allowed in the meeting. She had learned by experience how contagious and destructive bad attitudes could be. If they were taken home by the consultant they would affect their ability to be successful.

As believers, we are to walk confident in our salvation and hope. If we allow ourselves to become critical or negative, our witness is compromised and we lose our peace. More importantly, the Gospel we're sharing won't appeal to anyone.

When a negative thought enters your mind, refuse to give it space to settle in and make itself at home. Keep a mental basket at the door of your heart and dump negative thoughts in it immediately. Think about the good that God has done in your life and give him praise. Make a list of praises and positive thoughts and post it on the door of your heart so the enemy will see you are serious about it.

Father, help me keep negative thoughts and critical attitudes out of my mind today.

December 6

How does he get in?

"If you are then "risen" with Christ, reach out for the highest gifts of heaven, where your master reigns in power. Give your heart to the heavenly things, not to the passing things of earth."

Colossians 3:1-2 (Philips)

When my son Jeff was about seven years old, he climbed up a ladder to get to the roof of our bi-level home. He wanted to check out the chimney to see how Santa got in on Christmas Eve. We never figured out if he was beginning to question if there really was a Santa or if he actually wanted to see how the jolly old elf got in, but he was willing to take some risk to find out. He was seeking the source of his Christmas gifts.

During this busy, sometimes distracting holiday season, it takes effort to stay focused on what we are really celebrating. We are drawn to the light displays, the festive parties, buying and wrapping gifts and getting the house decorated. In all of the activity, which is not "bad", incidentally, the birth of our Savior may be put on the back burner until Christmas Day is almost here. He is the source of all we are or have.

Take some time every day this month to thank God for his wonderful gift to us. Ask him to help you stay focused on the wonder of this Babe who brought us saving grace and hope. Then you will truly have a blessed Christmas.

Redeemer Father, you are the source of all that is good. Help me stay focused on your incredible gift and how it has changed my life.

December 7

Facing fears

"God met me more than halfway, he freed me from all my anxious fears."

Psalm 34:4 (MSG)

When I was about six, one of my front teeth had become loose but wasn't quite ready to come out. My dad wanted to pull it, but he when he stood before me with a small pair of pliers in his hand, I refused to open my mouth. He assured me it wouldn't hurt but I was determined not to let him touch it. A few days later it still hadn't come out so my mother made an appointment with the dentist to have it pulled. I had never been to a dentist before and was apprehensive. When the dentist started to work on me, I again refused to open my mouth and he decided to give me a little gas to relax me. When I saw that mask coming toward my face I was terrified and began screaming. I carried on so much that the dentist gave up and my mother took me home, tooth still attached.

The Bible talks about dealing with fear in nearly every book. As far back as Adam and Eve in the garden after they had disobeyed God, fear has been something people have had to deal with. One after another, in every situation, God told them not to fear.

Once in a while we'll face situations that strike a paralyzing fear in us and we may not think rationally. We're told to run to God for his strength and reassurance, and trust in his promise that he will never leave us or forsake us. The One who calms the seas and controls the universe will calm us.

Lord, it's the unknowns that fill me with fear and dread. Strengthen my faith so I won't falter.

DECEMBER

December 8

Walking on the ice

"But when I am afraid, I will put my trust in you. I praise God for what he has promised. I trust in God, so why should I be afraid?"

Psalm 56:3-4 (NLT)

One really cold winter when I was about eleven years old, the river in my home town froze completely from bank to bank and the ice had become pretty thick. My mother, brother and I went to see it one afternoon. There were already a number of people out on the ice, a few even ice skating, and all were enjoying the adventure. At first I was intimidated by the thought of leaving the safety of the river bank and stepping on the frozen wonder. After a few minutes, I mustered up enough courage to try, and it was exhilarating. The ice was deep enough to hold all those people and it was an experience I will never forget.

Trusting God when you face a mountain that seems insurmountable is a little like stepping onto that frozen river. Sometimes he won't act on that need until you take that first step of faith and trust him. It can be frightening until you realize that you're not sinking. He holds you firmly with his strong arms and will meet every need you have. When you actually see how he works in your situation, you'll feel unbelievable joy and exhilaration, just as I did when I realized I was safe on the frozen river.

You are a Father who walks with me through every challenge I face. Thank you for your presence when I feel like I'm walking on thin ice.

December 9

Surrounded by darkness

"For you are all children of the light and of the day; we don't belong to darkness and night."

I Thessalonians 5:5 (NLT)

It's been over two years since our home and many others in the area were suddenly plunged into darkness following the November tornado outbreak. As a rule, when we lose power a few houses in the neighborhood will still have lights, so it was strange to look out the window to complete darkness. The moon hadn't risen yet so we couldn't see anything. Jack got out a lantern to light and we had a couple of flashlights, so we could find our way around the house. When you walk in complete darkness you run the risk of tripping over something or stubbing your toe. Having light gives you a feeling of security and safety for you can see where there is danger and risk. We don't realize how much we depend on flipping a switch to have all the light we need.

There are multitudes of people in this world who are walking in darkness spiritually. They're stumbling around in their lives not seeing the pitfalls in front of them, or even realizing what path their lives are on. They've rejected the light that could change their life and guide them safely down the right road. They don't know they will spend all eternity in darkness. If we let our little light shine around them, maybe they'll see what a difference it can make and reach out to the true Light of the world.

Lord, help me remember to be a light to those I come in contact with every day.

DECEMBER

December 10

Losing patience

"The Spirit, however, produces in human life fruits such as these: love, joy, peace, patience, kindness, generosity, fidelity, tolerance and self-control - and no law exists against any of them. If our lives are centered in the Spirit, let us be guided by the Spirit."

Galatians 5:22, 23, 25 (Phillips)

In the early 1990's I was a church secretary in Louisville, Kentucky. The 100-year-old church was in the process of being remodeled and the architect, who was a member of the church, was showing the electrician where the circuit breaker was located in the basement. For several hours I had been typing names and addresses into the computer for a new church directory. I was about three quarters finished but hadn't taken the time to save it. All of the sudden the power went out and the computer went blank. It came back on almost immediately, but all the work I had accomplished was gone. Of course I was very upset and fussed at the architect when he came by the office. It wasn't his actions but my own carelessness that cost me all my work. I did learn a valuable lesson and saved everything on a regular basis after that.

All of us face situations where our self-control is stretched to the limit as mine was that day. We have the Holy Spirit dwelling within us to direct our reactions, but we're sometimes slow to listen. I am so thankful God is more patient than I am. He has given us the means to grow more Christlike through the Spirit.

Lord, I don't like taking my frustrations out on others, but sometimes I do. Help me learn to be more patient.

December 11

Route 66

"For this God is our God for ever and ever; he will be our guide even to the end."

Psalm 48:14 (NIV)

"The Lord will guide you continually, giving you water when you are dry and restoring your strength. You will be like a well-watered garden, like an ever-flowing spring."

Isaiah 58:11 (NLT)

Occasionally when we're traveling we'll go through an area that's under construction and the road signs will be confusing. A map helps, but if it's out of date, the roads in some areas may have changed. We rely on our GPS as well, but we can't always count on it to be accurate. Once, at 2:00 a.m, our GPS led us down a dead-end street with no place to turn around. We were in our RV and Jack had to back up in the dark for almost a block to reach an intersection. Signs, maps and GPS devices are good when they get you where you want to go, but you can't always depend on them.

God gives us promises in his Word that he will guide us safely to our destination. His road map is in "Route 66" (the 66 books of the Bible) and if we study it carefully we won't get lost or on the wrong road. His directions are absolutely trustworthy and dependable, enabling us to travel this life with confidence and enjoy the scenery on the way.

Father, thank you for guiding me safely down my path in this life. Forgive me when I fail to check your road map for directions.

December 12

Being an Uncle Sam

"But, let me repeat, there is glory and honor and peace for every worker on the side of good, for the Jew first and then the Greek. For there is no preferential treatment with God."

Romans 2:10, 11 (Phillips)

"And the leaders of the church had nothing to add to what I was preaching. (By the way, their reputation as great leaders made no difference to me, for God has no favorites)."

Galatians 2:6 (NLT)

Our grade school put on a patriotic program when I was in the first grade. Our part was to be a line of marching Uncle Sams led by two little girls who got to wear little skirts, jackets and white boots. Of course I wanted to be one of the girls selected for that privilege, but ended up being an Uncle Sam, as were almost all the other children. All of us had cute costumes but I was so disappointed.

There are times when we want to be picked for a job, a position on a team, a part in a play, or just to be part of a group. When we're not asked it shakes our confidence and perhaps stirs up a little resentment or jealousy.

When God first chose the people of Israel to be his chosen nation, they were commanded not to mix with the Gentiles. After the resurrection of Jesus, God opened his arms to accept anyone who would believe in his Son. I am so grateful that God has no favorites and all are welcomed into his family.

Loving Father, I'm so grateful that you don't have favorites. Thank you for accepting me even with all my faults and failures.

December 13

Feeling thirsty

"Let me tell you why you are here. You're here to be salt-seasoning that brings out the God-flavors of the earth."

Matthew 5:15 (MSG)

"Jesus said, "Everyone who drinks this water will get thirsty again and again. Anyone who drinks the water I give him will never thirst-not ever. The water I give will be an artesian spring within, gushing fountains of endless life."

John 4:13-14 (MSG)

When I eat something that's especially salty, it creates so much thirst that I can't seem to get enough water. I don't normally drink a lot of water but I have learned that a glass of cool water quenches my thirst better than any other kind of drink.

As believers we're the salt of the earth. We have a responsibility, through our witness, to create a thirst in those with whom we have contact. If we're reflecting God's love and compassion, they'll see how their life could be different. Spread your salt around so others will thirst for the living water that Jesus offers.

Lord, help me mirror the love you so graciously bestowed on me so others can see you and have a thirst for what you offer.

December 14

Follow the leader

"Later, Jesus spoke to the people again and said: 'I am the light of the world. The man who follows me will never walk in the dark but will live his life in the light.'"

John 8:12 (Phillips)

One of my favorite games as a child was "follow the leader." I enjoyed mimicking everything the leader did, although sometimes it could be challenging. I was always relieved when they didn't do cartwheels or stand on their head because those were things I never mastered.

Teenagers are occasionally led into risky behavior when they pattern their life after a peer they think is really cool. Even as adults we're often influenced by the successful people we admire which can be dangerous because we run the risk of losing sight of who we are in the process.

As believers, there is only one leader we should follow and that is our Savior, Jesus Christ. When we imitate his love and compassion we can't lose, for he never did anything to compromise his relationship with his Father.

Father, it's so tempting to imitate the actions of people I admire, even when they don't display Christian values. Help me keep my eyes on Jesus, my true leader.

December 15

Decorating for Christmas

"Be strong and courageous. Do not be afraid, do not be discouraged, for the Lord your God will be with you wherever you go."

Joshua 1:9 (NKJV)

"The Lord looks down from heaven and sees the whole human race. From his throne he observes all who live on the earth. He made their hearts, so he understands everything they do."

Psalm 33:13-15 (NLT)

Each year at Christmas, as I unpack and put up our decorations, I'll take a trip down "memory lane" remembering times when the children were young. I think about my dad as I hang the old glass ornaments I inherited from him. Many of my treasured decorations hold special memories.

Then when Christmas is over, I pack them all away and wonder what the next Christmas will be like. Having survived a lot of personal storms, I realize that life can change in an instant, so I always know that the next year might be very different. But I also learned over the years that it can still be good even if circumstances have changed. I am so thankful for the memories of times gone by, but I know God controls my future and he will always be by my side to guide and strengthen me.

No matter what changes we will face in our faith journey this year, God is always constant. He promises us he will never leave us. We can rest in the security of his unrelenting love.

Father, you know what my future holds and my desire is to leave it in your loving hands.

December 16

On hold

"Morning, noon, and night I cry out in my distress, and the Lord hears my voice."

Psalm 55:17 (NLT)

"God met me more than halfway; he freed me from my anxious fears."

Psalm 34:4 (MSG)

A few years ago I called our cable company to get an issue resolved and I was put on hold. The recording said "all representatives are busy but your call is important to us and it will be answered in the order in which it was received." Then I had to listen to irritating music that was repeated over and over. After waiting half an hour I was tempted to hang up, but I didn't want to start the whole process all over again later; so, I continued to wait. It was over an hour before I was finally connected with a live person. They told me the best time to call was later in the evening.

How comforting it is to know that we are never put on hold when we call out to God. He receives millions of calls at a time but answers each one the minute he receives it. You don't have to wait or listen to music. You might be in a noisy room or in your bed at night - it doesn't matter. It can be anywhere, anytime - morning, noon or in the middle of the night - your call really is important to him!

Father, I am so thankful that you listen every time I call out to you.

December 17

Too involved

"...I have come that they may have life, and that they may have it more abundantly."

John 10:10 (NKJV)

Early in my faith journey I was preoccupied with being involved in everything our church had to offer and soon became so busy with activities that I wasn't getting acquainted with the One who gave me this new life. I was making new friends, serving on committees and was learning all the songs by heart. I had a full life but Jesus was offering me more than that. He wanted to give me an abundant life.

Gradually I learned to depend on God's guidance, and during that growth process, became more intimately acquainted with my Savior. My fellowship with him allows me to check in with him off and on all day for direction and strength. He is my constant companion and sustainer. What a blessing that is.

It's easy to get so caught up in serving that you lose sight of the One you're serving. Some of the responsibilities we take on consume a lot of time and attention and will often deceive us into thinking we're in the driver's seat. He offers us a life that is filled to the brim with the blessings that only he can give: peace, contentment, love, patience, and the comfort of sensing his presence all the time.

Father, I want to serve you, but sometimes I'm so busy being a Martha that I forget to stop and enjoy fellowship with you. Help me become like Mary so I will sit at your feet and worship.

December 18

A rock in my shoe

"So the Lord must wait for you to come to him so he can show you his love and compassion. For the Lord is a faithful God. Blessed are those who wait for his help. Your own ears will hear him. Right behind you a voice will say, 'This is the way you should go,' whether to the right or to the left."

Isaiah 30:18, 21 (NLT)

Sometimes when we're hiking, I'll get a little rock in my shoe. It is irritating but a lot of the time, I'm reluctant to untie my shoe and remove it, so I put up with it. However, I don't enjoy the walk as much and after a while the rock seems as though it's getting bigger.

Our irritations and problems can be like a little rock in our shoe. We can ignore them and put up with the distress they cause, but then we become so focused on the stress and pain that we lose our peace and closeness to our Lord. When we have these times it's best to deal with them quickly before they grow any bigger. No matter what it is, you can defuse it by turning to God for guidance and strength. Maybe it's an apology, forgiving someone, shedding anger and resentment or just letting go of past mistakes. This frees you so you can continue your journey without pain - walking peacefully with the Lord by your side.

Father, help me deal with the little irritations in my life before they become so big that they're like boulders in my path.

December 19

Handing out gifts

"In him we were also chosen, having been predestined according to the plan of him who works out everything in conformity with the purpose of his will."

Ephesians 1:11 (NIV)

We were on our way south for the winter and stopped for a few days to visit our daughter and her family in Lexington. All of the family had gathered for an early Christmas celebration, and when we finished dinner we retired to the family room to exchange Christmas gifts. I asked my 5-year-old great-grandson Riley if he would hand out the gifts we had brought. With the hint of a smile on his face and his eyes dancing with excitement, he stood before me, pleased to be chosen. As I handed him each bag, he carefully studied the name and delivered the gift to the recipient. I saved Riley's bag for last and he broke out in a big smile when he saw his name on the tag. He was happy to have a gift but his greatest joy was being chosen to pass them out.

As Christians, we have been chosen by our Heavenly Father to pass along the wonderful news of our Lord's amazing grace. What a privilege it is to be counted as someone he can use. We've already received that wonderful gift and we should feel honored that he has given us the mission of telling others how they can receive it too.

Gracious Father, the giver of peace and true joy, thank you for choosing me as a child who can pass on your wonderful news of grace to those who are empty and lost.

December 20

Getting a new outfit

"There are different kinds of spiritual gifts, but the same Spirit is the source of them all. There are different kinds of service, but we serve the same Lord. God works in different ways but it is the same God who does the work in all of us. A spiritual gift is given to each of us so we can help each other. It is the one and only Spirit who distributes all these gifts. He decides which gift each person should have."

I Corinthians 12:4-7, 11 (NLT)

When I'm shopping for a new outfit for a special occasion, I don't just pick something off the rack and purchase it without making sure it fits, is comfortable and appropriate. It helps if I like the way it feels on me, for then I can wear it with confidence.

God has an assortment of gifts to use in His kingdom. Not all of them will fit us. Like the outfit I choose when I shop, we need to try them on to see which one brings us joy and glory to God. He has a special gift for each of us but it won't be tagged with our name on it. We have to discover which one fits. With observations and advice of friends, along with our feelings about it, we can discover our personal gift, crafted to fit us perfectly.

It took me most of my life to find mine because I tried a few that didn't fit and then gave up when I couldn't find the right one. Now with my pen and some paper, I am finding great joy and a sense of God's guidance in writing. You too will find your own special gift when you search for it.

You are the Father of all gifts. Thank you for guiding me to the ones that fit and bring me joy in my serving.

December 21

Winter Solstice

"For everything there is a season, a time for every activity under heaven. A time to cry and a time to laugh. A time to grieve and a time to dance. A time to scatter stones and a time to gather stones. A time to embrace and a time to turn away. A time to search and a time to quit searching, a time to keep and a time to throw away."

Ecclesiastes 3:1, 4-6 (NLT)

Our years are divided into seasons. Spring brings new growth but can produce major storms and flooding. Summer offers sunshine and the opportunity to enjoy the outdoors but can bring extreme heat and drought. Fall bursts forth in color but we also witness the demise of plants and wind stripping all signs of life from the trees. On this day, winter officially begins; winter offers glistening white snow and time to spend with loved ones through Christmas, but it can also bombard us with relentless bad weather, sickness and seemingly endless days of gray.

Our lives have seasons as well. We'll have seasons of joy as we experience a discovered love or the birth of a baby. There'll be seasons of settling into routines when nothing out of the ordinary occurs. There are seasons of setbacks and challenges that cause us to reflect on our path. We have seasons of victory and a joyous connection with our Lord. We also have seasons of trials that seem to come one after another like the storms in the winter, and these are the ones that draw us the closest to our Savior. Do not be discouraged for all seasons come and go, and a new one is just around the corner.

Father, you set the seasons of our life in motion when we are born. Thank you for the season I'm in now, for I'm confident it will be filled with your presence and blessings.

December 22

Special letters and cards

"I always thank my God when I pray for you, Philemon, because I keep hearing about your faith in the Lord Jesus and your love for all of God's people. Your love has given me much joy and comfort, my brother, for your kindness has often refreshed the hearts of God's people."

Philemon 4, 5, 7 (NLT)

Every once in a while I pull out a box containing some of the letters and special cards I have received through the years and as I re-read them, a flood of memories washes over me. They remind me of friends and family members, some who have since died. The memories are mostly good mixed with a few painful ones but they are a part of the fabric of my life. These handwritten treasures can be held and read over and over. Today we have instant messaging, texts, emails, phone messages, posts on Facebook, twitter, etc. but once they are gone you cannot pull them up again.

How blessed we are that God chose a few faithful people to write down the words he gave them. Without the Bible where would we go to learn about his love and plans for our eternity?

The modern way of communication is fine for some things but don't neglect writing personal expressions in a form that can be held, saved and looked at again when others need a lift or encouragement. How encouraged Philemon must have been by Paul's letter!

Loving Father, how I treasure your inspired words. They bring me hope when I am discouraged, peace when I am afraid and joy at your incredible love for me.

December 23

Family heirlooms

"Tell your children about it, let your children tell their children, and their children and other generations."
Joel 1:3 (NKJV)

"A good man leaves an inheritance to his children's children……"
Proverbs 13:22 (NKJV)

As I unpack the Christmas ornaments each year, a few of them bring back special memories. One in particular is a card holder I made when my children were small, made of green felt trimmed in gold rick-rack and hung on the wall each year, laden with the Christmas cards we receive.

When I began my posts in 2013, I only wanted to have a record of my life, as I had lived it, to pass on to my family. I never dreamed it would eventually lead to a book. The stories we share with our children give them a legacy to build on. My maternal grandma shared many fascinating stories of my great-grandparents and their parents as well. However, my paternal grandmother never opened up about her background or told me stories about my dad's childhood. This left a hole in my perception of my dad's family, the personal side that I so longed to know.

It is important to pass on to your children where you came from and how you lived. This is as much an inheritance as the material things you leave them, and far more valuable; If God was a strong presence in the lives of your parents and grandparents, their lives steered you on the path that led you to where you are today. Your guidance and influence will have an impact on the coming generations long after you are gone.

Father of my past, present and future, thank you for the positive Christian influence left by those who walked before me. Help me live so that those who follow me will have my strong faith as an example.

December 24

What's your name?

"For unto us a child is born, unto us a Son is given, and the government will be upon His shoulder and His name will be called Wonderful, Counselor, Mighty God, Everlasting Father, Prince of Peace."

Isaiah 9:6 (NKJV)

Have you ever thought about how many names are used to identify you? Jack is known as Dad, Granddad, Papaw, Grandpa, Mister Jack, Grandpa Jack, Poppy, John (his legal name) and Jackson (when he's in trouble with me). It seems like all the grandchildren picked out the name they wanted to use. Even though he has all these different names, he is still the same person. His name doesn't change who he is and he answers to all of them.

Our Savior, Jesus Christ, is known by many names. To the Israelites he was their Jehovah God. In John's gospel he is introduced as The Word. Later in his ministry, John identified him as Friend. To Peter, he became Messiah. In the book of Revelation he is called the Lamb of God. He became our Savior. Isaiah 7:14 identifies him as Immanuel. Behind all those names is our Lord, the God of the Universe, the Great I Am. We can't understand all of it, but we accept with faith that our Savior and Friend has always been and will always be. He is the Alpha and Omega, The Beginning and The End.

God, you have so many names, but to me you are truly my Father.

December 25

The faith of a child

"At that same time Jesus was filled with the joy of the Holy Spirit, and he said, 'O Father, Lord of heaven and earth, thank you for hiding these things from those who think themselves wise and clever, and for revealing them to the childlike. Yes, Father, it pleased you to do it this way.'"

Luke 10:21 (NLT)

"Santa won't stop at our house if he sees that you're still up!" It was Christmas Eve and we were having trouble getting our grandson, Tyler, to settle down. To a four-year-old, this was the most exciting night of the year, so he didn't heed my warning. Finally, unnoticed by Tyler, his Papaw slipped out the back and went to the front porch, jingling some bells. As soon as Tyler heard the bells he scurried up the stairs and jumped into his bed, fearful that Santa would catch him still up.

How hard it is for us as adults to have that kind of faith. Tyler accepted without question the reality of Santa. We need the faith of a child in our Christian walk. We proclaim that we believe but often struggle with doubts and worry. Santa was make-believe, but our Lord is real! He can be trusted and he will never leave us nor forsake us. Santa only comes once a year, but our Lord is with us every moment of every day.

Father, help me to live my life with the faith of a child.

December 26

An immigrant

"But now that you have been set free from sin and have become slaves of God, the benefit you reap leads to holiness, and the result is eternal life. For the wages of sin is death, but the gift of God is eternal life in Christ Jesus our Lord."

Romans 6:22-23 (NIV)

A little over two hundred years ago, one of my Irish ancestors immigrated to America as a bond-servant. A farmer in Pennsylvania had purchased her ticket. As a bond-servant she was bound to serve in his home and farm until her service equaled the price of her ticket. How liberating it must have been for her when that debt was finally paid and she was free to plan her own future. She eventually migrated to Indiana and became part of my grandfather's lineage.

Before we accepted Jesus as our Savior, we were bound to Satan. We were more than bond-servants, though. We were slaves with no way to pay our debt. I'm so thankful for the unbelievable gift that was given to me by my Savior. His incredible grace has freed me and now I'm a willing servant to my Lord. I guess you could call me a slave, but I serve because I love him, not because I have no choice.

Father, you are my master and I rejoice that you chose me to serve as your slave.

December 27

Learning to knit

"For you created my inmost being; you knit me together in my mother's womb. I praise you because I am fearfully and wonderfully made; your works are wonderful, I know that full well."

Psalm 139:13-14 (NIV)

I learned to knit when I was a teenager. For a while all I attempted were dish rags and scarfs. After I developed the skill, I bought a sweater kit, complete with yarn and instructions. It had a cable stitch running through it and, even though it was difficult, I finished it, except for one thing. You had to crochet the trim, which was a skill I had never learned, so the almost-finished sweater went into a box and on a shelf in my closet.

God knit each one of us together before we were born. He had a special pattern for every person and then that pattern wasn't used again, so no two people are exactly alike. He carefully crafted every stitch to create his finished piece. What an awesome God we have - never running out of new patterns. Every baby born is given a special set of physical characteristics and then equipped with talents and gifts tailored just for them. Each one of us is unique.

Sometimes we'll question why God made us a certain way, but he had a reason and someday it will be clear to us. Let's just rejoice that he loved us so much that he designed each of us to be special.

Father, I stand in awe of the diversity of your creations. Thank you for making each of us special and unique.

December 28

Eyes in the back of my head

"The eyes of the Lord watch over those who do right; his ears are open to their cry for help."

Psalm 34:15 (NLT)

As a young parent, I could sometimes sense when one of my children was being naughty so I told them "I have eyes in the back of my head and I can see you." I don't think they really believed me, but they were a little more cautious about their behavior for a while. Most of the time though, I liked watching them as they grew and learned to do new things. New parents can sit and watch their baby for hours, drinking in every move the baby makes. Their love knows no bounds when it comes to this little bundle of joy that God has given them. It doesn't matter if the mother gave birth to the child or if she's adopted; the child is now their pride and joy.

Sometimes new Christians feel like God is watching every move they make and they fear his judgment and condemnation. They don't yet understand his unconditional love. God loves watching us the same way parents watch their child. We're his created children and his eyes are upon us constantly, not to judge us or to see if we're being obedient, but because he is proud of us and wants to be in on everything we do. I think he smiles when we do something funny and claps when we accomplish something difficult. He hurts for us when we grieve or stumble and fall in our walk. I feel like our Lord is eager for the day we will finally see him face to face. Then he will be like a proud papa as we receive our rewards in Heaven.

Father, help me do things that are pleasing to you and make you proud.

December 29

Being a light

"You're here to be a light, bringing out the God colors of the world. God is not a secret to be kept. We're going public with this, as public as a city on a hill. If I make you light bearers, you don't think I'm going to hide you under a bucket do you? I'm putting you on a hill top, or on a light stand!"

Matthew 5:14-15 (MSG)

I have a floor lamp with a three way bulb in my sitting room. Recently it has begun to flicker because the connection is not right. If I'm studying or writing, it can be very distracting. I need a steady light that I can depend on or I end up thinking about the flicker more than what I'm actually doing.

Jesus tells us we are to be lights to a lost and dying world. However, it seems like the light we're displaying is often flickering. When we complain and criticize or let the worries of this world undermine our trust and faith, our light begins to flicker. Will a seeker trust our Lord if we act as though he's not with us all the time? Perhaps our connection has become loose and we're no longer shining brightly all the time. I want my light to shine steadily every day and the only way I can maintain its glow is to keep God at the center of my heart.

Lord, help me to be a light that doesn't flicker. I want your love to shine through me with a steady, bright glow that will draw others to you.

December 30

The weather forecast

"Don't envy sinners, but always continue to fear the Lord. You will be rewarded for this; your hope will not be disappointed."

Proverbs 23:17-18 (NLT)

One thing Jack and I watch faithfully on TV every night is the weather forecast. I read the weather page in the newspaper and check the weather app. on my iPad as well. I'm not sure why we're so hung up on tomorrow's weather; we can't do anything about it. Sometimes our plans for the next day will depend on the forecast, but usually it doesn't affect us one way or the other. We've experienced some pretty bad storms that weren't predicted, so you can't really depend on the forecast anyway.

Most of the people in the world around us worry about what the future holds for them. Their jobs, their investments, their health - none of them are guaranteed. They hear dire predictions of doom and gloom so they have no hope. For them, nothing in their life is certain.

As believers, we love hearing about what is being predicted for our future. Unlike the world around us, though, we have been promised a future that has no clouds or storms in it. The light will come from our Lord and we can bask in it without fear of sunburn. Now, I love that forecast!

Lord, thank you that the forecast for your children is a bright future filled with Sonlight.

December 31

A new exercise program

"We can rejoice, too, when we run into problems and trials, for we know that they help us develop endurance."

Romans 5:3 (NLT)

I've noticed that a lot of people blame their emotional struggles on the way they were raised or because they were abused or neglected. They claim they're dysfunctional because of circumstances over which they had no control, and won't assume responsibility for their actions, saying "It's because of..."

When we're confronted with trials, whether we cause them or not, we have a choice to make. Challenges don't make us who we are, they define who we are! They can bring us down, or we can rise above them. No one else is responsible for how we react. The choice is ours.

God uses our trials to develop our character and help us grow spiritually, sort of a "spiritual exercise program." With prayer and the help of the Holy Spirit we can have victory over any challenge we face.

Lord, as I celebrate the beginning of another New Year, help me embrace with confidence the challenges I'll face, knowing that you alone have the keys to my future. Teach me to accept responsibility for my actions when I stray out of your will.

Final Thoughts

I would like to thank you for spending time with God through my devotional. I hope you found your own story in some of my joys, victories and struggles. Take some time to reflect on your faith journey and remember God's faithfulness.

If you have any questions, comments or requests, I can be reached at: wandahood536@yahoo.com

Additional copies may be ordered from your favorite Christian bookstore, Encourage Books, Amazon, or you can contact me.

For immediate shipment of single book orders, visit Encourage Books at www.encouragebooks.com or through the contact information below.

Bookstores, churches or other groups wanting multiple copies or to make a tax exempt purchase should contact the publisher directly to receive a generous discount:

Encourage Publishing
info@encouragebooks.com
812-987-6148

www.ingramcontent.com/pod-product-compliance
Lightning Source LLC
Chambersburg PA
CBHW071143300426
44113CB00009B/1061